The Beth Chatto Handbook

Beth Chatto's descriptive list of
unusual plants

The Beth Chatto Handbook

Published by The Beth Chatto Gardens Ltd. April 2015.

Copyright © The Beth Chatto Gardens Ltd.

All rights reserved. No part of this publication may be reproduced, stored
in a retrieval system, or transmitted, in any form, or by any means,
electronic, mechanical, photocopying, recording or otherwise without
either prior permission in writing from the publisher or a
licence permitting restricted copying.

British Library Cataloguing in Publication Data.
A catalogue record for this book is available from the British Library.

ISBN
978-0-9932496-0-0

Typeset, prepared for press and printed by Smith & Watts Limited,
Ipswich Road,
Colchester, C04 OAD.

Cover designed by Amanda Sebborn-Connelly.

Contents

Introduction

Since the last publication of 'The Beth Chatto Handbook, a descriptive catalogue of unusual plants', we have seen many ageing copies, most are well thumbed and often covered in scribbled notes, a few still pristine. But whatever their condition all are loved and treasured as being written by a gardener for gardeners.

With an eye for detail and an uniquely engaging style, Beth Chatto's written descriptions are the result of personal experience and close observations gleaned from a lifetime of living among her plants.

We are therefore thrilled to publish this revised and updated handbook. It must no longer be considered a catalogue, but rather a bringing together of the plants that Beth Chatto has used over the years to create her gardens.

Not all of the plants in this handbook are available from the nursery but the majority of the plants we now offer are included.

As we no longer publish a static annual price list, we would encourage you to visit our comprehensive website where we have a much wider and more flexible range of plants on offer, all with images and up-to-date stock availability: www.bethchatto.co.uk

The Nursery and Mail Order

Towards the end of the 1960s the farm was sold and, to help carry on and develop the garden, Beth Chatto decided to start a small nursery. Like the garden it began modestly with one girl and a Saturday helper, but eventually acquired a total of just over 6 hectares, including the garden. Over the years the staff has also grown, their enthusiastic, knowledgeable and dedicated support is obvious to all our valued customers. The plants are classified according to their growing conditions where they can be seen growing in their required habitat in the garden. Today there is an extensive choice of over 2,000 different kinds of mainly herbaceous plants, bulbs, ferns and grasses. The majority of these are propagated and grown on site. New plants are constantly added to the range and if a visit to the gardens is not convenient then our range of plants and garden related gifts can be seen and ordered online at: www.bethchatto.co.uk

Our method of mail order packing has evolved over the last 30 years and is carried out by our team who ensure the quality and reliability of our plants. Their expertise was rewarded in 2013 by being awarded 'Editor's Choice' for Mail Order Plants by 'The English Garden' magazine. With the advent of the internet and improvement of delivery services we have established an excellent relationship with our carriers, the vast majority of orders leave our nursery one day and arrive safe and sound the next.

By reading your letters and receiving your orders, we are aware that we have a special relationship, based on our mutual love of plants.

"I received my plants yesterday and would like to say thank you for what I think is an exceptional mail order service for plants. They arrived in tip top condition and were packed beautifully. I was out when they arrived but they were placed exactly where I had asked for them to be – an unusual thing in my experience. Excellent service from beginning to end. THANK YOU."
M.F. Brentwood, Essex. September 2013.

Notes on The Beth Chatto Gardens

The garden began in 1960. A shallow depression of three or four acres lay neglected and overgrown between two farms. A few fine oaks and hollies rose above a confused tangle of willow, blackthorn and bramble, while buried in its depth was a spring-fed ditch that ran down the centre of the hollow. This trickle of water, which never dried up in the severest of Essex droughts, was the source of inspiration for a water-garden, with dreams of primulas and marsh marigolds, normally impossible in flat and drought-troubled Essex. The surrounding land provided hot, sun-baked gravel facing south-west, while the opposite north-east slope had some shade from the old farm-boundary oaks, and a cool, water-retaining, fine silty soil. Overall the soil was acid. We marked several oaks and hollies worth preserving and put a bulldozer through the twenty-feet-high bramble tangles, the willow swamps and tall bracken beds.

We hoped to make an informal garden that would harmonise with the surrounding countryside, and would eventually be beautiful and interesting all the year round. With such differing aspects and conditions we had in mind three distinctly different types of garden. Around the house, situated on the warm gravel slope, we decided to plant only those plants and shrubs, which can stand prolonged drought and hungry soil. This we called our Mediterranean garden, since many of the plants and shrubs are found growing wild in those southern countries of Europe.

The sites facing north-east, where the soil was better, have become our shade gardens. We planted larger-leafed trees and shrubs to add to the shade, where we can now grow those plants that have been collected from the temperate forests of the world.

Finally we made the Bog garden. Over a period of several years we have made five large ponds by damming the spring-fed ditch. The clay was dragged up to form four dams across the floor of the valley, so flooding the low marshy area, while the shallow edges provide moist beds for bog plants. The dams have been levelled and grassed to make green walks across the water, splendid vantage points to enjoy the lush water plants, the busy ducks and moorhens, and the host of red-finned rudd that surge around, hoping to be fed.

In the beginning, apart from the few magnificent oaks and the varying levels, there were no features, no backgrounds and no sheltered corners. We lost too many plants in our impatience to possess them, because we had not achieved the proper growing conditions. Often plants were shrivelled by the desiccating east wind which blows endlessly it seems all spring and half the summer, or we planted too soon in ill-prepared soil, and in no time at all our treasures were swamped by rampant natives. As well as the need for shelter, we also learnt the value of good planting. Fortunately, the stacked mounds of rotted weeds provided rich, fibrous compost, so, following the great gardener, Gertrude Jekyll, I like to plant almost everything in a large hole, filled up with this sweet-smelling, spongy mixture. From another enterprising gardener, I have learnt one can compost almost all household waste. Surround a shallow pit with concrete blocks, make a wire-netting lid to cover it, and into this pile sink-waste, old newspapers, letters, and waste material other than man-made plastics or fibres. It all rots down, and over the year can be scraped out and sandwiched between layers of a compost heap that is being turned. We have the advantage of using a forklift on the front of a tractor to turn our heaps. We also use well-rotted muck, but mostly as a top-dressing.

Over the past years we have learnt the value of mulching, as much for its labour saving effect as for its moisture-retaining properties. Now, when we have made a new bed, or are remaking an older one, and have finally planted it, we then cover all the bare earth with a 5cm layer of crushed bark. This sterile layer acts like a carpet, stifling the millions of weeds that are struggling to germinate out of my compost. Where there would have been a green film of weeds like sown mustard and cress, there may be here and there a recalcitrant clump of grass or chickweed, which are a comparative pleasure to pull out. Running menaces like creeping thistle or bindweed, or deep-rooted perennials like docks or dandelions, if not previously exterminated, are hand painted with a diluted solution of systemic weedkiller.

To supplement this weed-suppressing mulch, there must be a growing covering of foliage. This carpet of leaves of various shapes and sizes gives me greater pleasure than almost any other feature in the garden. The endless patterns, forms and textures, the wide range of subtle or dramatic colours continue to create interest for much of the year. Not all remain throughout the winter, of course, but all do make a valuable contribution to the design and furnishing of the garden for many months. In one season, a newly planted bed can be almost grown over with ground-cover plants if carefully planned.

Although I have mentioned that the soil is acid, practically all the plants in this handbook are lime tolerant. The most notable lime haters are members of the family Ericaceae, the rhododendrons, summer-flowering heathers and their relatives. Whatever your soil you can grow almost anything if you achieve reasonable depth that is both aerated and containing some humus. Those people who are unable to obtain enough humus will find many of the plants listed under Hot, Dry Conditions will survive or even thrive, especially the silver foliage plants, which can readily rot where the soil is heavy and the rainfall too generous. I must confess that I cannot offer such an easy way out for those owners of cold sticky clay. Although plants such as roses and other strong tap-rooted plants seem able and willing to thrust their way through, I myself try to bury the clay beneath mixed layers of compost, sand, leaf mould and anything I can find, to make a medium in which I can work.

Finally a thought on design in the garden. I like to plant in groups, which will eventually grow to form roughly asymmetrical triangles. On a large scale, the low places, or gaps, created by these visually interlocking shapes, reveal new views beyond, which are pleasing. Even groups of small plants arranged on this principle look more interesting. A group I enjoy in the Dry Garden, for example, has for height the soft, brown, cloudy bronze fennel, surrounded by bushes of the purple sage and the golden *Salvia officinalis* 'Icterina', leading down to mats of scented thyme on the ground.

Whatever the scale of planting, some plants with large simple leaves are a 'must' to provide an area of rest for the mind and eye. They act as a full stop at the end of a sentence. After enjoying many fascinating things in a border, it is a relief to come to a big bold shape and rest there for a bit. Bergenias and hostas are ideal for this purpose, while on a larger scale, perhaps in a bay among fussy-leaved shrubs, an imposing clump of the ornamental rhubarb (*Rheum palmatum*) can be guaranteed to refresh.

So, to simplify, these are my basic principles of gardening:

1. To provide plants as far as possible with the kind of conditions for which nature has fitted them.

2. To plant in planned groups and not dotted like pins in a pincushion.

3. To cover the ground with foliage for as long as possible.

4. To provide relief with the occasional bold plant.

The Gravel Garden

Many years ago visitors to the garden will remember parking on the grass on the area of land, which lies in front of the house and nursery entrance. We now have a new and larger grassed car park outside the leylandii hedge. What could I do with the old car park surrounded by tree and shrub borders? In the winter of 1991-92 the site was prepared to make a new Gravel Garden. The land, about a third of a hectare was ploughed and then sub-soiled to break up the hard compacted layer after years of parking cars. Next, using several long hosepipes, I laid out the design. I had in mind the picture of a dried-up river bed, so I made the main path to wind through the centre of the irregular rectangle, forming long curving borders on either side, with room here and there for the odd island bed.

We dug a wide and deep hole to study the sub-soil. After a shallow layer of topsoil we found orange sand and gravel, hungry and dry. With our low rainfall, 50cm a year on average, this site could only support plants adapted by nature to drought, and droughts for us in Essex are a regular feature, not an occasional disaster.

Watching the poor stony soil fall through the tines of the fork I knew we must incorporate all the organic material we had been collecting for this project. Home-made compost, well-rotted farmyard manure, and bought-in mushroom compost were all used, spread thickly over the areas to be planted and then rotavated in, and allowed to settle. This preparation was necessary, even for drought-tolerant plants because I do not intend to irrigate the area. Plants will have been given a good start, but then must get their roots down and survive, or not, as the case may be. If some unwisely chosen plants die, in long weeks of drought, they will not be replaced, except by plants better adapted to this hard discipline.

By this experiment we are learning which plants will survive and look well in spite of the hosepipe bans imposed over many parts of the country when water supplies are threatened. We hope our visitors from such areas will be encouraged to see a wide range of plants, which look neither shabby nor distressed after weeks without rain or watering.

During July and August 1994 we had no measurable rainfall together with high temperatures. This caused signs of stress in some plants. Those worst affected we cut back, (using the secateurs rather than the hosepipe), and to our relief once the rains came, they soon made fresh growth, some flowering again in autumn.

All the plants and shrubs in this garden recovered well with cooler conditions, showing no gaps or other signs of stress. Overall the Gravel Garden has become our best winter feature, with so much contrast of textures and colour from good overwintering foliage, while late autumn bulbs lead us gently into a short winter with spring bulbs making an early appearance in the warm, well-drained soil.

Since making the Gravel Garden we have had comparatively mild winters, temperatures seldom dropping below -6°C and that not lasting for any length of time. So far there has been little noticeable frost damage even though this garden is on an open exposed site. Some protection is afforded by a 3m tall leylandii hedge, which checks the cruel north-east winds. The mulch of 10mm gravel, spread over all the borders 5cm deep, the same as that used for the paths, now also affords some protection to roots and bulbs and presents a good appearance since there are no hard edges to the borders; the plants advance and retreat like the tide with the ebb and flow of seasonal growth.

How to use this Handbook

I hope you will not skip by these introductory remarks in your enthusiasm to find treasures buried in the main body of this handbook. If you are an experienced and knowledgeable gardener you will know what you are looking for and what to do with it when you have found it, but for those less sure of what to put together I would urge you to consider first the soil and aspect of your garden and then to study the classified lists that are at the beginning of the handbook and select those nearest your conditions. Almost any of the plants listed for specified conditions will create a picture when planted together.

I am sometimes asked how one decides to put plants together to create a harmonious whole. My reply goes something like this. Designing the garden is like learning to speak. You begin with odd words, learning the individual plants. Then you create a simple phrase, finding two or three plants that look well together, next comes a sentence and finally the complete story, with embellishments still to come. In your garden the theme of your story will be governed by your site, whether it is open and sunny, a cool shady border, or a bit of damp land, which might become a bog garden.

Another analogy is to consider your garden as an outside room. It will need a background (curtains and wallpaper) provided by a tree (or trees according to space), wall shrubs or climbers. Next bulky shrubs take the place of large pieces of furniture like bookcases, wardrobes or armchairs, and then you must provide a floor covering with ground cover plants. Finally you will need occasional plants or star performers representing your standard lamp, pieces of china or pictures.

We do not supply trees and only a few of the less commonly known shrubs, but once you have made the woody framework of your garden we can supply plants for any kind of situation, helping, we hope, to solve most problems with regard to soil and site.

Soil types and weather vary so much, even within a few miles. Each of us must learn by experience the varying conditions that exist even in the smallest garden. You will know where the sun strikes most of the day, whether your soil needs a good rain every week, which corner remains cool and dark most of the year. None of these situations need be a problem if you find plants which are adapted by nature to those very conditions.

With experience you come to appreciate the value of good foliage. It is possible to create an attractive and long-lasting effect providing contrast in colour, texture and form by considering foliage alone, while most of those plants will flower also in their season. This type of planting prolongs the live season of the garden. With thoughtful planning it is possible and pleasurable to enjoy a furnished garden every month of the year, rather than contemplate the bleak aspect that can result if borders are planned for flower colour alone.

We must put up with our rainfall, be it too little or too much, but in either situation we can do much to improve the soil, thereby ameliorating adverse conditions. Even the best soil needs pampering. We must put back what is being taken out by cutting down of remains, or removal of weeds.

Apart from feeding the micro-organisms, which turn vegetable waste into available plant food, we can also do much to improve the texture of the soil. Old beds sometimes need to be partially emptied and deeply dug to aerate the compacted soil. If, on the other hand you have liberally mulched the soil with humus over many years a thriving population of earthworms will have kept the soil well aerated with their tunnelling.

Heavy sticky soil is improved if generous shovelfuls of pea-sized grit (not sand) are thrown across the face of your trench as you dig. Autumn is a good time before the soil is too wet, and you can add well rotted compost or manure then as well.

Starved sandy soils or gravels constantly need additional humus so consider garden compost, well rotted manure or mushroom compost but not if you wish to grow lime-hating plants, since spent mushroom compost contains chalk.

Once beds are planted and weed-free, a good mulch spread at least 2-5cm thick and left undisturbed, will cut down tremendously the number of germinating weed seedlings, as well as help to conserve moisture. Pulverised bark is most easily obtained. I also use straw, bought in bales after the harvest, and spread it thickly in the centre of large beds, beneath trees and shrubs and large coarse plants. A light dressing of nitrogenous fertiliser is scattered over the mulch in spring.

Mulches do not need to be re-applied every year. The second time round your plants will have covered much of the bare soil, and only where the mulch has blown thin, or you have disturbed it, will you need to add a few bucketfuls here and there.

Plants are very accommodating. Many will survive without all this care and attention, but I am constantly surprised and delighted by the response of my plants when I have done my best for them.

Grow contented plants and you will find peace among them.

BETH CHATTO

Drought Tolerant Plants

I have used plants from this list in making the Gravel Garden. Many small and low-growing plants for hot, dry conditions can easily be overgrown, so I have designed a new scree-garden for them, a series of slightly raised beds over the same gravel sub-soil as we have in the Gravel Garden. In these beds I am using small plants.

The following two lists contain plants which in my experience stand long periods of drought and full sun without dying. Most require well-drained soil, they will not survive being waterlogged in winter. Plants destined for very poor sand or gravel soils will be grateful for additional humus, either when planting or as a mulch. An additional mulch of weed-free material overall will help prevent excessive evaporation and suppress weed seedlings. In good garden soil all these plants will flourish like weeds. All tolerate lime.

Small and low-growing plants for hot, dry conditions

Acaena
Achillea – (dwarf forms)
Anemone × *fulgens*
Anemone pavonina
Antennaria
Anthemis – (dwarf forms)
Arabis
Armeria
Artemisia – (dwarf forms)
Asperula aristata
Aubrieta
Aurinia
Belamcanda
Calamintha
Cerastium
Chamaemelum
Cotula lineariloba
Dianthus
Diascia
Erigeron karviskianus
Eriophyllum
Erodium
Erysimum
Euphorbia cyparissias
Euphorbia myrsinites
Fritillaria (not *F. melengris*)
Gypsophila – (not *G. paniculata*)
Haplopappus
Helianthemum
Hypericum – (dwarf forms)
Iberis

Ipheion
Iris 'Green Spot'
Iris unguicularis
Leptinella squalida
Libertia peregrinans
Lychnis flos-jovis
Melissa
Muscari macrocarpum
Oenothera macrocarpa
Origanum
Osteospermum
Phlox douglasii
Phlox subulata
Potentilla calabra
Raoulia
Rhodanthemum hosmariense
Saginia
Saponaria
Scilla peruviana
Sedum – (dwarf forms)
Sempervivum
Serratula seoanei
Silene uniflora
Stachys byzantina
Teucrium × *lucidrys*
Thymus
Tulbaghia violacea
Urospermum dalechampii
Verbena 'La France'
Zauschneria

Bulbs

Allium – (dwarf forms)
Arum creticum
Ipheion

Nerine
Ornithogalum
Tulipa sprengeri

Grasses to use with some of the plants listed above

Elymus magellanicus
Festuca
Holcus mollis

Koeleria glauca
Pennisetum
Stipa tenuissima

Medium to large plants for hot, dry conditions

Acanthus
Agapanthus
Alstroemeria ligtu hybrids
Anaphalis margaritacea
Anthemis cupaniana and 'Tetworth'
Anthericum
Artemisia
Asphodeline
Asphodelus
Ballota
Bupleurum falcatum
Centaurea
Centranthus
Cichorium
Cistus
Commelina
Convolvulus cneorum
Crambe
Crinum
Cynara
Dictamnus
Echinops
Eryngium
Euphorbia characias subsp. wulfenii
Euphorbia corallioides
Euphorbia epithymoides
Ferula

Foeniculum
Gaura
Gladiolus papilio
Glaucium
Grindelia
Gypsophila paniculata
× Halimiocistus
Iris – bearded
Lavandula
Libertia grandiflora
Linaria
Linum
Lychnis coronaria
Nectaroscordum siculum subsp. bulgaricum
Nepeta
Onopordum
Parahebe perfoliata
Perovskia
Phlomis
Romneya coulteri
Salvia
Santolina
Sedum
Senecio
Stachys
Verbascum

Bulbs

Allium

Gladiolus

Grasses to use with some of the plants listed above

Ampelodesmos mauritanica
Eragrostis curvula
Helictotrichon
Leymus arenarius

Melica altissima
Oryzopsis miliacea
Poa labillardieri
Stipa

Shade Loving Plants

Many of these plants prefer to be protected from direct sunlight, for part, if not all, of the day. None like to be starved or dried out, either by lack of rainfall or root competition. Shade, or part shade from trees or buildings will provide good sites together with shelter from drying wind. Poor soils which suffer from low rainfall should have plenty of moisture-holding material well incorporated before planting. Plants with yellow leaves need enough light to keep their foliage bright, but not direct sunlight which will scorch them. Plants grown primarily for flower, such as primula or violas will need more sunlight than those grown for large and handsome foliage. Provided these points are kept in mind none of these plants are difficult, none require drenched peaty soils or high humidity, both conditions unattainable in our garden here in East Anglia.

Small and low-growing plants for shade

Adonis 'Fukujukai'
Ajuga
Alchemilla conjuncta
Alchemilla erythropoda
Androsace geranifolia
Anemone – (low forms)
Aquilegia – (dwarf)
Arisarum
Aruncus aethusifolius
Asarum
Astilbe – (dwarf forms)
Cardamine
Chiastophyllum
Convallaria
Corydalis flexuosa
Cryptotaenia
Dactylorhiza
Dicentra formosa
Disporum
Epimedium
Epipactis gigantea
Ficaria verna
Fragaria
Galium odoratum
Geranium – (lower growing forms)
Haquetia epipactis
Hepatica
Heuchera
× *Heucherella*
Lamium
Leptinella
Liriope
Lysimachia nummularia

Mentha
Mitella
Omphalodes
Ophiopogon planiscapus 'Nigrescens'
Oxalis sp ex Mount Stewart
Pachysandra
Persicaria affine
Phlox divaricata
Phlox stolonifera
Polygonatum curvistylum
Primula denticulata
Primula polyneura
Primula vulgaris
Pulmonaria
Reineckia
Roscoea cautleyoides
Sagina
Saxifraga
Solidago caesia
Symphytum – low forms
Tanacetum parthenium
Tellima
Teucrium
Thalictrum kiusianum
Tiarella
Tolmeia
Trifolium
Uvularia perfoliata
Vancouveria
Veronica gentianoides
Vinca
Viola
Waldsteinia

Bulbs

Arum italicum
Colchicum
Erythronium
Fritillaria camschatcensis

Galanthus
Leucojum vernum
Narcissus

Ferns to use with some of the plants listed above

Adiantum pedatum 'Imbricatum'
Athyrium filix-femina 'Minutissimum'
Athyrium niponicum var. pictum

Blechnum penna-marina
Cystopteris fragilis

Grasses to use with some of the plants listed above

Carex oshimensis
Deschampsia 'Tatra Gold'
Hakonechloa
Holcus

Luzula
Milium effusum 'Aureum'
Molinia caerulea 'Moorhexe'

Medium to large plants for shade

Heavy soil lightened with 10mm grit, lighter soil enriched with compost, or good leaf mould type soil – all will suit the following plants together with shade or part-shade provided by walls or trees. They must not be waterlogged in winter or leaf scorched and dried out in summer. Some, like digitalis will stand dry shade but are repeated here as they add much to this group and thrive in better conditions.

Aconitum
Actaea
Alchemilla mollis
Anemone – border forms
Angelica
Aquilegia
Artemisia lactiflora
Aruncus dioicus
Astilbe
Astilboides tabularis
Astrantia
Brunnera
Cenolophium denudatum
Datisca cannabina
Delphinium
Digitalis
Diphylleia cymosa
Filipendula ulmaria 'Aurea'
Fuchsia
Hedera

Helleborus
Hosta
Kirengeshoma
Lamprocapnos spectabilis (Dicentra spectabilis)
Ligularia
Lysimachia
Maianthemum racemosum
Myrrhis
Pachyphragma
Paeonia
Persicaria
Polygonatum
Pulmonaria
Rheum
Rodgersia
Trachystemon
Tricyrtis
Trillium
Veratrum
Zantedeschia

Ferns to use with some of the plants listed above

Blechnum chilense
Blechnum spicant

Matteuccia
Polystichum

Grasses to use with some of the plants listed above

Carex elata 'Aurea'
Deschampsia
Melica uniflora f albida

Miscanthus
Panicum
Pleiobastus

Dry Shade

This is a difficult situation for plants but it can be planted successfully. Usually there is adequate moisture in spring, but the soil becomes dried out by tree or shrub roots as the season progresses. Additional humus plus mulching if possible will help.

Ajuga
Alchemilla
Arum
Bergenia
Brunnera
Cyclamen
Dicentra formosa
Digitalis
Epimedium
Euphorbia a. robbiae
Euphorbia cyparissias
Geranium endressii
Geranium macrorrhizum
Geranium nodosum
Geranium × oxonianum
Geranium phaeum
Hedera
Helleborus foetidus
Hypericum androsaemum
Lamium
Liriope
Lunaria
Melissa
Pachysandra
Polygonatum
Pulmonaria
Rubus
Symphytum
Tellima
Teucrium
Thalictrum
Tiarella
Tolmeia
Trachystemon
Valeriana
Vinca
Viola riviniana
Waldsteinia

Ferns to use with some of the plants listed above

Dryopteris filix-mas

Polystichum setiferum Acutilobum Group

Grasses to use with some of the plants listed above

Carex
Holcus mollis 'Albovariegatus'

Milium

Plants for Waterside and Bog

These plants like full sun, but they will not stand soil which dries out. Soil conditions vary in borders made along ditch sides or pond edge. Water does not travel far into heavy soil sideways, so the soil becomes drier the further you go from the source of water. Although needing regular moisture, some plants will not tolerate saturated soil, especially in winter when they will rot. These include astilbes, gunnera and rheum. Others, like myosotis, acorus, and houttuynia are amphibians, and will climb in or out of the water.

This first list indicates plants which will thrive in water or water-logged soil.

For shallow water, i.e. marginal plants

Acorus
Caltha
Cardamine pratensis
Houttuynia
Iris 'Gerald Darby'
Iris laevigata
Iris pseudacorus

Iris versicolor
Lysichiton
Lythrum
Myosotis scorpioides
Pontederia
Zantedeschia

Grasses or grasslike plants for water edge

Butomus umbellatus

Carex elata 'Aurea'

Ferns for water edge

Onoclea sensibilis

Plants for constantly damp, but not water-logged soil, in full sun

Astilbe
Darmera
Eupatorium
Euphorbia palustris
Filipendula
Gunnera
Helianthus
Hemerocallis
Hosta
Inula
Iris ensata
Iris sibirica
Ligularia
Lysimachia

Lythrum
*Myosotis scorpioides
Persicaria
*Petasites
Primula bulleyana
Primula florindae
Primula japonica
Primula pulverulenta
Ranunculus acris 'Flore Pleno'
Ranunculus constantinopolitanus 'Plenus'
Rheum
Rodgersia
Valeriana pyrenaica
Verbena corymbosa

Grasses or grasslike plants to combine with above

Carex pendula
Deschampsia
*Glyceria maxima
Luzula sylvatica
Miscanthus

Phalaris arundinacea var. picta 'Feesey'
*Sasa veitchii
Uncinia uncinata

*Invasive plants.

Ferns to combine with above

Matteuccia struthiopteris. (prefers shade)
Onoclea sensibilis

Osmunda regalis

Plants for Retentive Soil in Sun

The following plants will flourish in average garden conditions, that is, well prepared, reasonably retentive soil which sees plants through all but abnormal drought. They could suffer under conditions which the first two lists will tolerate but in suitable circumstances, (with adequate rainfall) some plants from these two classifications could be combined.

Small and low-growing plants for retentive soil in sun

Ajuga
Alchemilla conjuncta
Alchemilla erythropoda
Androsace
Anemone multifida
Aquilegia – (dwarf forms)
Arctanthemum arcticum
Arthropodium candidum
Aruncus aethusifolius
Astilbe – (dwarf forms)
Bergenia – (dwarf forms)
Buglossoides purpurocaerulea
Ceratostigma plumbaginoides
Chrysogonum virginianum
Coreopis
Erigeron
Geranium – (dwarf forms)
Geum
Hemerocallis – (dwarf forms)
Heuchera
× Heucherella
Iris graminea
Iris innominata
Iris japonica
Jasione laevis 'Blaulicht'

Kalimeris
Lychnis viscaria
Nepeta nervosa
Omphalodes
Ophiopogon
Origanum vulgare 'Aureum'
Parahebe
Persicaria – (dwarf forms)
Phlox – (dwarf forms)
Potentilla neumanniana
Potentilla × tonguei
Pratia
Primula pubescens
Primula denticulata
Prunella
Pulsatilla vulgaris
Serratula seoaneii
Silene
Sisyrinchium – (dwarf forms)
Stokesia laevis
Symphotrichum (Aster) – (low growing forms)
Trifolium
Viola
Zigadenus

Bulbs

Arum creticum
Colchicum
Erythronium

Fritillaria meleagris
Leucojum

Grasses to use with some of the plants listed above

Alopecurus
Carex
Holcus
Imperata
Luzula

Melica
Molinia
Pennisetum
Phalaris

Medium to large plants for retentive soil in sun

Achillea – (border types)
Aconitum
Agastache
Alchemilla mollis
Amsonia
Angelica
Anthemis tinctoria
Anthericum
Aquilegia
Arctanthemum arcticum
Artemisia lactiflora
Aruncus dioicus
Aster
Astilbe
Astrantia
Baptisia
Bergenia – (large forms)
Buphthalmum
Camassia
Campanula
Canna
Cenolophium denudatum
Centaurea
Cephalaria
Chaerophyllum
Chelone
Chamaemelum angustifolium var. album
Chrysanthemum
Cirsium rivulare
Crocosmia
Delphinium

Dierama
Dipsacus inermis
Echinacea purpurea
Elsholtzia stauntonii
Eupatorium
Euphorbia griffithii
Euphorbia palustris
Euphorbia sikkimensis
Eurybia (Aster)
Fagopyrum dibotrys
Filipendula
Fuchsia
Geranium
Gillenia trifoliata
Gypsophila 'Flamingo'
Hedychium densiflorum
Helenium
Helianthus
Helleborus
Hemerocallis
Hesperantha (Schizostyllis)
Houttuynia
Incarvillea
Inula
Iris ensata
Iris sibirica
Kalimeris
Kirengeshoma
Knautia
Kniphofia
Leucanthemum × superbum

Liatris
Libertia
Ligularia
Limonium platyphyllum
Lobelia
Lychnis chalcedonica
Lysimachia
Lythrum
Macleaya
Monarda
Morina
Nepeta govaniana
Nepeta sibirica
Nerine
Origanum 'Rosenkuppel'
Papaver orientale
Patrinia
Penstemon
Persicaria
Phlox – (medium to large forms)
Physostegia
Polemonium
Potentilla 'Gibson's Scarlet'
Potentilla nepalensis
Potentilla rupestris

Ranunculus aconitifolius
Ranunculus acris 'Flore Pleno'
Rheum
Rudbeckia
Salvia uliginosa
Sanguisorba
Scabiosa caucasica
Scrophularia auriculata 'Variegata'
Sidalcea
Sinacalia tangutica
Solidago caesia
Stachys macrantha
Stachys officinalis
Symphytum 'Hidcote Pink' and 'Hidcote Blue'
Thalictrum
Thermopsis lupinoides
Tradescantia
Tricyrtis
Tritonia
Trollius
Valeriana officinalis
Vernonia
Veronicastrum virginicum
Zigadenus

Grasses to use with some of the plants listed above

Calamagrostis
Carex pendula
Chasmanthum latifolium
Cortaderia
Deschampsia cespitosa 'Goldschleier'
Luzula sylvatica

Miscanthus
Molinia
Panicum
Sorghastrum
Spartina

Plants for Clay Soils

The big problem with clay soil is the close texture which impedes drainage, so it lies cold, sticky and wet in winter, often setting like concrete in summer. Young plants can be lost, unable to penetrate such soil, before they become established. I find that sharp pea-grit, bought from a local gravel pit, spread thickly, and dug in, together with whatever vegetable waste (muck, garden compost) I can find makes a much more friable texture in which to plant.

Where our land has suffered waterlogging, trenches dug about 45cm to 60cm deep, half-filled with coarse stone, then in-filled have also helped tremendously.

This work needs to be done in autumn, ready for planting the following spring. Once planting is completed a mulch (straw under shrubs, crushed bark or leaf mould among plants) has also helped tremendously to maintain a better soil structure, and prevent hard capping in summer. This kind of preparation may be impossible for everyone, but even a small effort, adding something to each hole when planting, will be rewarded by a real improvement in plant health and vigour. Plants with fine soft roots, adapted to ferreting through leaf mould will not succeed in clay soils.

Once a raw soil has been well worked and humus added over a number of years many more plants requiring good moisture-retaining soil, e.g. astilbe, primula, etc. can be added. When established the following will flourish:

Acanthus
Alchemilla
Anemone × *hybrida*
Aruncus
Bergenia
Brunnera
Caltha
Darmera
Epimedium
Eupatorium
Euphorbia a. var. *robbiae*
Hedera
Helleborus
Hemerocallis
Hosta
Inula
Kniphofia

Lamium
Petasites
Polygonatum
Primula – (some)
Prunella
Pulmonaria
Ranunculus
Rheum
Rodgersia
Rubus
Salix
Saxifraga 'Aureopunctata'
Symphytum
Trachystemon
Vinca
Waldsteinia

Grasses to use with some of the plants listed above

Alopecurus pratensis 'Aureus'
Carex
Deschampsia
Fargesia – (Bamboo)
Miscanthus

Molinia
Panicum
Pleiobastus – (Bamboo)
Sasa veitchii – (Bamboo)
Spartina

Plants for Naturalizing

For many years my plant lists have suggested the desirability of grouping plants in the garden as they grow together in nature. Difficult places – hot and dry, wet or shady – become advantageous when you know the plants to use to transform once shabby areas.

I hope the following lists will help home-gardeners and landscape designers anxious to create both a labour-saving, and a more natural style of planting. A run down orchard or meadow, roadsides, or areas in urban parks – anywhere where conventional herbaceous borders can no longer be maintained – these are some of the places I have in mind.

Ornamental grasses should be given an important role in the overall scheme, as their graceful outlines last for most of the season. They give much needed contrast, and create a softness and naturalness among many flowering and handsome foliage plants. The combined effect evokes the same emotions we feel when we see a flowering bankside or meadow in England, or see colourful alpine meadows.

If this style is to be adopted in freshly prepared soil, then a certain amount of maintenance will be needed to weed out undesirable local 'weeds' until the intended planting covers the area, making its own weed control. A mulch in the first season would be helpful. Once the introduced plants have established themselves, native plants can be allowed in and will all together, enhance the natural effect. Eventually seeding and natural increase will achieve a much prettier effect than rigid detailed planning. Future maintenance will only require cutting down and tidying up in autumn, always watching out for unwanted rogues like oak and bramble seedlings, nettles or docks.

If you contemplate planting in existing grass, then please do prepare adequate holes, deep and wide enough with improved soil added if existing soil is starved. Robust plants such as acanthus, fennel, gunnera in damp soil, indeed most of those listed below will flourish and reappear from strong crowns, tubers, or bulbs, with no further assistance except the addition of a light annual dressing of well-made compost to take the place of herbaceous material removed in tidying up.

It is not necessary to use many different plants to achieve a good effect. In the early stages of my present garden I planted a few bold plants, *Aruncus dioicus, Leucanthemella serotina* and *Rheum palmatum,* in roughly mown grass, around groups of young trees, alongside a close mown grass walk. The effect was an immediate improvement and involved no extra work. More recently I have been naturalizing bulbous plants and others suited to the conditions, in grass, in shade and part shade, among oak trees.

These lists are by no means exhaustive. It would be worthwhile trying other strong growing plants, according to soil and conditions.

Plants for naturalizing in well-drained, medium soil, in sun

Acanthus
Achillea
Asphodeline
Asphodelus
Centaurea macrocephala
Crambe cordifolia
Crocosmia
Echinops ritro
Eryngium
Euphorbia cyparissias
Foeniculum
Geranium
Knautia
Kniphofia
Lathyrus latifolius
Liatris
Macleaya
Papaver orientale
Pulsatilla
Salvia × superba
Verbascum

Grasses to use with some of the plants listed above

Helictotrichon
Holcus mollis 'Albovariegatus'
Koeleria glauca
Leymus arenarius

Melica altissima
Stipa calamagrostis
Stipa gigantea

Bulbs

Such as crocus and lilies could also be used.

Plants for naturalizing in retentive to damp soil in sun

Alchemilla
Artemisia lactiflora
Aruncus dioicus
Aster
Astrantia
Campanula lactiflora
Cephalaria gigantea
Datisca cannabina
Dipsacus inermis
Eupatorium
Euphorbia griffithii
Euphorbia sikkimensis
Eurybia - (Aster)
Filipendula
Gunnera

Hemerocallis sp.
Inula hookeri
Inula magnifica
Iris pseudacorus
Leucanthemella serotina
Ligularia
Lythrum
Packera
Persicaria
Petasites
Phytolacca
Rheum
Rudbeckia
Veratrum

Grasses to use with some of the plants listed above

Alopecurus pratensis 'Aureus'
Carex elata 'Aurea'
Carex pendula
Deschampsia caespitosa 'Goldschleier'
Miscanthus
Molinia

Panicum
Pennisetum alopecuroides
Sasa veitchii –
    an invasive but handsome bamboo
Spartina

Bulbs

Colchicum
Camassia

Galanthus
Narcissus sp.

Plants for naturalizing in part shade, or light woodland, but not too dry

Aconitum
Actaea
Ajuga

Anemone nemorosa
Aquilegia
Arum italicum

Astrantia
Cardamine
Convallaria
Datisca cannabina
Dicentra
Digitalis lutea
Digitalis purpurea f. *albiflora*
Epimedium
Euphorbia amygdaloides var. *robbiae*
Filipendula ulmaria
Galium
Hedera
Helleborus
Hosta
Lamium
Liriope

Maianthemum
Pachyphragma
Pachysandra
Phlox stolonifera
Polygonatum
Primula polyneura
Primula vulgaris
Pulmonaria
Symphytum
Tellima
Tiarella
Tolmeia
Trachystemon
Tricyrtis
Vinca
Viola riviniana

Grasses and grass-like plants to use with some of the plants listed above

Luzula
Melica

Milium
Panicum

Bulbs

Anemone nemorosa
Cyclamen

Erythronium
Galanthus (Snowdrops)

Ferns to use with some of the plants listed above

Dryopteris filix-mas
Matteuccia struthiopteris

Polystichum

Ground-covering Plants

It is possible to have a great deal of the hard work of keeping the garden clean and tidy done by the plants themselves. This involves planting suitable types which gradually, or rapidly according to needs, cover the ground so densely that few weeds penetrate. Many of these plants are evergreen, or ever-grey, and so provide a welcome furnishing throughout the bleakness of winter.

However, it would be most unwise to plant ground-cover on 'dirty' soil. All perennial weeds must be eliminated before planting. It is possible to have a great deal of the hard work of keeping the garden clean and tidy done by the plants themselves. This involves planting suitable types which gradually, or rapidly according to needs, cover the ground so densely that few weeds penetrate. Many of these plants are evergreen, especially running root-stocks such as twitch grass and sorrel, must be eliminated before planting. The easiest way to do this, apart from careful digging, is to use on the unplanted ground, one of the recommended weedkillers. But, it is most important to obtain expert advice before you buy. The number and complexity of weed-killing materials today is very confusing, and they can do much damage to all forms of life. Nevertheless they are a boon if used carefully and intelligently. Certain perpetual nuisances such as bind-weed and thistle can be dealt with after planting by dabbing the growing tips with a systemic weed killer on a paintbrush. This will eliminate them, although it may take several doses.

During the first year the newly planted bed will require some weeding of annuals and small seedlings. But if these are dealt with promptly the next year's weeding will be very much less, and the spaces for weeds rapidly become smaller.

Acaena
Achillea
Ajuga
Alchemilla
Anaphalis
Anthemis
Arabis
Arctanthemum arcticum
Arenaria montana
Armeria maritima
Aurinia
Ballota
Bergenia
Brunnera
Campanula – (some)
Ceratostigma plumbaginoides
Chiastophyllum
Cistus
Crambe cordifolia
Darmera peltata
Dianthus
Diascia
Dicentra
Epimedium
Erigeron
Eriophyllum

Euphorbia
Festuca
Filipendula
Fragaria 'Chaval'
Geranium
Geum
Gunnera – (dwarf forms)
Hebe
Hedera
Helichrysum 'Schweffellicht'
Helleborus
Heuchera
Holcus
Hosta
Hypericum
Lamium
Luzula
Lychnis
Lysimachia
Marrubium
Melissa
Mentha
Monarda
Myosotis
Nepeta
Omphalodes

Onosma
Origanum vulgare 'Aureum'
Osteospermum
Pachyphragma
Pachysandra
Persicara – (most)
Petasites
Phlomis
Phlox – (Rock-garden species)
Phuopsis
Phyla nodiflora
Potentilla
Pratia
Prunella
Pulmonaria
Rubus tricolor
Salvia officinalis
Santolina
Saponaria

Saxifraga – (some)
Sedum
Senecio
Stachys
Symphytum
Tanacetum densum
Tellima
Teucrium scorodonia
Thymus
Tiarella
Tolmeia
Trachystemon
Trifolium
Verbena corymbosa
Veronica
Vinca
Viola
Waldsteinia

Evergreen Plants

Plants which keep their leaves in winter are often worth more than flamboyant neighbours which disappear completely when conditions are grim. They give pleasure all the year round, give a reason for walking in the garden in winter and help to present a picture from the house.

Hot sandy or gravel soils which cause concern in dry summers often provide the most furnished areas in winter, apart from an absence of flowers in several winter months, the view from my office window scarcely changes, being predominantly 'Mediterranean' plants, planted in gravel. The following list includes a few shrubby plants as well as:

Plants which keep their leaves in warm well-drained soils

Achillea – (some)
Anthemis punctata subsp. cupaniana
Anthemis tinctoria
Arabis
Artemisia (not A. lactiflora)
Aurinia
Ballota
Bergenia
Dianthus
Dierama
Eryngium agavifolium
Eryngium eburneum
Euphorbia – (drought loving kinds)
Grindelia
× Halimiocistus
Hebe
Helianthemum
Helichrysum
Hyssopus

Iberis
Lavandula
Marrubium
Othonna
Phlox douglasii
Potentilla calabra
Raoulia
Rhodanthemum hosmariense
Ruta
Salvia officinalis
Santolina
Sedum oreganum
Sedum spathulifolium
Sedum spurium
Sempervivum
Senecio – (grey-leafed forms)
Stachys byzantina
Thymus

Grasses

Festuca
Helictotrichon
Koeleria
Poa
Stipa gigantea

Plants which keep their leaves in retentive soil, in sun

Ajuga
Bergenia
Geranium – (some)
Hebe
Helleborus
Heuchera
× *Heucherella*
Iris innominata
Libertia
Limonium
Lychnis viscaria
Ophiopogon
Persicaria affinis - retains its leaves which turn reddish-brown and remain all winter.
Phlomis russeliana
Phlox subulata
Potentilla neumanniana
Primula pubescens
Viola

Plants which keep their leaves in cooler shady conditions

Alchemilla conjuncta
Alchemilla erythropoda
Arum italicum subsp. *Italicum 'Marmoratum'* – not evergreen but appears in November and is one of the best winter foliage plants.
Cardamine trifolia
Carex oshimensis
Chiastophyllum
Digitalis parviflora
Epimedium
Euphorbia amygdaloides var. *robbiae*
Geum rivale
Hedera
Helleborus
Heuchera
× *Heucherella*
Holcus mollis
Lamium
Leptinella
Liriope
Mitella
Ophiopogon
Pachysandra
Phlox stolonifera
Polystichum
Pulmonaria
Reineckia
Saxifraga – (some)
Symphytum
Tanacetum parthenium
Tellima
Teucrium scorodonia 'Crispum Marginatum'
Tiarella
Tolmeia
Vinca
Viola
Waldsteinia

Handsome Foliage Plants

As well as needing large and elegant leaves to set off handsome flower arrangements in the house, so the garden design is improved if groups of foliage are used in contrasting scale, colour, and texture. Many types of plant are needed to make harmonious patterns. The less conspicuous, unobtrusive background or cover plants are most important to set off the brilliant blues, reds and yellow of the flowering plants among them. Perhaps less obvious than a plant in flower, but of great value are the colourful patterns that can be made with the base plan of foliage alone. Each of these plants may contribute a brilliant patch of colour in turn, such as the snowpatch of *Parahebe catarractae* white form or the lime sprawl of *Euphorbia myrsinites,* but for the rest of the year it is the quiet and satisfying pattern of the many textured greens, grey, bronze and purple leaves which provide the longest-lasting pleasure in the garden. The following plants I value particularly for their outstanding foliage effect:

Acaena
Acanthus
Acorus
Aegopodium p. 'Variegata'
Ajuga
Alchemilla
Alyssum s. 'Dudley Nevill Variegated'
Artemisia
Arum italicum subsp. *italicum* 'Marmoratum'
Arundo donax var. *versicolor*
Astilboides tabularis
Astrantia major 'Sunningdale Variegated'
Ballota
Bergenia
Brunnera
Calamagrostis
Canna
Carex
Convallaria majalis 'Albostriata'
Crambe
Cynara
Darmera
Disporum sessile 'Variegatum'
Elymus magellanicus
Epimedium
Eryngium agavifolium
Eryngium bourgatii
Eryngium variifolium
Euonymus
Euphorbia
Fargesia
Festuca

Filipendula ulmaria 'Aurea'
Fuchsia
Geranium
Glaucium
Grindelia
Gunnera
Hedera
Helleborus
Heuchera
Hosta
Imperata cylindrica 'Rubra'
Iris pallida forms
Lamium
Libertia
Ligularia
Liriope
Luzula sylvatica 'Aurea'
Lysichiton
Lysimachia nummularia 'Aurea'
Marrubium
Melissa officinalis 'Aurea'
Mentha suaveolens 'Variegata'
Milium effusum 'Aureum'
Onopordum
Onosma
Ophiopogon
Origanum vulgare forms
Petasites
Phlox paniculata variegated forms
Physostegia virginiana 'Variegata'
Pleiobastus – (Bamboo)
Polygonatum

Pulmonaria
Rheum palmatum
Rodgersia
Rubus
Ruta
Salvia argentea
Salvia officinalis
Sasa veitchii – (Bamboo)
Saxifraga fortunei 'Rubrifolia'
Saxifraga 'Dentata'
Sedum
Senecio cineraria 'White Diamond'
Sisyrinchium
Stachys

Symphytum 'Goldsmith'
Tellima grandiflora
Thymus 'Bertram Anderson'
Trachystemon
Trifolium repens 'Purpurascens'
Trillium
Valeriana phu 'Aurea'
Verbascum bombyciferum
Veronica gentianoides 'Variegata'
Veronica prostrata
Vinca
Viola riviniana
Zantedeschia

Seed Heads

Too prompt tidying-up of dead flower heads deprives the garden and the flower arranger of another season of interest. Of course not all plants are beautiful when in seed, but those that are, continue to outline the framework of the garden, retaining architectural shapes against the skyline. And when autumn frosts rime the standing stems the garden suddenly flowers again. The flower arranger is provided with endless opportunities for creating new designs. Whether used green, for those popular green arrangements, or when dried to many and varying shades, from straw, tan, russet and chestnut to darkest brown, these carved shapes are invaluable.

Personally I love the natural look of my drieds so well that I dislike the practice of paint and glitter. But when some magician with Christmas decorations shows me 'frosted' primula heads or gilded sea hollies I am almost tempted.

All of this needs to be combined with common sense of course. To leave opium poppies to seed everywhere is the greatest source of irritation, while a wind and rain-battered mass of tattered remains is depressing. The following make good seed heads:

Acanthus
Achillea
Aconitum
Agapanthus
Allium
Anaphalis
Armeria
Aruncus
Asphodeline lutea
Asphodelus
Ballota
Baptisia
Carex pendula
Carlina
Cortaderia
Crocosmia

Cynara
Dierama
Digitalis
Diplarrhena
Echinops
Eryngium
Galtonia
Helichrysum 'Schweffellicht'
Heuchera
Hosta
Incarvillea
Iris innominata
Iris sibirica
Limonium
Lotus
Lychnis

Lysimachia ephemerum
Lythrum virgatum
Malva moschata
Miscanthus
Morina
Nectaroscordum
Phlomis russeliana
Physalis franchetii

Primula bulleyana
Primula florindae
Pulsatilla vulgaris
Stachys byzantina 'Cotton Boll'
Thalictrum aquilegifolium
Verbascum chaixii
Verbascum bombyciferum
Zigadenus

Grasses

Chasmanthum latifolium
Cyperus eragrostis
Deschampsia
Luzula nivea
Melica altissima

Miscanthus
Panicum
Pennisetum
Spartina pectinata
Stipa

Flowers for Cutting

I have listed below those flowers which last reasonably well in water. Very small flowers which may make tiny posies I have not listed, nor those which drop quickly.

Acanthus
Agapanthus
Alchemilla mollis
Allium
Alstroemeria
Anaphalis
Anemone – (border forms)
Angelica
Anthemis tinctoria
Aquilegia
Arctanthemum
Asperula aristata
Aster
Astrantia
Bergenia
Campanula
Catananche
Centaurea
Chelone
Chrysanthemum
Convallaria
Cortaderia
Crocosmia
Cynara
Dephinium
Dianthus

Dicentra
Dierama
Digitalis
Echinops
Eryngium
Erythronium
Euphorbia
Galtonia
Helichrysum 'Schweffellicht'
Helleborus
Hermodactylus
Hesperantha
Heuchera
Iris
Kniphofia
Leucanthemella serotina
Liatris
Libertia
Ligularia
Linaria
Liriope
Lobelia
Lychnis
Lysimachia
Lythrum
Monarda

Narcissus
Nerine
Papaver orientale
Penstemon
Persicaria
Phlomis
Phlox – (border forms)
Phytolacca
Plantago
Polygonatum
Primula
Pulmonaria
Pulsatilla

Ranunculus
Salvia haematodes
Salvia × superba
Saponaria officinalis
Sedum telephium
Sedum 'Herbstfreude'
Sedum 'Ruby Glow'
Stachys byzantina 'Cotton Boll'
Tellima
Thalictrum
Tricyrtis
Veronicastrum virginicum 'Album'
Zigadenus

Plants for Seaside Gardens

Provided some thought is given to shelter from the worst winds, and the soil has been suitably prepared, i.e. humus has been added to dry sandy soil, or grit and humus have been added to lighten very heavy soil, the following plants should prove reliable.

Achillea
Agapanthus
Allium
Alstroemeria
Anemone
Anthemis
Anthericum
Armeria
Artemisia
Atriplex halimus
Bergenia
Campanula (low growing)
Catananche
Centaurea
Crambe
Crocosmia
Dianthus
Dierama
Echinops
Erigeron
Erodium
Eryngium
Euphorbia
Filipendula hexapetala
Geranium
Gypsophila
Hesperantha
Heuchera

Iris
Kniphofia
Libertia
Limonium
Linaria
Lychnis flos-jovis
Melissa
Mimulus
Morina
Nerine
Oenothera
Origanum
Penstemon
Physostegia
Potentilla
Pulsatilla
Ruta
Salvia (low growing)
Santolina
Scabiosa
Sedum
Sisyrinchium
Stachys
Stokesia
Tritonia
Veronica
Zantedeschia

Trough and Sink Plants

It is astonishing what can be grown in small containers by people who are prepared to take care of them. Like all forms of gardening it can take years to learn the art, both how to grow, and what can be grown in trough gardens. I am sure many people find out by experimenting, sometimes with very unexpected results. One year I left a seedling of *Clematis orientalis* in a seed tray in an open frame. It was watered occasionally, but otherwise must have starved. Instead of yards of feathery growth I had a cluster of yellow lanterns, like a posy, for weeks. Definitely not an alpine but showing very clearly the effect of root restriction and poor diet, result – plenty of flower, very reduced growth.

Androsace
Antennaria
Arabis procurrens 'Variegata'
Armeria juniperifolia 'Bevan's Variety'
Artemisia glacialis
Dianthus arvernensis
Draba
Hypericum coris
Hypericum reptans

Iberis sempervirens 'Weisser Zwerg'
Raoulia
Sedum hispanicum 'Aureum'
Sedum lydium
Sedum spathulifolium
Sempervivum – we have a large selection
Thymus serpyllum 'Minor'
Thymus neiceffii

Plants which dislike Lime

Baptisia australis
Carex pendula
Dicentra
Fritillaria camtschatcensis
Iris innominata

Lithodora
Maianthemum racemosum
Osmunda regalis
Pachysandra

Herbs for Cooking

Allium schoenoprasum (Giant chives)
Artemisia dracunculus (French tarragon)
Foeniculum vulgare (Fennel)
Mentha piperita (Peppermint)
Origanum vulgare 'Aureum' (Marjoram)

Salvia officinalis 'Purpurascens' (Purple sage, can be used as common grey sage)
Thymus 'Golden King' (attractive and edible)
Thymus 'Silver Queen' (attractive and edible)

Aromatic Plants for Pot Pourri

Acorus calamus 'Variegatus'
Agastache foeniculum
Aloysia triphylla
Angelica archangelica
Artemisia – (most forms)
Calamintha grandiflora
Calamintha nepeta
Foeniculum vulgare
Geranium macrorrhizum
Houttuynia cordata
Hyssopus

Lavandula
Melissa
Mentha
Monarda
Morina
Origanum vulgare
Perovskia
Salvia officinalis
Santolina
Thymus

Scented Flowers

Cestrum parqui
Convallaria
Crinum × powellii
Dianthus
Gladiolus tristis
Hemerocallis lilioasphodelus
Houttuynia cordata
Iris graminea
Lilium regale

Lunaria rediviva
Maianthemum racemosum
Monarda
Phlox pilosa
Primula vulgaris
Tellima grandiflora odorata
Viola 'Maggie Mott'
Viola 'Moonlight'

Plants Attractive to Bees

Achillea
Agastache
Allium
Alstroemeria
Alyssum
Anemone
Anthemis
Armeria
Aster
Calamintha
Camassia
Campanula
Centaurea
Coreopsis
Darmera
Delphinium
Dictamnus

Echinacea
Echinops
Eryngium
Eupatorium
Filipendula
Fuchsia
Galtonia
Geranium
Geum
Helianthemum
Helleborus
Heuchera
Hypericum
Hyssopus
Kniphofia
Lamium
Lavandula

Lavatera
Liatris
Ligularia
Limonium
Linaria
Lysimachia
Lythrum
Malva
Marrubium
Monarda
Melissa
Mentha
Nepeta
Oenothera
Onopordum
Origanum
Papaver
Persicaria

Petasites
Phlox
Plantago
Polemonium
Potentilla
Pulmonaria
Salvia
Saxifraga
Scabiosa
Sedum
Sidalcea
Solidago
Stachys
Thymus
Verbascum
Veronica
Viola

Plants Attractive to Butterflies

Achillea
Anaphalis
Arabis
Armeria
Aster
Ajuga
Calamintha
Centaurea
Centranthus
Cephalaria
Ceratostigma
Chrysanthemum
Dianthus deltoides
Echinacea
Echinops
Eupatorium
Erigeron
Erysimum
Hebe
Hyssopus

Iberis
Inula hookeri
Knautia
Liatris
Ligularia
Lunaria
Lychnis
Lysimachia
Melissa
Mentha
Nepeta
Persicaria
Phlox
Phuopsis
Primula
Scabiosa
Sedum spectabile (not S. 'Herbstfreude')
Solidago
Thymus (not yellow leafed forms)
Verbena bonariensis

Plants for which I have not noted specific growing conditions will thrive in reasonably fertile soil in mainly open situations.

The height of plants may vary according to growing conditions, such as in high or low rainfall areas, in cooler northern counties or the warmer south. It is not possible to be precise, therefore we give approximate heights under average growing conditions. Overall size of mature plants can be classified under three simple headings: small, medium or large. See classified lists.

Plant List

ACAENA affinis. Forms a mat of filigree, blue-grey leaves contrasting with red stems. Good to sprawl over paving. 13cm.

anserinifolia. Soft pewter-blue foliage, larger than *A* 'Blue Haze', denser than *A. affinis*. Desirable ground-cover, not a menace. 5cm.

inermis 'Purpurea'. Spreads flat carpets of tiny, rose-like purple leaves, coated with a faint grey bloom. Effective against paving or pale gravel. 5cm.

microphylla. Forms a carpet of moss-like, green-bronze foliage, smothered in summer with large rosy-red spiny burrs. 5cm.

saccaticupula 'Blue Haze'. Less rampant than *A. affinis* and with much more finely cut leaves of pewter, tinged mauve on bronze stems. 8cm.

sanguisorbae. The correct name for the plant I have previously listed as *A.* 'Pippa'. Soft pewter-blue foliage, larger than *A.* 'Blue Haze', denser than *A. affinis*. Desirable ground cover, not a menace. 5cm.

ACANTHUS dioscoridis var. perringii. From southern Turkey, requiring a hot, well drained situation. Clumps of short basal leaves give rise to short spikes of disproportionately large pink flowers. Height 40cm.

hirsutus subsp. syriacus. Fascinating pointed buds emerge to unfurl spiny yet soft foliage soon stiffening up. Flowering spikes of creamy-yellow flowers below reddish brown bracts over midsummer. 75cm.

mollis. The flower-spikes of this sculptural plant are very similar to those of *A. spinosus*, but the handsome glossy leaves are broader, less cut and not prickly. Flowers late summer. 1.2m.

mollis 'Hollard's Gold'. Forms a late winter-early spring feature, with lax leaves, less deeply cut to form broad, wavy-edged lobes in shades of yellow, conspicuous in shape and colour. Reverts to pale green in summer. 1m.

spinosus. A striking foliage plant of architectural value in the garden. From rich glossy deeply cut leaves rise stately stems bearing strange flowers, purple-hooded and white lipped. Good seedheads. 1.2m.

spinosus Spinosissimus Group. Even more finely cut, each leaf reduced almost to veins and spines, more silver than green. Revels in hot dry soil. Best where foliage can be admired, less free flowering. 75cm.

ACHILLEA – Border Forms.

Achilleas thrive in an open sunny site in reasonable soil conditions. They perform better if lifted and young pieces are replanted in refreshed soil every second year. Apart from *A. chrysocoma*, most will have a second flowering if cut down after the first flush.

'Apfelblute'. A reliable and long lived form with charming flowers in shades of pale pink. Needs a good soil in full sun. Cut back after flowering for a second flush in September. 75cm.

ageratum 'W.B. Childs'. Said to be of Swiss origin. In spring it forms neat, tidy, non-running clumps of fresh green finely cut leaves. By June it is a white bouquet swaying elegantly on the edge of a border. Each wide lace-like head is made of many flowers held in a flat loose cluster, poised on thin stalks, furnished with finely fretted leaves. Each composite flower has a dark green eye which slowly turns to greenish-white, surrounded by chalk-white ray florets. There is nothing daintier or more prolific for picking in armfuls for a June wedding or enjoying as it stands. If cut down when faded there will be a second crop. 75cm.

chrysocoma 'Grandiflora'. A grand impact plant for back of the large border, or in the wild garden where it can tower above lower plants, and show off its tall stems, clothed from top to toe with handsome pale-green, finely divided leaves topped in midsummer with domed heads, 15cm across of tightly packed, small daisy-like flowers. 1.8m.

'Credo'. Tall strong stems carry very large domed heads of clear yellow flowers, ageing to cream, with side branches flowering simultaneously, forming a foam of yellow. Has handsome, grey, finely cut aromatic leaves. Among many good achillea this plant is outstanding and was selected by Ernst Pagels who has such an eye for a good plant. Average soil, sun. July-August. 1.2m.

'Fanal'. Opens flat heads of guardsman's red tiny daisy flowers fading to curry-yellow. Midsummer. 45cm.

'Feuerland'. Dense flat head of tiny daisy flowers open cherry-red with yellow centres slowly fading through shades of burnt orange to brownish-yellow, all shades seen together. Sturdy stems retain good-shaped plant. Mid-late summer. 90cm.

filipendulina 'Gold Plate'. Well known with its tall, stiff stems bearing flat heads of tiny yellow flowers. Dries excellently, retaining its colour. Flowers midsummer. 1.4m.

'Inca Gold'. A short sturdy plant holding together well, topped with wide heads of lemon-yellow daisy flowers with greyish centres, a cool effect mid-late summer. 75cm.

'Lachsschönheit'. Flowers open coral-red, fade to soft-peach, both colours seen on plant at same time, very attractive. 75cm.

'Lucky Break'. A sport from *A.* 'Taygetea', occurring at Great Dixter, Christopher Lloyd's garden. A stronger, more vigorous form, carrying wide flat heads of cool-lemon flowers above feathery-grey leaves. If cut down after midsummer flowering will produce a second crop in autumn. 90cm.

'Martina'. A plant of great presence. Makes strong clumps of very finely cut scented foliage topped with branching stems carrying wide flat heads of sharp lemon-yellow flowers. One is a treat. En masse is stunning. If cut down when fading a second crop will follow. 75cm.

millefolium 'Cerise Queen'. Very effective near the front of a sunny border, with massed flat heads of cherry-red flowers, standing 70cm tall from a base of ferny-green leaves.

millefolium 'Lilac Beauty'. Finely cut, leafy stems topped with flat heads of lilac flowers, good to cut. Midsummer. 60cm.

millefolium 'Red Velvet'. Has densely packed heads of small, cherry-red flowers with pale centres, much admired. 75cm.

'Moonshine'. Similar to *A.* 'Taygetea', but larger, with beautiful feathery foliage of silver-grey. Branching stems, bright yellow flowers. Midsummer. 60cm.

ptarmica 'Nana Compacta'. Quite distinct for the edge of a sunny border. Each plant creates a dome of blossom carried on short, stiff, leafy stems, each flat head composed of many individual daisy-like flowers with white petals surrounding conspicuous grey-green centres. Good to pick, remains fresh for weeks in the garden. Mid to late summer. 30cm.

ptarmica 'Perry's White'. A non-floppy version, with somewhat larger, chalk-white button flowers, on shorter, stiffer stems. Full sun, average soil. 60cm.

ptarmica The Pearl Group. Is invasive but invaluable for cut flowers. Good strong stems topped with branched heads of pure-white, double button-like flowers. Midsummer. 75cm.

'Summerwine'. Slender branching stems carry lacy clusters of small wine-velvet flowers fading slightly to give a two-tone effect. Mid-late summer. 75cm.

ACHILLEA – Smaller Forms

ageratifolia. Spreading tufts of narrow, silvery leaves, covered with flat heads of tiny white daisies. 15cm.

× **lewisii 'King Edward'.** Rosettes of narrow, ferny, grey-green leaves form neat, low mounds topped with flat heads of sulphur-yellow flowers, long season. 13cm.

tomentosa. Delightful tiny yarrow for edgings. Its woolly, ferny foliage sets off its flat flower heads of golden-yellow. A very neat plant. 15cm.

ACIS autumnale. syn. *Leucojum autumnale*. After the grassy leaves have died down bunches of bare stems carry little white bells, stems and calyxes wine-tinted. Attractive little late summer bulb. 25cm.

ACONITUM - CAUTION TOXIC IF EATEN

carmichaelii 'Arendsii'. The species is found in stands of large herbs on the borders of damp meadows and woods with filipendula, veratrum and huge umbellifers in Kamchatka and Amuria. *A. carmichaelii* 'Arendsii' is a fine garden form, superb in late September and October with large shadowed-blue flowers. Close inspection shows kinship with the buttercup family. If you lift the top petal, which looks like a hooded cowl, you will find it is sheltering the stigma while the rest of the petals form the familiar innocent face of the buttercup surrounding the central boss. Lovely with *Persicaria amplexicaulis.* In good soil grows 1.5m.

compactum 'Album'. Stiffly upright stems clothed in rounded, finely-cut leaves carry spires of closely-set monkshood flowers, white, opening from large pale green buds. Midsummer. Retentive soil, sun or part shade. 1m.

'Ivorine'. Exquisite plant for cool conditions. Branching stems closely set with ivory-white hooded flowers. May-June. 75cm.

lycoctonum subsp. vulparia. From woods and damp shady places in the mountains of Europe and north Asia to China. I have seen it massed in a grassy gulley in the Pyrenees, with mauvy-rose fluffy heads of *Thalictrum aquilegiifolium*. Tall, about 1.5m, the slender branching stems carry yellowish-green flowers, not unlike little delphiniums. It flowers for weeks in late summer.

'Spark's Variety'. Navy blue buds held on wide airy spires open in late summer, dark midnight-blue hooded flowers. Stems are lightly clad with dark-green, deeply-cut leaves. 1.2m.

'Stainless Steel'. Good contrast to the midnight-blue forms, this lovely plant carries tall spires of pale silvery-blue flowers above finely divided foliage. 1m.

ACORUS calamus 'Argenteostriatus'. Handsome sword-like leaves boldly variegated cream and green with rose-pink bases in spring. Grows in bog or shallow water, with long, narrow blade-like leaves attached to rhizomes, very much like an iris. The roots and leaves are spicily scented, valued when earth floors were strewn with sweet-scented rushes. They have been used medicinally, for their perfume and for their restorative qualities. Dried they are still used as flavouring, among other things in toothpaste, gargles and gin. 90cm.

gramineus. Grows in wet places around ponds and along streams from India to China and Japan. It is much smaller and makes neat grass-like tufts, ideally suited for small ponds, sink gardens if kept moist, or even an aquarium. 15cm.

gramineus 'Variegatus'. Has leaves brightly variegated cream and green. 13cm.

ACTAEA. These woodland plants are admired for their graceful habit, delicately cut foliage and clusters of berries which are poisonous, hence the name Baneberry.

We originally called some of these plants *Cimicifuga.* In my garden these are choosy plants, only thriving in precious areas of moist shade. Moist soil in full sun will not do; the leaves, especially of *A. simplex*, scorch horribly. Well grown they are among the most elegant and beautiful of late summer-autumn plants.

cimicifuga. A lovely wild bugbane from Cally Gardens. Leafy clumps of fresh dark green foliage from which arise head-high spikes of tiny starry creamy-white flowers. Attractive in seed too. 2m.

matsumurae 'Elstead'. Differs in having purplish stems and buds, which open creamy-white with pink stamens. 1.4m.

matsumurae 'Frau Herms'. Differs from *A. matsumurae* 'White Pearl' in having dark stems and larger tapers of creamy-white fluffy flowers. Flowers open a week or so in advance of other cultivars. 1.2m.

matsumurae 'White Pearl'. For a cool shady place, not dry. A most elegant plant in autumn. Branching stems carry snowy-white bottle brushes 13cm long. These develop into a most desirable lime-green seedhead. All flower October-November. 1.2m.

pachypoda. Dolls eyes. Elegant clumps of stiff slender stems are furnished with light-green, divided leaves. Spires of fluffy white flowers become spikes of pea-sized white berries in late summer. Each white berry carries a conspicuous black dot and is fastened by a short red swollen stem. 75cm.

rubra. From the woods of north east America, makes far better plants and berries in gardens if grown in part shade, when it is the most showy *Actaea,* with large clusters of smallish berries. They are attractive in July when jade-green, and gradually turn to gleaming scarlet, remaining handsome for weeks into early autumn. 75cm.

simplex var. simplex Atropurpurea Group. Unlike most others whose leaves can be scorched in full sun, this colours best in an open situation in retentive soil, when the deeply cut leaves and stems become dark purple, topped in early autumn with slender spires of small, sweetly-scented cream flowers. A north or east facing border suits it well. 1.8m.

simplex 'Brunette'. This selected form has very dark, purple-black foliage and stems, providing dramatic contrast for the tall, slender spires of sweetly scented, small, white flowers. Needs moist retentive soil, in sun or part shade; flowering in late autumn. 1.8m.

simplex 'James Compton'. Another named form selected for its dark foliage, which develops after the first season. A shorter growing form with white, scented flowers. 1.2m.

simplex 'Pink Spike'. Charming new pink flowered contrasting well with dark green leaves which emerge darkest purple in spring. Upright growth, flowering during September. Best in part shade and sheltered from drying wind. 1.4m.

simplex 'Prichard's Giant'. Above mounds of glossy-green foliage, dense spires of creamy-white flowers. In autumn forms good seedheads, lasting throughout winter. A superb vertical, up to 2m tall.

spicata. The British and European form, from cool conifer forests, has clusters of small black berries at the tip of 45cm leafy stems.

ADONIS 'Fukujukai'. Semi-double golden buttercup-like flowers open from bronze buds nestling in a ruff of feathery-bronze leaves. These change to green, dying down by midsummer. 25cm.

amurensis 'Pleniflora'. Among nests of ferny foliage crouch double, shining flowers with green centres. 15cm.

vernalis. Found in the meadow steppes of Russia, with cowslips, the shining single saucer-like flowers are ruffed with fretted leaves. 25cm.

AEGOPODIUM podagraria 'Variegatum'. This attractively variegated form of the pestilential weed, Ground elder. After growing it for several years, I must admit it does travel, although not uncontrollably so. Its bright, handsome cream and green leaves transform the poorest piece of soil in dull corners , i.e. confined at the base of a north or east facing wall. 60cm.

AGAPANTHUS. Blue African lily. The following forms offered are all hardy in well-drained but well-fed soil. All flower throughout August, good seedheads in September. In very cold situations a winter mulch is advisable.

'Albatross'. This magnificent form was given to me by James Russell. Large white flowers held on individual stems of varying lengths form large open heads, very effective. Green seed pods also decorative. Broad strap leaves. For a warm site, well-drained soil. Excellent in tubs. July-August. 1.2m.

Ardernei hybrid. Large, well-shaped heads of white flowers faintly touched with flecks of rose and purple on tips of petals, with black dot-like anthers. 90cm.

'Blue Moon'. Large, densely packed heads of pale blue flowers, another of Eric Smith's cultivars. Appears to be hardy in well-drained soil. Flowers late when the others are setting seed. 1.2m.

campanulatus var. albidus. From clumps of strap-shaped leaves come smooth bare stems carrying round heads of close-set, white, trumpet-shaped flowers. All the agapanthus pick well, as flowers, and make good seedheads, either green or dried. 75cm.

campanulatus 'Chatto's Blue'. syn. *A. campanulatus* 'Cobalt Blue'. An extra fine cobalt blue form, selected by us. 60cm.

campanulatus 'Profusion'. Very free-flowering, with almost a striped effect in petals of light and dark blue. 90cm.

campanulatus variegated. The strong cream variegation is best in early summer, almost faded when the rich blue flowers are making a good show in August. 60cm.

'Cedric Morris'. Similar to *A.* Ardernei hybrid, white flowers faintly tipped with lilac, more densely packed in large rounded heads, with black dot-like stamens. Another late flowerer. 1.2m.

'Enigma'. Dark green strap like leaves, white petals darkening to pale blue at the throat, a pleasing combination. Likes full sun and moist but well drained soil. 60cm.

'Evening Star'. Purple stained stems carry heads of dark buds which open wide paler blue flowers, each petal bearing a dark central stripe with the overall effect of light and dark-blue very attractive. 60cm.

'Flore Pleno'. Above broad strap leaves stand upturned heads of double flowers, shaded light and dark blue. Needs sheltered position and good drainage. August. 50cm.

Headbourne hybrids. Fine strain, good heads of blue shades. 90cm.

'Isis'. More narrowly tubular flowers than *A.* Headbourne hybrids, but very effective with well-spaced buds and dark blue flowers. 75cm.

Johannesburg hybrid. Originally grown from seed sent to us, collected in the wild. Has survived here many winters outside in well-drained soil. Such magnificent appearance one might think it to be a conservatory plant. Forms huge heads of large, light-blue, open, bell-like flowers, each petal marked with dark central vein, giving a striped effect. Each head creates a light airy effect since individual flowers are poised on long slender stems attached to a central point. Occasionally a second tier of flowers is held above the lower one. Flowers last longer than many other forms, well into August. We believe this to be an exceptional introduction. 1m.

'Kingston Blue'. Blue-black buds open to the darkest royal-blue. Good edge-of-the-border plant. July-August. 60cm.

Lewis Palmer hybrid. A grand hardy plant, reminiscent of the large agapanthus customarily grown in conservatories, has overwintered here in well-drained soil for several years. Handsome, upstanding, strap-shaped leaves support tall stems, carrying large heads of cool, lilac-blue flowers. 1-1.2m. This plant is not to be confused with those we list under *A.* Headbourne hybrids. It is distinctly different; we propagate it by division.

'Lilliput'. Above neat tuffets of narrow leaves stand rounded heads of rich-blue flowers, opening star shaped, showing dark central veins and blue stemmed stamens. Midsummer. 45cm.

'Loch Hope'. Named after a lake in Scotland. It is one of the last to flower, in autumn, bearing large, pale-blue pendulous flowers on 1.2m stems.

'Midnight Blue'. One of the darkest blue, low-growing varieties of agapanthus. Ex Daisy Hill Nursery in Northern Ireland. 45cm.

'Midnight Star'. Another good form with dark blue buds opening rich blue flowers forming large heads on tall stems, overall effect darker than *A.* 'Evening Star'. 75cm.

white dwarf hybrids. Small heads of white flowers with green veins and slight lilac tips. Counter-part of *A* 'Lilliput'. Midsummer. 45cm.

'Windlebrooke'. Outstanding colour. Deep indigo buds open to form globular heads of dark blue flowers, intensified by dark central veins, freely produced above tidy clumps of narrow leaves. This came from John Bond, Savill Gardens. 70cm.

AGASTACHE 'Blue Fortune'. Creates a good vertical effect from July to October. Stout branching stems carry many spires of soft lavender-blue flowers held in whorls of dark bracts; close-packed to form slender bottle brushes 15cm long, held above fresh green pointed leaves, all spicily scented and attended by bees. For sun and retentive soil. 1m.

'Firebird'. This graceful shrubby plant clothed in small grey leaves is aflame with salmon tubular flowers appearing in endless succession from June onwards. Not hardy. Superb in pots or bedded out. 45cm.

rugosa. Very upright branching stems carry scented mint-like leaves, each stem topped in autumn with thimble-shaped dense clusters of tiny dusky-mauve flowers. 90cm.

rugosa 'Golden Jubilee'. An exciting new introduction. Bushy plants are clothed in quantities of pale lemon-yellow leaves, topped with short spires of lavender-blue flowers in autumn. 75cm.

'**Spicy**'. Branched stems carry long spires of violet-blue catmint-like flowers held in whorls around the stem, more widely spaced than in *A. rugosa*, the effect deepened by dark calyxes. August-October. 75cm.

AGERATINA ligustrinum. Forms medium-sized rounded shrub clothed in shining evergreen privet-shaped leaves. For weeks in autumn it is crowded with wide lacy heads of small fluffy, pinkish-green flowers accented by dark stems. Needs good soil and sheltered site. Can be cut down by hard frost, but returns from the base like fuchsias. 1.2m.

rugosum 'Chocolate'. Many branching stems create a compact bushy plant clothed from tip to base with pointed leaves strikingly stained purple, topped with fuzzy white flowers in late summer-autumn. A splendid accent plant for retentive soil, in sun or light shade. 1.2m.

AJUGA. Ajugas make eye-catching carpets of flower in May-June when their densely packed flowers emerge from over-wintered leaf rosettes. After flowering, new trailing stems flow to make ground cover, the good coloured leaf forms creating another colour harmony among surrounding plants. They will not tolerate very dry soil. Watch should be kept too for attack by aphids and mildew, both of which can spoil the clean foliage effect.

pyramidalis. From mountain meadows and open woods in central Europe to the Altai and China. It does not run alarmingly but makes dense, slowly spreading clumps of dark green smooth leaves. Spikes of small vivid gentian-blue flowers are held in whorls of navy-blue bracts, looking like little pagodas in spring. 15cm.

reptans 'Atropurpurea'. Makes rosettes and runners of shining beetroot-coloured leaves with short spikes of deep blue flowers in spring. 13cm.

reptans 'Burgundy Glow'. Beautiful foliage suffused rose and magenta, regularly edged with cream. Vivid carpet all winter. Flowers blue. 15cm.

reptans 'Catlin's Giant'. The flower stems are 30cm tall and bear 15cm long heads of rich blue flowers, the effect deepened by purplish-brown calyxes. After flowering, new rosettes of large glossy leaves, twice as large as other ajuga, assume this same dark hue.

reptans 'Jungle Beauty'. Larger than most with loose rosettes of round green leaves, wavy edged, sometimes tinted purple-red, setting off the spikes of gentian-blue flowers. 25cm.

reptans 'Multicolor'. Bronze foliage curiously splashed with pink and cream; only looks good when well suited in rich leaf-mould soil in semi-shade. 10cm.

reptans 'Pink Surprise'. Although ajugas tend to fade away in our dry sandy soil we shall do our best to please this new introduction from Holland. Very impressive with dark purple foliage contrasting with spikes of pink flowers in April. 15cm.

reptans 'Purple Brocade'. Deeply veined purple leaves with ruffled edges make a contrast in texture as well as colour, with spires of blue flowers in spring. 20cm.

reptans 'Variegata'. The least strong-growing, best in shade or on north-facing borders. Grey-green leaves are boldly edged with cream. 5cm.

× **ALCALTHAEA.** These introductions to the garden are greatly admired and desired. A cross between a hollyhock and a mallow.

suffrutescens 'Parkallee'. Having stems clothed with delicate semi-double creamy apricot-pink flowers. Best in full sun. 2m.

suffrutescens 'Parkrondel'. It has rosette shaped flowers, composed of an outer circle of cyclamen-pink, translucent petals whose thread-like veins merge to form a dark centre filled with curled and crumpled inner petals, held in clustered buds up and down the branching stems, ensuring a display from midsummer until the frosts. Lasts well picked. Prune tips in spring to make a bushier plant. 1.5m.

ALCHEMILLA conjuncta. Closely related to *A. alpina*. It differs in that the individual leaflets, which compose the little parasol-shaped leaves, appear to be seamed halfway to the centre. The top side of each leaf is smooth dark green, the back appears to be lined with shimmering silk which just shows as a silver edge. Both leaves and small sprays of tiny green flowers are valued by flower arrangers, particularly for pressed flower pictures. In the garden the plant makes a neat low cushion, valued for its attractive foliage. 10cm.

erythropoda. Was discovered in a piece of mountain turf brought home from Turkey by J.R. Mar. Small scallop-shell leaves of soft blue-green are set off by sprays of tiny lime-green stars which turn coral-red as they age; a pretty foliage plant by the edge of a cool walk. Midsummer. 15cm.

erythropoda Turkish form. This has proved a distinct and worthwhile plant soon forming low clumps with much greyer foliage than the type. Excellent for the borders edge. 15cm.

mollis. Lady's Mantle is found in east European mountain meadows, making a far larger plant than the other two. The downy, rounded leaves may be 10-13cm across, the radiating veins prolonged into gentle scallops whose fine serrated edges exude pearls of moisture on still humid mornings. All June and into July long sprays of frothy lime-green stars cool the wealth of colour that comes with midsummer. The floppy flower stems are 60cm.

mollis 'Robusta'. Differs in having sturdier stems, so many remain upright. Large in leaf also. Produces second crop of flowers in autumn. 60cm.

ALLIUM – Ornamental Onions

ampeloprasum. Wild leek. Differs from other ornamental onions in having wide, blade-like, grey-blue leaves. Tall strong stems carry in midsummer, large round buds held in pointed papery cases, like candle snuffers. These split off to release large heads of tightly packed silvery-pink flowers. The whole plant forms a dramatic vertical for months, from bud stage to seedhead. They dry well, best picked in mature flower before seeds are formed. 1.5m.

atropurpureum. Darkest of all the ornamental onions, blackish-purple flowers in dense heads. 90cm.

carinatum subsp. pulchellum. Charming and valuable in late summer, especially among silver-foliage plants, when many dusty-lilac bells dangle from massed slender stems. Retains its colour when dried. 40cm.

carinatum subsp. pulchellum f. album. The exquisite white form of the above. 40cm.

cernuum. Graceful stems carry nodding heads of rose-magenta bells. Midsummer. 45cm.

cristophii. Amazing globular heads, the size of a small football. Each made of up to 80 metallic lilac-purple stars. They dry in perfect shape, the delicate spoke-like stems remaining purple. Midsummer. 60cm.

'Firmament'. A hybrid between *A. atropurpureum* and *A. cristophii*, combining the beauty of both parents in producing impressively large round globes of glistening deep purple flowers on tall stems, about 80cm. Early summer.

flavum. A very distinctive little onion with tight clumps of almost blue foliage, set off by heads of small citron-yellow bells. Mid to late summer. 40cm.

hollandicum. Rising above the greys and silvers, slender, bare stems carry globular heads, the size of an orange, formed by tightly packed lilac-purple stars. They fade to straw-coloured perfectly shaped seedheads. 1m.

hollandicum 'Purple Sensation'. Has larger heads of darker flowers, a rich rosy-mauve, dramatic above mounds of grey ballota, lavender or rue. May-June. 1.2m.

karataviense. Usually two, dark, purplish-grey, wide curving leaves cradle a soft, pinky-beige flower head the size of an orange. Still effective in midsummer when it forms a good seedhead. Best in groups. May-June. 20cm.

karataviense 'Ivory Queen'. Forms globular heads of densely-packed, creamy-white flowers almost at ground-level, all eye-catching among mat-plants in full sun. 20cm.

lusitanicum. Taller and bolder than *A. senescens* subsp. *montanum*. Above grass-green leaves sway bright green stems carrying globular heads of soft-lilac flowers, full of bees. Long season, early-late summer. 60cm.

nigrum. Commonly known as Black garlic, oddly so, as it has white flowers (it's the ovaries that are black). Produces heads of starry white flowers each with a darker green eye. A useful early summer flowering bulb for a sunny spot. Bulbs tend to produce prodigious amounts of offsets which are almost impossible to weed out so be sure you plant it in the right place from the outset. 70cm.

obliquum. Stiff, slender stems, clasped by narrow, blue-green leaves, carry round heads of closely-packed lemon-yellow flowers. 75cm.

oreophilum. Charming seen in drifts on open sunny edges. Clustered heads of rich rose-pink flowers, followed by attractive sun-bleached white seedheads. July. 15cm.

'Rien Poortvliet'. Stout stems carry globular heads packed with lavender flowers, a lovely soft colour. 90cm.

rosenbachianum 'Album'. Tall bare stems carry globular heads of tightly packed starry flowers, each pinned with a green eye. Having narrow petals means you can see light through them. As they mature the green eyes become seed cases held on wire thin stalks like spokes of a wheel, the whole creating a pale diaphanous effect. It creates an exciting vertical, especially when grouped, standing 1.2m.

schoenoprasum. Giant chives. Forms closely packed clumps of fresh green foliage valued for flavouring salads and soups. The round heads of small mauve flowers are very attractive. 25cm.

schoenoprasum f. albiflorum. Draws the eye for weeks, from the first sight of tight pale green buds, until they open pure white flowers in early summer. By midsummer stiff bleached stems holding neat seedheads are still effective. 25cm.

schoenoprasum 'Forescate'. This very attractive form of giant chive holds globular heads of bright rose-red flowers on 25cm stems, flowering in June-July.

senescens subsp. montanum. Above clumps of upright twisting leaves stand rounded heads of soft-lilac flowers tipped with dark purple anthers supported on stiff slender stems, swaying in the wind. Mid-late summer. 45cm.

senescens subsp. montanum var. glaucum. Quickly forms interesting clumps of swirling leaves, with round heads of lilac flowers in late summer. 15cm.

sphaerocephalon. On thin stalks, these plum-shaped wine-purple heads are most effective in late summer, among the silver foliage plants. 75cm.

tuberosum. Dainty heads of white starry flowers. Useful for cutting. Latest of all the alliums to flower in September. 45cm.

ursinum. Ransomes. Comes from the moist woods of temperate Europe and far into Asia, often in wide drifts. This wild onion, the bulbs of which used to be eaten by the gypsies, sends up flat heads of white, starry flowers, about 25cm high, above two broad, shiny leaves, rather like those of Lily-of-the-Valley. As they seed and multiply readily, they soon form a carpet, and can be a nuisance in the garden, but are attractive in open woodland.

ALOYSIA triphylla. Lemon verbena. Long slender branches bear deliciously lemon-scented leaves, dried they make herb tea or pot pourri. Panicles of tiny violet and white flowers in August are not without charm. Needs shelter of warm wall. Normally cut down by severe winters, but shoots again. 1.2m stems in one season.

ALSTROEMERIA – MAY CAUSE SKIN ALLERGY
ligtu hybrids. Tall stems carry large heads of many small lily-like flowers exquisitely veined, in shades of pink to apricot. Pot-grown plants. July to August. 75cm.
Princess Frederika 'Starbronza'. We have grown a few of the princess lilies series outside in our dry sunny gravel garden for several years where they seem perfectly hardy and always put on a show from early summer onwards. 80cm.
psittacina. From Brazil, also called parrot lily on account of its colouring. Narrow lily-shaped flowers are dark crimson with bright green tips, streaked with black. Needs a warm well-drained site, decorative for months from July onwards as it constantly makes fresh stems while the first crop bears seed pods admired by flower arrangers. Makes an unusual tub plant. 90cm.

ALYSSUM montanum. Is a delight on a raised bed or draped on a rock. Sometimes flat, sometimes a low mound of wiry branches set with small, neat, grey leaves, smothered in spring with thimble-sized clusters of bright yellow, tiny flowers which are scented. 15cm.
spinosum 'Roseum'. Low round bush of wiry stems, tiny grey leaves, smothered in small rose-pink flowers. June. 20cm.

AMSONIA hubrichtii. Has very finely cut, willow-like leaves along entire length of stem, topped with clusters of narrow indigo-blue buds, opening pale, grey-blue starry flowers in June. Intense golden, butter-yellow autumn colour. 75cm.
orientalis. From Turkey. Slowly produces a clump of slender stems clothed in narrow, willow-like, grey-green leaves. Topped in midsummer with clustered heads of small starry grey-blue flowers, it always draws attention. 60cm.
tabernaemontana. From north east America. Will grow in half shade, or in full sun in moist soil. The charm of this plant lies in the curious colour of the flowers. At the top of many slender wands, set with narrow, willow-like leaves, sit dark-stemmed clusters of thin green and dark-blue pointed buds which open small slate-blue stars. The effect of greenish-blue in these modest heads is appealing. They flower from June to early July. 60cm.

ANAPHALIS margaritacea var. yedoensis. Is a plant of warmer climates. I am familiar with the name *Anaphalis yedoensis,* which belongs to the form from Japan, where it is found in sunny places along rivers. Thin branched white-felted stems stand 75cm-1m, bearing broad oval dark grey leaves with pale backs and white edges, topped with loose clusters of small chalk-white everlasting daisies. Stripped of leaves, hung upside down to dry they make excellent `drieds'. *Anaphalis margaritacea,* in its other varieties from north east America and north east Asia, is similar in habit with narrower green leaves. They both flower from August to October.
triplinervis. Found by rocky stream-sides in the Himalayas, sometimes with mats of pink *Persicaria affinis.* Ideal for the edge of the border, it makes low, neat mounds of very white, felted leaves which are buried beneath white sprays of crisp white daisies, slightly larger than those of *A. m.* var. *yedoensis.* Flowers July to October. 30cm.
triplinervis 'Sommerschnee'. This slightly more dwarf form of *A. triplinervis* makes spreading clumps of felt-grey foliage topped with clusters of pearly-white everlasting daisies. Late summer. 25cm.

ANAPHALOIDES bellidioides. Makes quick-spreading flat stems covered with tiny grey and silver leaves, crowded with surprisingly large papery-white daisies, in early summer. Must have good drainage in winter. 2.5cm.

ANDROSACE geraniifolia. From northern India and Tibet. Rounded, scallop-edged leaves form rosettes each carrying long-stemmed clusters of small primula-like white flowers in midsummer. New leaf rosettes on long stems arch over to touch the soil and make new plants. Creeps around in semi-shade, in leaf-mould soil. 13cm.

sempervivoides. Small evergreen rosettes spread gradually in well-drained soil, carry heads of pink flowers on short stems. Midsummer. Trough or raised bed. 6cm.

ANEMONE – Smaller forms

apennina. Tuberous rhizomes produce deep blue starry flowers, similar to those of *A. blanda* but with narrower petals. For well-drained soil in a cool situation. Will succeed in the grassy floor of light woodland; flowering March-April. 20cm.

apennina double flowered. This exquisite plant is a rarity since it is slow to propagate. Perfectly formed double flowers, combine shades of blue and mauve unfolding from green centres. Spring. 25cm.

apennina var. albiflora. Above low cushions of finely cut leaves stand crowds of palest blue daisy-shaped flowers, open to the sun, showing hearts filled with white stamens around a green ovary. 30cm.

× **fulgens.** Clear scarlet, perfect with yellow-green euphorbias. March-April. 20cm.

× **lesseri.** A lower growing anemone which never fails to draw attention to upturned light wine-coloured flowers in midsummer. 30cm.

× **lipsiensis.** In April from thin, horizontal rootstocks emerge pale, sulphur-yellow flowers of good size, held above finely cut bronzed leaves. 15cm.

multifida. Neat clumps of dark green, cut leaves are a setting for cool lemon-yellow flowers in spring, followed by large, woolly seedheads. 30cm.

nemorosa. Wood anemone, of moist forests of Europe and north-west Asia. They grow almost anywhere, preferably in part shade under trees or shrubs, in light or heavy soil but are best left undisturbed to colonise the floor of shrubbery or wood. There are several good named cultivars, which include the following forms:

nemorosa 'Alba Plena'. In early summer above spreading carpets of finely cut leaves stand tiny 'Victorian posies', each flower having an outer circle of large sepals surrounding a centre of overlapping, tiny white petals. 10cm.

nemorosa 'Allenii'. A lovely blue form of our wild wood anemone. Nodding buds, stained purplish-rose on the reverse, open to the sun in spring, breathtaking flowers filled with yellow stamens. Best in peaty or leaf-mould soil, in part shade. 20cm.

nemorosa 'Blue Eyes'. Most unusual, a fringe of double-white, finely shredded petals are pinned with a green eye, circled with dark blue, in April. 10cm.

nemorosa 'Bracteata Pleniflora'. The outer petals (or bracts), have divided to make a double layer, like a white ruff, centred with a green knob and yellow stamens. April. 15cm.

nemorosa 'Buckland'. Extra large flowers with deeper plum staining on the backs of the petals, giving a warmer blue effect. 25cm.

nemorosa 'Lady Doneraile'. Large white flowers filled with yellow stamens flutter over bold-cut foliage, on dark stained stems. April. 15cm.

nemorosa 'Lychette'. Six creamy-white broad petals with rounded tips form a bowl filled with yellow stamens. Similar to *A. nemorosa* 'Lady Doneraille' but flowers later. 15-18cm.

nemorosa 'Robinsoniana'. Differs from *A. nemorosa* 'Allenii' in having light blue flowers with silvery-white backs to the petals. 20cm.

nemorosa 'Royal Blue'. Smaller than some forms of our wild wood anemone but opens intense blue flowers to the sun. 15cm.

nemorosa 'Virescens'. Slowly spreads clumps of divided leaves entirely covered in late March with curiously attractive green flowers. Instead of the normal white flower, each consists of overlapping layers of modified calyxes, all finely divided. Intriguing to look down on, irresistible to a flower arranger. Later the 'flowers' will be flecked with white. 15cm.

pavonina. Similar to *A.* × *fulgens* but has jewel-like flowers in many shades, deep rose, crimson red, cherry, and salmon pink often with navy-blue eyes, while others, creamy-white are stained coral on reverse. Given to me by Cedric Morris. Grown from seed so any colour possible. 20cm.

ranunculoides. From damp open woods of Europe to the Caucasus. Has smaller flowers but creates a pretty effect with yellow pointed starry petals. 10cm.

ranunculoides 'Pleniflora'. A tiny wood anemone with bright yellow, semi-double flowers. Spring. 10cm.

trifolia. From woods and upper slopes of the southern Alps, this is a firmer-leafed version of *A. nemorosa*, forming cushions covered with flat, white starry flowers whose purity is emphasized with white stamens around a green ovary. 15cm.

ANEMONE – Border Forms

There are many forms and hybrids of the autumn flowering anemone. All are garden worthy but not all differ markedly. We offer the following as being distinct:

hupehensis 'Hadspen Abundance'. Free flowering, a good edge-of-border plant. Each flower is attractively deformed with alternate dark and light pink petals, the dark being slightly smaller. This is the true form, which I am told is hard to find, propagated from root cuttings. 75cm.

hupehensis var. japonica 'Pamina'. A delight. Slender, dark-stained, branching stems carry long succession of neat, semi double flowers in shades of rose-pink, centred with a ring of golden stamens. Autumn. 75cm.

hupehensis var. japonica 'Prinz Heinrich'. Has a seemingly double layer of petals, narrow, slightly twisted and quilled, in a deep pink shade. 75cm.

× **hybrida.** I take refuge under this title with the many beautiful cultivars, which have been produced from among these species. Some are larger, paler in colour, or deeper. Some are double. Personally, I prefer the single forms with perfectly formed round cupped petals.

× **hybrida 'Honorine Jobert'.** Unsurpassed, this lovely old variety has pure white flowers filled with yellow stamens, elegant on tall branching stems above dark green leaves. Flowers for weeks in autumn. 1.2m.

× **hybrida 'Königin Charlotte'.** A fine plant, has large blooms of rich rose-pink with well-formed rounded petals. 1.2m.

× **hybrida 'Montrose'.** Interesting Japanese anemone with mature basal leaves distinctly ruffled. I had this as *A* × *hybrida* 'Crispa', maybe that's its correct name? Bears large single pink flowers over a long period from late summer. 80cm.

× **hybrida 'Whirlwind'.** Differs from *A.* 'Honorine Jobert' in having a double layer of white petals, giving a more fluted effect. 75cm.

narcissiflora. The stems of this anemone rise to a height of 40-60cm, according to where it grows, from a clump of much-cut leaves. At the top, each bears a cluster of white flowers, usually with rosy backs, above a green ruff of leaves.

rivularis. From the damp, rocky sub-alpine meadows of the Himalayas to the mountains of west China. A close relative of *A. narcissiflora*. The white petals are backed with metallic-blue, which is repeated in the blue anthers. 60cm.

sylvestris. Dangles delicate white flowers (like over-large snowdrops), which turn into bundles of cream fluff containing seeds. Colonises light soil, more restricted in heavy soil. Flowering begins in spring, continuing intermittently throughout summer. For sun or part shade. 45cm.

tomentosa. From Tibet, flowering earlier than the Japanese hybrid anemones. Large and handsome in leaf, petals rounded, pale pink within, dark on the reverse, one of the best. 1.2m.

'Wild Swan'. A long and free-flowering windflower with typical white flowers but which have a distinct lavender-blue shading to their backs. Best in a humus rich soil and part shade and needs to be kept moist in dry spells. Chelsea Flower Show plant of the year in 2011. 60cm.

ANEMONOPSIS macrophylla. From mountain woods in central Japan only, and rare even there. This beautiful plant has leaves twice cut into threes, and its stems grow some 60-75cm tall. They bear open heads of nodding, waxy flowers like those of an anemone, purple outside and lilac within. It needs humus rich soil in a cool climate, sheltered from drying winds. Height varies with conditions.

ANGELICA archangelica. A great plant valued both for its architectural effect and delicate flavour. In its second year there rises from the broad divided leaves a stout branching stem ending in wide heads of cow parsley flowers. The green seedheads are most decorative. The young hollow stems can be preserved in sugar. Unfortunately, it is biennial, but well worthwhile to carefully place a few seedlings. Late summer. 2m.

gigas. This biennial was sent to me from the United States. It produces domed umbellifer flower heads astonishingly deep beetroot red on thick branching stems. If it sets, then save the seed. Mid to late summer. 1.2m.

ANTENNARIA dioica 'Rubra'. Fluffy rose-pink 'everlasting' heads over mats of silver-grey, flat rosettes. A useful paving plant. Midsummer. 8cm.

ANTHEMIS 'Grallagh Gold'. Very attractive plant. Bright yellow daisies on stiff slender stems over ferny, green foliage, flower for weeks in midsummer. Cut down as soon as faded to encourage fresh basal shoots. 90cm.

marschalliana. A gem. Low mounds of exquisite, finely-cut silver foliage with large daisy-flowers of clear yellow. Midsummer. 15cm.

punctata subsp. cupaniana. Invaluable for the new garden since it quickly makes low sprawling mounds of finely cut, pale-grey leaves covered in midsummer with chalk-white daisies. After flowering and the spent stems are tidied away, the foliage becomes almost white as it protects itself with fine, white hairs, while, in winter you may be surprised to find it has thrown off its protection and the leaves become fresh green. Can be damaged by too much winter wet, but thrives in poor, well-drained soil, in full sun. 40cm.

'Tetworth'. This hybrid (*A. tinctoria* × *A. punctata* subsp. *cupaniana*) is an excellent introduction. Less prostrate than *A. punctata* subsp. *cupaniana*, its woody framework supports bushy plants clothed in soft grey finely-cut leaves, crowded with very neat white daisy flowers throughout the summer. For most soils (excepting soggy) and sun. 45cm.

tinctoria. Collected form, ex Ala Dag, Turkey. Makes low bushy plants whose wiry stems are minimally clothed with small fretted leaves, topped with unusual daisy flowers. They have large yellow centres surrounded by a short frill of petals, produced in joyful profusion throughout summer. Designed for hot dry position. 40cm.

tinctoria 'E.C. Buxton'. One of my best ten garden plants. Above a low neat mound of ferny, green leaves, thin, stiff stems carry creamy-yellow daisies endlessly throughout summer until the frosts. Invaluable in the garden or picked. 45cm.

tinctoria 'Wargrave Variety'. Much admired for its cool, lemon-yellow flowers, looking well with *Euphorbia griffithii* 'Fireglow'. 90cm plus in good soil.

All forms of *Anthemis tinctoria* need to be cut down after flowering and replanted occasionally in refreshed soil to retain vigorous, free-flowering clumps.

ANTHERICUM liliago var. major. Like a miniature Madonna lily, but much easier to grow and flower. From dense tussocks of strap-shaped leaves rise quantities of slender stems clothed from top to bottom with small ivory-white lily-shaped flowers, lasting for weeks during April-May, forming a graceful vertical rising above lower plants. 75-90cm.

ramosum. From low clumps of narrow grass-like leaves rise tall slender stems, branching in the upper half, carrying myriads of star-like white flowers, elegant and dainty. Midsummer. 90cm.

ANTHRISCUS sylvestris 'Ravenswing'. This irresistible form of Queen Anne's lace has dark, brownish-purple leaves, perfect contrast for lacy heads of white flowers which continue in succession for several weeks in early summer. Comes true from seed. Easy in sun or shade. 75cm.

APONOGETON distachyos. Water hawthorn or Cape pond weed, from South Africa, is a very attractive aquatic. From a tuberous rootstock rise many green strap-shaped leaves which lie on the surface of the water creating a round, tray-like shape supporting a long succession of short spikes of tightly packed, sweet-smelling white flowers with jet-black anthers. It will grow in a few centimetres of water or up to a depth of 1m. Good for shady ponds unlike water-lilies.

AQUILEGIA – HARMFUL IF EATEN

alpina. From the Alps and north Italian mountains, in rocky bushy places. Deep blue, sometimes blue and white. 75cm.

canadensis. From the north eastern United States and Canada in rocky woods, this plant is similarly coloured to *A. formosa* var. *truncata* but smaller, and with a larger central yellow bell of petals. 60cm.

chrysantha. Found in open woods of the southern Rockies. All soft yellow with long spurs, it is one of the species from which the long-spurred hybrids were raised, and is a vigorous plant, growing up to 1m high.

flabellata var. pumila. Exceptional among a beautiful genus. The bold bluish foliage is arresting, while the large, soft blue and white flowers are irresistible in early summer. 20cm.

flabellata var. pumila f. alba. Creamy-white flowers shadowed with green. 20cm.

formosa var. truncata. Grows in the shade or part shade of wood openings in the Californian mountains and the Rockies south from Alaska. One of the daintiest, with multitudes of nodding flowers, brilliant scarlet and yellow on much-branched stems. The pistil and stamens extend well below the pointed scarlet sepals giving a sharp dart-like effect as the long spurs end in a very short circle of petals. May-August. 75cm-1m.

longissima. From partially shady rocky slopes on the last spur of the Rockies in west Texas. The flowers are almost white, with very long spurs. July-October. 75cm.

vulgaris. Found in woods and thickets in the Alps, Europe, Siberia and the Himalayas. These crosses include many shades of blue, rich plum, soft pink and white. The blue-green foliage is as handsome as the flowers, especially late in the year when tinted with shades of purple. Excellent in shade or semi-shade, to follow spring bulbs.

vulgaris 'Adelaide Addison'. This lovely old-fashioned double form has blue outer petals while the inner white petals are edged with blue. June-July. 75cm.

vulgaris 'Nivea'. Light green leaves set off creamy-white flowers, true from seed, lovely in small colonies. June-July. 75cm.

vulgaris var. stellata 'Nora Barlow'. Is a curiously fascinating old variety. Stiff stems carry many nodding heads of fully double flowers which combine red, pink and green narrow petals and sepals in subtle harmony, from May to July. 75cm.

vulgaris var. stellata 'Ruby Port'. Anemone flowered double purple. Neat upturned flowers. Sun or part shade. Will seed around. 50cm.

vulgaris Vervaeneana Group. Leaves appear cream from a distance, but are marbled in shades of gold, white and russet tones. Pink flowers. June-July. 60cm.

vulgaris Yellow leafed form. Retains an even shade of yellow, setting off pink columbine flowers. 60cm.

ARABIS alpina subsp. caucasica 'Flore Pleno'. Charming with its stems of double white flowers, like tiny stocks. Spring. 25cm.

alpina subsp. caucasica 'Variegata'. Forms spreading mats of green rosettes, edged with cream. Looks good in winter. 13cm.

× arendsii 'Rosabella'. Rose-pink single flowers over fresh evergreen rosettes. 20cm.

procurrens 'Variegata'. An individual little plant. Forms tight rosettes of shining leaves, splashed with more ivory than green. Many sprays of white flowers in spring. 7cm.

ARCTANTHEMUM arcticum. In warm well-drained soil this plant can be breathtaking in October when it produces quantities of large chalk-white daisies over low mounds of dark green foliage. 40cm.

ARENARIA montana. Makes a snowdrift in summer with its sheets of small rich green leaves simply smothered by large saucer-shaped white flowers. Indispensable. 8cm.

ARISAEMA candidissimum. From rocky slopes and cliff ledges in west China. The great plant collector, G. Forrest, first found it on the sides of the upper Yangtze gorge in Yunnan. One of the latest plants to appear through the soil. Not until June do the bare pink stems appear, opening into the narrow spathe which is white-veined and shadowed with pink and green on the outside, pink and white candy striped inside. The pointed tip overhangs the white spadix, sheltering it from the rain. Neatly wrapped round the base of the stem is a single leaf which unfolds surprisingly large, three-lobed, like a great clover leaf. A mound of them is very handsome, especially in autumn when they turn the colour of chamois leather. This plant will grow in an open situation, provided it is planted in good retentive soil, but is best sheltered from wind. Flowers 20cm. Leaves 25cm long and wide.

consanguineum. Found in moist wood openings and among bushes, from the Himalayas to the west and central Chinese mountains. Like a very elegant umbrella, supported on 45cm long slender stems mottled green and brown. The green hooded flower, striped with brown, extends a long thin brown tail from the tip of the spathe to hang down in front. Does better in the moist and warm gardens of the west country.

jacquemontii. Dark purple stems emerge from the leaf mould wrapped in a transparent sheath, palest green, pencilled irregularly with thin purple slashes. Each stem up to 90cm tall holds at its tip a large, deeply divided round parasol-like leaf, sheltering a sturdy purple and green striped flower.

tortuosum. From woodland slopes of the lower Himalayas. It startles the unwary when they come face to face with its pale hooded flower standing about 1m tall above lower plantings. From a large underground tuber there rises a thick purple-stained stem; halfway up two pedate leaves appear, while above them is poised a snake-like hooded head, a narrow green spathe, which from the tip of the curved lid flickers the long, thin brown tail of the spadix. There are many of these strangely fascinating plants to be found, they need part-shade and deep retentive soil, well enriched with rich leaf-mould soil. Sheltered site. Midsummer. 90cm.

triphyllum. Jack-in-the-pulpit. From rich woods in the eastern United States north to Nova Scotia. For cool shady places. The markings on the spathe vary in intensity. Basically green, the stripes inside are light or dark purplish-brown, lit with palest green. Intensifying the colour is the dark spadix protected beneath the overhanging spathe tip. Orange-red berries seed themselves in favourable sites. June-July. 30cm.

ARISARUM proboscideum. From shady moist slopes in the Apennines. The Mouse-tailed arum is well named. Long thin tubers increase readily beneath humus-rich soil, sending up dense clusters of small shining green leaves. Hidden within them are tiny flowers, white inside with brown backs, the spathe tips extended into long thin tails which poke out among the leaves as though tiny mice had dived in, head first, to hide leaving their round backsides on view. Best in shade, near the edge of a path where you can stoop to see them. May. 10cm.

ARMERIA alliacea. Collected in Portugal. Tall drum-sticks of pale pink flowers in bloom all summer. 30cm.

juniperifolia 'Bevan's Variety'. A gem. Tiny, tight hummocks of dark green leaves are studded with pink, almost stemless thrift flowers. 5cm.

maritima 'Alba'. Neat grassy mounds covered with small drum heads of pure white. Very good ground-cover. Midsummer. 15cm.

maritima 'Corsica'. Short grassy tussocks studded with little thrift heads of unusual brick-red. Midsummer. 15cm.

maritima 'Düsseldorfer Stolz'. Continuous show of large flowers on short stems, light wine-red. 13cm.

maritima 'In the Red'. A valuable addition with purple tinted foliage during the summer, turning more intense as the cold weather sets in. Pink flowers contrast well. 15cm.

ARNICA montana. From alpine and sub-alpine turf in the mountains of central Europe and northern Asia, this plant produces handsome orange daisy flowers, long petalled and strangely scented. A distillation produces Tincture of Arnica, used to soothe bruises. June. 30cm.

ARTEMISIA. With their beautiful silver, highly aromatic foliage, these plants are invaluable as ground cover or background plants in the hot, dry garden.

abrotanum. Southernwood or Lad's love. Put this deliciously aromatic plant beside a path or sitting area. It makes a bushy plant densely set with whorls of feathery, sage-green foliage, lovely contrast for *Salvia officinalis* or cistus Spring pruning keeps it well-shaped. 75cm.

absinthium 'Lambrook Silver'. This does not run, but forms a woody stem from which cascade boldly cut silver leaves, followed by long sprays of yellow mimosa-like flowers. 45cm.

alba 'Canescens'. Very distinctive in form. Low bushes of upturned stems carry the whitest wisps of filigree foliage. At its best midsummer-autumn. 45cm.

arborescens. Strikingly beautiful silver filigree foliage covers a quick-growing elegant shrub, for well drained soil in southern counties. Well worth putting a cutting in a cold frame or cool greenhouse. 90cm. Taller in warm areas.

dracunculus. The true French tarragon. Narrow green foliage adds very distinctive flavour to salads, chicken and fish dishes. 60cm.

glacialis. Ground-hugging mats of silvery-white thread-like foliage, useful among small bulbs. 5cm.

lactiflora. Grows in moist meadows and forest clearings in the mountains of western China, often with tall anemones, aruncus, *Astilbe rivularis* and others. It is the odd man out in a family, most of whom are adapted to drought conditions. I value this as a strong vertical in cool retentive soil. Tall, stiffly-upright stems carry dark green, jagged foliage, topped in August with large, loose heads of small creamy-white flowers. Good against a dark background or behind blue *Aster × frikartii* 'Mönch'. 1.2m.

lactiflora Guizhou Group. Dark purple branching stems carry creamy-white fluffy flowers. Eye-catching. 1.2m.

ludoviciana subsp. ludoviciana var. incompta. Low mass of woody stems erupt into a froth of feathery, felted leaves which whiten with drought. Runs about, but that adds to its charm among stouter plants. 30cm.

ludoviciana 'Silver Queen'. Tall stems up to 1m clothed in white felted foliage, carry narrow branching spires of pearl-grey buds. Lovely contrast to rounded bushes in garden design. Dries well hung upside down.

ludoviciana 'Valerie Finnis'. Came to me many years ago from Valerie Finnis when I called it after her. This plant is highly valued for its new young shoots, terminating in large rosettes of startling whiteness, like silver flowers. 75cm.

pontica. Forms a miniature forest of stiff, upright stems clothed in finely-cut silver-grey scented foliage. Excellent feature and ground cover in dry sunny places. Spreads by underground stems. 45cm.

'Powis Castle'. Not unlike *A. aborescens*, which is probably a parent, but altogether sturdier, forming a low mound of silver fine-cut foliage, much admired here on dry gravel. 60cm.

schmidtiana. For edges, or among small bulbs this plant makes low cushions of silky, finely-cut silver foliage. 10cm.

stelleriana. Bold handsome foliage, looking like chrysanthemum leaves cut out of white felt, sprawls on lax stems to make an effective edging to a dry, sunny border. 20cm.

ARTHROPODIUM candidum. Produces low clumps of pinky-buff, grass-like foliage. Above this stand wiry branching stems starred with tiny white flowers in midsummer, still worth looking at in October when full of tiny black seeds. Good among cyclamen or contrast for the black, strap-shaped leaves of *Ophiopogon planiscarpus.* 'Nigrescens'. 25cm.

ARUM creticum. From fat underground tubers glossy spear-shaped leaves emerge early in winter. In spring, sweet-scented flowers appear above and among them, clear yellow, goblet-shaped spathes folding backwards at the tip to reveal long, thin spadices. This treasure is best in sheltered, sunny situations, in well-fed soil. Has survived many years at Hidcote in Gloucestershire and Great Dixter, Sussex. 45cm.

italicum subsp. italicum 'Marmoratum'. These exotic leaves unroll from the leaf-mould in late autumn, continuing to grow throughout the winter, bowing beneath bitter frost, but standing undamaged immediately it thaws. By April they are full height, dark glossy green, spear-shaped, and veined with ivory. In September, above the bare earth, appear stems of red berries. Alas it has now done rather too well in my garden and has now to be meticulously dug out to keep it in check. 40cm.

ARUNCUS aethusifolius. Produces low clumps of fresh green leaves as finely cut as chervil but with more substance. A forest of wiry flower stems arise 30cm, carrying tiny astilbe-like heads of small creamy-white flowers in June. By September they are still attractive, with barren heads tinted light chestnut, while seed-bearing heads are dark, shining brown, and foliage develops pink and reddish autumn tints.
dioicus. Goat's beard. Grows in mountain woods and along shady stream-sides from central Europe to China and Japan; also in North America. Makes a superb garden plant from the moment its elegant sprays of light green pinnate leaves emerge in spring. I like it best just as the flowers are opening. Long tapering spires of tiny green buds become cream seed pearls, finally bursting into a plume of creamy frothy blossom, towards the end of June. Male plants make superior flowers, but females produce graceful chestnut-brown seedheads. 1.8m.
dioicus 'Glasnevin'. For smaller gardens with creamy-white flowers. Up to 1m.
dioicus 'Kneiffii'. Flowers similar to *A. dioicus* but daintier, as is the whole plant. The leaves look as though they have been eaten to the veins by some creature but perversely (perhaps because it is the natural state) these thread-like segments appear delicately attractive. Flowers slightly later. 75cm.
'Woldemar Meier'. Stands up to 1m tall with very open spires of tiny cream flowers in June, above a mound of finely cut leaves, both dainty and elegant.

ASARUM caudatum. From deep conifer woods in the well-watered mountains of British Columbia. The matt-green leaves are somewhat larger than the European form, while curious reddish-brown flowers with three tail-like whips lie flat on the ground, hidden among the leaves, which form weed-smothering, evergreen carpets in shade. 25cm.
europaeum. Covers the floor of central European, Scandinavian, Russian and west Siberian woods, as ivy does in British woods. Round kidney-shaped leaves of rich glossy green on slowly creeping surface shoots eventually make almost evergreen carpets. Dull brown flowers crouch unseen except by fertilising flies and beetles. 10cm.

ASPERULA aristata subsp. scabra. Forms gypsophila-like mounds of meshed wiry stems, carrying fresh green linear leaves, sparkling with myraids of tiny white starry flowers. Charming in a mixed bouquet, effective on the border edge. Ordinary soil and sun. 40cm.

ASPHODELINE liburnica. Slender willowy stems clothed in needle-like grey-green leaves carry spires of six-petalled star-shaped flowers each marked with a central green vein. Not open till mid-afternoon so unspoilt by midday heat. Midsummer. 1m.
lutea. Tall stems, bear whorls of grey-blue, grassy leaves. Strap-petalled, star-like flowers of bright yellow. The seed pods form a wand of bright green cherries which eventually dry to crinkled brown, still useful. 90cm.

ASPHODELUS aestivus. Similar to *A. albus.* Carrying slightly pink-flushed flowers in early summer, forming handsome seedheads in late summer. 1.5m.

albus. Seen everywhere around the Mediterranean on dry, stony soils. From fleshy roots it produces a huddle of long narrow leaves above which stand tall, smooth, strong branching stems topped with spires of long narrow buds which open in early summer to starry-white flowers, warmed by a soft brown vein running down the centre of each petal. Dormant by late summer. 1.5m.

ASTER. Many now have a new identity. See *Doellingeria, Eurybia* and *Symphytotrichum*
amellus. From rather dry open woods and rocky grasslands of central Europe to Asia Minor and the northern meadow-like steppes of Russia. The wild form is scarcely known, but many named selected forms exist, varied in quality. The general habit is low growing with rough leaves and clusters of large flowers in many shades from lavender to violet, including various pinks. Some stand well, others flop untidily.
amellus 'King George'. This old variety is still a firm favourite with its long-lasting show of large violet-blue flowers on compact plants, which need no support and are resistant to mildew. For full sun or part shade. 45cm.
amellus 'Sonia'. Produces shortish stems stiffly upright, holding in autumn heads of broad-petalled, mauvish-pink flowers about 5cm across illuminated with greenish-yellow centres. 40cm.
amellus 'Veilchenkönigin'. An excellent old variety of striking colour. Stiff dark stems carry open heads of intense violet, well-shaped flowers throughout autumn. 40cm.
× frikartii 'Mönch'. Each individual stem produces seven or eight side branches starting from the base, all carrying further branching heads of flowers. An established clump will send up many such stems resulting in a wide-spreading elegant bouquet of flowers which lasts for months from late July-October, somehow never looking untidy with dead flowers. Individual flowers are 6cm across, warm lavender-blue with yellowish-green centres. Absolutely the best daisy, for long display and sheer beauty: does not need staking, and is not affected by mildew. Deserves the best soil and position in the garden. 1m.
laevis 'Calliope'. I had this from David Shackleton's garden in Ireland. Stout purple-black stems carry open pyramidal heads of lilac-blue daisies 2.5cm across, in autumn, will stand 1.5m tall in deep, retentive soil.
pyrenaeus 'Lutetia'. One of my favourites. Makes a loose mound of interlaced branching stems smothered to the ground with pale lilac-blue flowers, with finely-rayed petals 5cm across. Lasts for weeks in the garden, perfect to soften the outline of mixed autumn arrangements. Mildew free. 50cm.
tataricus. I had this variety from Michael Wickenden of Cally Gardens in Scotland. In an open situation, in deep retentive soil, it makes a strong clump of tall, erect stems clothed from top to bottom with fresh foliage, forming a handsome column of green, topped in October with branched heads of blue daisy flowers. For the back of the border. 1.8m.
tongolensis 'Napsbury'. This plant is a selected variety of an alpine from the mountains of south west China. Over mats of hairy, dark green leaves stand purple-blue daisies lit with orange eyes, lovely in midsummer. Needs planting in fresh soil every 2 to 3 years. 25cm.

ASTILBE 'Bronce Elegans'. A beautiful dwarf hybrid. Green foliage, less finely cut than *A.* 'Sprite', darkened with bronze shadows, makes a perfect base for arching sprays of tiny flowers which combine cream and salmon pink. July-August. 30cm.
'Cattleya' (× arendsii). Above bronze-stained foliage stand elegant spires of deep rose pink flowers on dark slender stems. 1.2m.

chinensis var. pumila. A selected garden variety, ideal for moist edges. Narrow branched spikes of densely set, rose flowers with blue anthers produce a mauve-pink effect. I like the narrow, stiffly upright silhouettes, which continue until winter as buff seedheads. Carpets of broadly spreading foliage make useful ground-cover. 45cm.

chinensis var. taquetii 'Purpurlanze'. Standing tall and elegant, narrow pyramidal heads of dark buds open vivid, light-purple fluffy flowers. 90cm.

chinensis var. taquetii 'Superba'. Flowering when other astilbes have finished. This Astilbe, and *A. chinensis* var. *davidii*, can do with less moisture (but not drought) and will take more sun than the others, but they will also flower and look superb in partial shade. *A. chinensis.* var. *taquetia* 'Superba' has smallish crinkled leaves tinged with bronze. Tall stately stems held well above the foliage carry dense spires of fluffy rosy-mauve flowers which look well near rudbeckia or the lovely pale lemon *Lysimachia ciliata*. 1.2m.

× **crispa 'Perkeo'.** Finely divided leaves create an almost parsley-like effect, bronze when young, maturing dark green. Bronze stems carry narrow spires of rose-pink flowers. 30cm.

'Dunkellachs'. Enchanting for edge of damp border in sun or part shade. Wide sprays of light and dark pink flowers almost smother neat basal foliage. 30cm.

'Elsie Schluck' (× arendsii). Almost guardsman's red. Well-shaped spires of fluffy flowers, a good clear colour without a touch of mauve. 60cm.

'Fanal' (× arendsii). Dark stems and leaves set off spires of deep red flowers. 60cm.

'Federsee' (× arendsii). Above fresh green foliage stand broadly, pyramidal heads of fluffy flowers, deep rose-pink. 60cm.

'Grete Pungel' (× arendsii). Above finely-cut bronze-tinted foliage stand narrow, pyramidal heads of densely set flowers, opening rose-pink fading to pale pink on dark stained stems. Very distinctive. 90cm.

'Professor van der Wielen'. Slender, red stained stems carry widely spaced drooping sprays of creamy-white flowers with flower heads up to 50cm long, the massed effect is outstanding above pale green divided foliage. 1m.

rivularis. Growing in lush valley meadows and wood edges from the Himalayas to the west Chinese mountains, this giant astilbe is for the wild garden, or for large-scale water-side planting (not in the bog). Great stems of broad divided leaves, glossy above, bristly beneath, are so heavily veined they produce a quilted effect. In August it is over topped with huge arching plumes of small greenish-white flowers which last long as nut-brown seedheads. Underground shoots could be a nuisance in a restricted area. 2m.

'Rosa Perle' (× arendsii). Massed stems of narrowly pyramidal flower heads appear like pale flames; cream buds opening pale, shrimp-pink, flowering later than *A.* × 'Venus'. 90cm.

'Sprite'. Much-divided leaves, chocolate-bronze when young, slowly changing to very dark green, the setting for wide triangular sprays of pale, shell-pink, fluffy flowers. They last for weeks, imperceptibly deepening to chestnut and finally reddish-brown seedheads, most welcome in the autumn border. August-November. 45cm.

'Venus' (× arendsii). From cream buds open graceful plumes composed of pale powdery-pink tiny flowers, always admired. 90cm.

'Weisse Gloria' (× arendsii). Has dense pure white plumes above dark foliage. 60cm.

ASTILBOIDES tabularis. Large, round, simple leaves, the size and shape of a dinner-plate (or a tea-tray, in very moist soil), dimpled in the centre where they are attached to the stem. The leaf edges are slightly scalloped. One of the most beautiful and calming of leaves for a shady place. A strong flower stem carries heavy drooping clusters of star-shaped creamy-white flowers in late summer. 90cm.

ASTRANTIA. Astrantias prefer retentive soil improved with leaf-mould in partial shade. Dead heading will extend the flowering season into autumn, and prevent unwanted seedling, which are unlikely to come true from selected forms.

'Buckland'. Has white outer 'ray' petals, green-tipped, filled with a posy of quivering tiny pink flowers, the overall effect pale-pink. Very free flowering, for weeks in summer. 75cm.

'Hadspen Blood'. Among several named varieties of wine-coloured astrantia this is one of the finest. 60cm.

major alba. Looking like old-fashioned posies are many up-turned heads, each made of many narrow segments, green tipped, filled with quivering creamy centres. Perfect, pressed flat, for dried picture making. Mid to late summer. 75cm.

major 'Claret'. A fine wine coloured variety selected by Piet Oudolf. Plants grown from seed come very close to type. Mid summer. 60cm.

major Gill Richardson Group. Named after a fine plantswoman. Strong growing form flower colour does seem slightly variable with at best deep wine red flowers on robust stems. Grow in this and all other wine coloured forms in as much light as possible to maximise the intensity of the flower colour. 80cm.

major 'Madeleine van Bennekom'. Once established produces large green tipped white flowers during midsummer. Shorter than some at 60cm.

major subsp. involucrata 'Shaggy'. Can produce flowers more than 5cm across with long narrow white `petals', more widely separated with green pointed tips. 75cm.

major 'Sunningdale Variegated'. Possibly the most beautiful variegated foliage plant in spring, irresistible for garden design or flower arranging. Large, hand-shaped and pointed leaves are elegantly marked with yellow and cream. Branching stems of white, flushed-pink posy flowers are an added bonus during summer-autumn. 75cm.

maxima. Each flower resembles a Victorian posy. The graceful branching stems are topped with strawberry-pink broad-petalled flowers, filled with quivering masses of pink stamens. Mid-late summer. 75cm.

'Roma'. Another Piet Oudolf selection with delightful heads of clear pink pincushion like flowers. Repeat flowering and a useful addition. 50cm.

'Stonehouse Surprise'. Taller than *A.* 'Buckland'. Deep pink buds open to show the central dome of crimson stems carrying turquoise-green ovaries tipped with pink anthers, all surrounded by the outer ruff of bracts pencilled with green and crimson veins, sharply tipped green. Phew! a Catherine wheel effect. Midsummer-autumn. It came to us unnamed from Stonehouse Cottage Nursery. 1m.

ATRIPLEX halimus. Tree pursalane from southern Europe. Handsome foliage-shrub for full sun in dry, well drained soils, where its vigorous bright appearance makes bold contrast among cistus and lavender. Furnished with heavily silvered shield-shaped leaves. To control shape and size and ensure plentiful fresh foliage, prune in spring, and again lightly in July. Flowers insignificant, buff and late. 2m x 1.6m wide.

AUBRETA 'Silberrand'. Another good plant from Ernst Pagels, Germany. Small, shining-green, wedge-shaped leaves are sharply outlined in creamy-white, creating a good effect all the year round. Blue flowers are a bonus in spring-early summer. 8cm.

AURINIA (Alyssum).
saxatalis 'Citrina'. Forms a sprawling mound of grey-green leaves buried beneath sprays of tiny, cool-lemon flowers in spring. 25cm.

saxatalis 'Dudley Nevill Variegated'. Forms a striking contrast among silver plants in well-drained soil, every soft, grey leaf broadly margined with cream, alas prone to revert. Then it becomes *A. saxatilis* 'Dudley Nevill'. The Soft apricot flowers are a welcome change from the usual yellow. 25cm.

BALLOTA acetabulosa. Similar to *B. pseudodictamnus*, but slightly daintier, and appears whiter in drier conditions. Each leaf has a faintly scalloped edge, and the green 'bobbles' along the curved flowering stems are larger. 75cm.

pseudodictamnus. One of the loveliest greys. From a woody base spring long curving stems of round leaves clothed in grey-white felt. The drier the better. 75cm.

pseudodictamnus subsp. ex. Crete. This attractive form was collected many years ago by one of my staff, Ian Stanton. Smaller in all its parts than the other forms, ideal for the border edge, or rock garden. 40cm.

BAPTISIA australis. A superior lupin-like plant needing deep, preferably lime-free soil where its long roots can be left undisturbed. You will be rewarded with slim spires of rich blue flowers, while autumn frosts leave behind dramatic clusters of black swollen seed pods on dark, stiffly-upright stems. 90cm.

BARBAREA vulgaris 'Variegata'. This variegated form of land cress makes attractive rosettes in rich soil, heavily mottled cream and green. Comes true from seed. 30cm.

BELAMCANDA chinensis. Blackberry lily. A bulbous plant producing fans of iris-like leaves which clasp the lower half of the stems. Above them bare branches form a zig-zag pattern to display bright narrow-petalled flowers, yellow heavily spotted with orange, developing by October, into large oval seed pods which split wide to reveal a cluster of shining black seeds, very like a blackberry. Needs a warm, well-drained site, or can be lifted and replanted in spring. 60cm.

BELLIS perennis 'Dresden China'. In early summer the pale pink pom-poms of this little double daisy are irresistible. Needs regular dividing. 8cm.

BERGENIA. These plants are among the most valuable as ground-cover, or for flower arranging. Being evergreen they are always a feature. The following are not to be confused with the commonly grown variety *B. schmidtii*, they are superior in flower and leaf. In the design of the garden, well placed groups of bergenia are as important in drier areas, as hostas are in richer, cooler soil. Place them in full sun and resist the temptation to tuck them in the shade and many of the following will repay you with rich winter colour. Severe winters may damage some, but all quickly produce fresh leaves in spring, creating a bold feature all the year round. Except for the dwarf forms most foliage clumps are about 30-50cm tall. Flower stems eventually stand well above at 45-60cm. All flower in April-May.

BERGENIA – Species

cordifolia 'Purpurea'. A superb plant, ideal for ground-cover and contrast with large rounded wavy leaves. Occasionally in summer one turns bright red or yellow, while winter frost burnishes them all to a purplish-red. Tall rhubarb red stalks carry vivid magenta flowers intermittently throughout summer. 45cm.

cordifolia 'Rosa Schwester'. Another form showing excellent winter colour in exposed situations. Mid-pink flowers during April. 50cm.

crassifolia 'Autumn Red'. Smaller leaves than *B. cordifolia*, flat and spoon-shaped. Turn vividly red in winter. Soft pink flowers, early summer. 30cm.

purpurascens 'Irish Crimson'. Given me by Helen Dillion. Rosettes of small oval leaves stand bolt upright, evenly stained light-reddish bronze in winter. Compelling on the border edge penetrated with low winter sunlight. 25cm.

stracheyi. A smaller bergenia from Afghanistan and west Himalayas. Among the small rounded leaves huddle short-stemmed clusters of rose-pink flowers. 15cm.

stracheyi Alba Group. The purity of white flowers held in small tight posies is enhanced by green calyxes. Small oval leaves are held upright in neat clumps. March-April. 15cm.

BERGENIA – Hybrids

'Abendglocken'. Medium-sized spoon-shaped leaves form good rosettes, assuming tints of bronzed enamel in late autumn-winter. 30cm.

'Abendglut'. Forms neat rosettes of roundish leaves, crinkle-edged, richly coloured maroon and plum-red in winter. Semi-double flowers are vivid rose-red in spring. 30cm.

'Admiral'. Oval, upstanding, weather resistant leaves, one of the best for bright winter colour with bronze and crimson tints. Cherry-pink flowers held well above leaves in spring. 30cm.

'Baby Doll'. Large flowers, soft pink, very free-flowering. Forms dense cover of medium-sized smooth, round leaves. No winter colour. 30cm.

'Ballawley'. Largest of all; shining fresh green leaves all summer are bronzed and reddened by frost. Branching heads of rose-red flowers on tall stems in spring and a few in autumn. 60cm.

'Beethoven'. An Eric Smith hybrid. Large dense clusters of white flowers ageing to pale pink and held in coral red calyxes. May-June. 30cm.

'Blickflang'. Means eye-catcher! Large heads of light-rose flowers densely packed stand on short stems, just above medium-sized leaves. Striking effect. Late flowering. 60cm.

'Bressingham Ruby'. Makes neat clusters of medium-sized spoon-shaped leaves with finely serrated edges. Winter colour superb, polished dark burgundy surfaces contrast with lighter crimson reverse. Tall stems carry spires of deep-rose, drooping bells in spring. Overall smaller in scale than B. 'Eric Smith'. 60cm.

'Bressingham Salmon'. Adds an unusual shade to our range of oh-so useful elephants ears. Winter foliage colour a pleasing burnished olive-green. Large salmon-pink flowers in April. 45cm.

'Bressingham White'. One of the best free-flowering forms. Opening pure white before expanding to the palest pink. Winter foliage not remarkable. 30cm.

'David'. A distinct cultivar with paddle shaped upright olive green foliage the backs of which colour well during winter. Deep pink flowers during spring. More upright habit than many others. 40cm.

'Eric Smith'. This superb form was raised by Eric Smith of 'The Plantsmen'. Undoubtedly the best for winter effect; large, rounded, crinkled leaves have polished bronze-tinted surfaces while backs, caught in low sunlight, glow rich carmine-red. 45cm.

'Eroica'. Curved branching flower stems carry open cups of vivid rose-pink lit with pale blue stigmas and cream anthers poised well above leaves on slender red-stained stems. Colours well in winter cold, bright cherry surface, maroon-stained undersides. April-May. 60cm.

'Jo Watanabe'. Smallish oval leaves stand upright to show glistening rose-red backs, an outstanding winter colour. 20cm.

'Margery Fish'. (Honouring Mrs Fish, who valued this family long before its worth was recognised as it is today). I value it for its distinctive foliage, large new leaves are glossy, fresh green and deeply veined. Above them stand tall reddish stems carrying heads of upturned rose-pink flowers with dark centres, retaining good colour and form well into May. 75cm.

'Morgenröte'. Large rosettes of rounded leaves produce dense heads of cherry-pink flowers in spring followed by an impressive second flowering in June. 45cm.

'Mrs Crawford'. Named after a friend who collected it in Kashmir, Mrs. Crawford, a member of the Frinton-on-Sea Flower Arranging Club. Neat rosettes of medium-sized leaves, very good autumn colour, rich plum and crimson tones. Narrow heads of white flowers in green calyxes in spring. 30cm.

'Pugsley's Pink'. A large planting of this along our car park entrance delights winter visitors when its large glossy leaves are suffused with dark bronze-red tones, accentuated by crimson stems, making outstanding contrast with evergreen shrubs. 60cm.

'Rosi Klose'. Spoon-shaped, medium-sized leaves, not particularly well-coloured in winter, but one of the best in flower, open bell-shaped flowers of an unusual salmon shade. 30cm.

'Schneekönigin'. Another interesting German hybrid with extra large flowers, palest shell-pink, almost white. Foliage remains green. 40cm.

'Silberlicht'. Strikingly beautiful with large trusses of pure white flowers in late spring, flushed pink with age or weather conditions. 30cm.

'Sunningdale'. Bright coral red flower stems carry fine heads of vivid rose-pink flowers. Foliage has good autumn and winter colour. 30cm.

'Wintermärchen'. A small-leafed bergenia. Narrow pointed leaves slightly twisting to reveal both the polished surfaces and light carmine backs, some leaves brilliant scarlet. Red stems carry narrow heads of deep-rose flowers. 30cm.

BRUNNERA macrophylla. In spring, long sprays of tiny forget-me-not blue flowers are followed by robust clumps of basal leaves, each huge and heart-shaped, making good ground-cover in shade. 45cm.

macrophylla 'Betty Bowring'. Has sprays of pure white forget-me-not like flowers above large matt-green leaves. 45cm.

macrophylla 'Dawson's White'. Heart shaped leaves boldly variegated, deep-green and creamy-white, some almost entirely white. Needs careful placing, protected from sun scorch or wind damage, in soil that never dries out. 30cm.

macrophylla 'Hadspen Cream'. Large, light-green leaves are irregularly bordered with primrose which dissolves partially into the centre. Gentler colouring than *B. macrophylla* 'Dawson's White' and easier to grow well, needs partial shade and retentive soil. 45cm.

macrophylla 'Jack Frost'. Heart-shaped leaves almost totally silvered, enhanced with a fine network of green veins and edged with a narrow green rim, form a setting for sprays of blue forget-me-not like flowers throughout spring and early summer. They are followed by new, much larger basal leaves which make dramatic contrast with green-leafed plants until autumn frosts if grown in part-shade and good soil. 50cm.

macrophylla 'Langtrees'. Large rough-textured dark green leaves are bordered with a pattern of silvery-grey spots, as if a paint brush dipped in aluminium paint had been used. Long sprays of forget-me-not blue flowers hover above them for weeks in spring. 45cm.

BUDDLEJA crispa. Prolonged drought intensifies the white felted coating which protects leaves and stems. Pendulous clusters of furry white buds open tiny lilac flowers. Forms medium to large shrub. Best against a warm wall in a well drained soil.

lindleyana. This elegant shrub flowers well into autumn, with a fountain-like effect when every branch tip carries drooping slender spikes of small violet flowers opening from grey velvety buds. Up to 2.5m tall in fertile soil. Makes attractive feature in a tub.

BUGLOSSOIDES purpurocaerulea. Needs sun and well drained soil, will tolerate chalk. Thrives here in open spaces in the poor sand of my woodland garden, where it makes good ground cover, sending out long trails of dark green matt leaves sprinkled with gentian-blue flowers. Good cover for taller bulbs. 40cm.

BUPHTHALMUM salicifolium 'Alpengold'. Low branching stems stained purple, crowded in summer with warm yellow daisies, unobtrusive foliage. Very good for edge of border. 60cm.

BUPLEURUM falcatum. Creates a soft haze of yellowy-green, for weeks, in midsummer when most euphorbias are over. Tiny, cow parsley-like heads on thin wiry branching stems seed harmlessly among stouter more colourful neighbours. A biennial for the dry sunny garden. 60cm.
fruticosum. Forms an evergreen shrub clothed in leathery blue-green foliage, creating a foil for the curiously attractive wide heads of tiny lime-green flowers in late summer, unexpectedly related to cow parsley. 1.2m.
longifolium. Has framed a cluster of tiny, yellow flowers in large round bracts, so it looks not unlike a buttercup in shape, going from green to lovely coppery-bronze tones, held on slender branching stems. 60cm.

BUTOMUS umbellatus. Grows in shallow water. Sheaves of stiff grassy leaves make fine verticals among clumps of round leafed caltha (Marsh marigolds). Flower stems carry umbels of rose-pink flowers in midsummer. 1.2m.

CALAMINTHA grandiflora. Useful for edge of border, neat little bushes of fresh green foliage, dotted with rose-pink blossoms all summer. 25cm.
nepeta. Charming in late summer with clouds of tiny pale blue flowers on bushy aromatic plants. Loved by bees. 45cm.
nepeta subsp. nepeta 'Blue Cloud'. This form has deeper blue flowers, the two planted together in groups create a pretty shaded effect. 45cm.

CALLA palustris. Bog arum. Useful round pond margins where its long scrambling rootstock makes floating rafts of small shiny heart shaped leaves. Small greenish-white arum like flowers in May.

CALTHA – HARMFUL IF EATEN
palustris var. alba. The lovely white form of the marsh marigold. From early spring to midsummer. 15cm.
palustris 'Flore Pleno'. The double marsh marigold whose golden flowers come as early as the single form but last longer. Spring. 30cm.
palustris var. palustris. Impressive foliage plant for damp soil or pond side, where it creates large rafts of rich shining leaves. Flowers fewer, larger and earlier than *C. palustris*. 60cm by as much space as available.

CALYSTEGIA hederacea 'Flore Pleno'. An exotic Japanese variety of giant bindweed. Long, narrow, arrow-shaped leaves clothe scrambling stems. A bud in every leaf axil opens a large, fully double, pale-pink flower, like a camellia or double old rose. June-August. 1.2m.

CAMASSIA. Bulbous plants from rich prairie land of north west America. They produce the finest flowers in well-fed cultivated soil, forming valued vertical features in early summer, tucked behind or between low shrubs or plants where their long lax leaves can be concealed. They look stately, naturalized in grass, when it begins to run to flower.
cusickii. Strong flower stems, carry spires of ice-blue, narrow petalled star-shaped flowers. May. 75cm.
leichtlinii 'Plena'. Still uncommon but very dramatic. Closely set rosettes of double cream flowers are carried on stout stems. Needs rich soil. Does not set seed. May-June. 1.2m.
leichtlinii subsp. leichtlinii. Tall, strong, bare stems carry spires of cream starry flowers taking up little space among other rounded plants or shrubs. Seeds freely if not dead-headed. May-June. 90cm.
leichtlinii subsp. suksdorfii Caerulea Group. Carries spires of rich-blue, star-shaped flowers on the upper two thirds of stout bare stems. Forms clumps of short, less lax leaves. 1m.
leichtlinii subsp. suksdorfii 'Electra'. Flowers twice as large as any other camassia are a rich amethyst-blue, arising on stout stems from clumps of strap-shaped leaves produced by fist-shaped bulbs. Outstanding in May-June. 90cm.
quamash. Has shorter stems of dark blue flowers. Untidy foliage so grow it lower covering plants. 30cm.

CAMPANULA alliariifolia. A handsome plant, with heart-shaped hairy leaves sending up long arching stems, hung with drooping white bells. Midsummer. 50cm.
'Burghaltii'. Deep purple-blue buds contrast with the large palest-blue open bells which dangle from slender stems. An irresistible plant. Early summer, and again in autumn. 45cm.
glomerata var. alba 'Schneekrone'. Forms weed-smothering patches, with useful spikes of pure white bells clustered in whorls round the stem. Midsummer. 40cm.
glomerata 'Caroline'. A welcome colour form, with lovely soft lilac-pink flowers in early summer. 30cm.
glomerata 'Joan Elliot'. Clusters of rich violet-blue flowers on lax 30cm stems. Not such large heads as *C. glomerata* 'White Barn', but flowers over long period, intermittently, till autumn frosts.
glomerata 'White Barn'. Dense rounded heads of violet-purple bells on short spikes, clumps slowly spreading. Fine for edges. Midsummer. 30cm.
lactiflora. A splendid sight when stout, leafy stems are crowned with great heads of powder-blue bell flowers. Well placed among shrubs, especially shrub roses. Mid and late summer. Cuttings from a particularly fine form. 1.5m.
lactiflora 'Alba'. The much admired white form. Grown from cuttings. 1.2m.
lactiflora 'Loddon Anna'. Large heads of soft dusky-pink flowers in midsummer. 1.2m.
lactiflora 'Pouffe'. Well named. Low green mounds are smothered with light blue open bells. 25cm.
lactiflora 'Prichard's Variety'. Much sought after, this well-selected form has much deeper, richer blue flowers than the type, grows shorter too, about 1m.
latifolia. Makes a fine feature plant. From basal clumps of rich green foliage ascend straight, stiff leafy stems topped with spikes of large, blue, tubular flowers. Seeds freely, best to remove seedheads. 1m.

latifolia var. macrantha alba. A stately plant of distinction. Tall, stiff stems carry large, pure white bells, impressive against a dark background. The fretted seedheads are interesting, bleached for dried arrangements. Midsummer. 90cm.

latiloba 'Percy Piper'. Slowly makes an evergreen patch of green rosettes. The strongest send up stiff straight stems closely set with wide saucer-shaped flowers of rich lavender-blue, flowering mid to late summer. 75cm.

persicifolia. The Peach leaved bellflower. An old-fashioned cottage garden flower of great charm and seemingly determined to pop up anywhere here in our gardens. Clumps gradually increase to form spreading ground cover from which arise spikes of blue, bell-like flowers in early summer. Doesn't seem to fussy but flowers best in full sun. 75cm.

poscharskyana 'Stella'. Desirable on sight. Makes dense mats of neat green leaves, picottee edged, buried in midsummer, beneath rich-blue star-shaped flowers. 8cm.

'Sarastro'. This stunning hybrid (between *C. punctata* and *C. trachelium*) sports narrow, pleated navy-blue buds, which open silky violet-blue, bell flowers in profusion on 38 stems. Great effect near yellow such as the ribbon-like grass *Hakonechloa macra* 'Aureola'. Height varies 45-75cm. Any soil, in sun or part shade.

takesimana. Where there is room to spread, this impressive bellflower with heart-shaped leaves, produces armfuls of arching spires hung with long narrow white bells, flushed lilac with darker insides. Midsummer. 60cm.

carpatica var. turbinata. Turban bellflower. A gem amongst campanulas. Free flowering, tidy clumps smothered beneath rich blue saucer-shaped flowers. Mid to late summer. 30cm.

carpatica var. turbinata f. alba. Exquisitely palest blue, almost white with deeper central point. 30cm.

CANNA indica 'Purpurea'. Bold simple leaves shaded purple and held on stout stems form an upright column topped in late summer with narrow, lily-like flowers tinted red and orange, late summer-autumn. 1.5m.

Cannas make dramatic feature plants in rich soil in sunny mixed borders. They must be lifted (except in very warm counties), in late autumn, and stored, but remember to check them as they come into growth in spring, pot them then, and grow on until safe to plant them out.

CARDAMINE heptaphylla. Forms a colony of bare stems topped with an umbrella of much-divided leaves above which stand clusters of chalk-white four petalled flowers during April. 70cm.

kitaibelii. Above handsome foliage, divided into pairs of pointed, tooth-edged leaflets stand bare stems carrying wide trusses of pink flushed buds, opening white, 4-petalled flowers in March. For part-shade, in moist, leaf mould soil. 25cm.

pentaphylla. A spring delight for cool soil. Fine cut leaves and nodding flower stems unroll together, the flowers soft lilac, like large cuckoo flowers. 30cm.

pentaphylla 'Albus'. Above low clusters of light green palmate leaves, stand handsome trusses of chalk- white crucifier flowers. For part shade. 30cm.

pratensis 'Flore Pleno'. The double Lady's smock. From rosettes of dark green deeply cut leaves rise dainty spires of pale lilac double flowers. A delightful spring flower for damp soil. 25cm.

quinquefolia. It is a welcome surprise in late February-March to find a vigorous patch of bright green sharply cut, tooth-edged flowers against the icy cool of snowdrops. It spreads slowly but disappears early, like celandines, the space covered by late-comers such as hostas. 25cm.

raphanifolia. Useful ground-cover by the water's edge. Spikes of cool lilac flowers are a beautiful contrast with spring-fresh foliage. 30cm.

trifolia. Neat edging in part shade, close packed trifoliate leaves, evergreen tinged purple in winter, covered with heads of tiny white, cress-like flowers in early summer. 18cm.

CARLINA acaulis subsp. simplex. Dark green very cut prickly foliage has dramatic thistle flowers on short stems, each a wide pale disc surrounded by silvered 'petals', in late summer. It dries perfectly. 30cm.

CARYOPTERIS × **clandonensis 'Arthur Simmonds'.** Very desirable autumn flowering small shrub. Soft blue flowers in terminal spires, arching stems of grey-green foliage. Up to 1m.
× **clandonensis 'Heavenly Blue'.** More upright in habit than *C.* × *clandonensis* 'Arthur Simmonds', deeper blue flowers with grey foliage. Up to 1.2m.
× **clandonensis 'Worcester Gold'.** Pale yellow-green leaves make a striking contrast with pale blue flowers in late summer-autumn. Up to 1m.

CATANANCHE caerulea. Clumps of narrow grey leaves send up branching stems of silver scaly buds which open as lavender-blue daisies, dark-eyed, in midsummer. 60cm.
caerulea 'Alba'. This white flowered form of cupid's dart is outstanding. Both forms require a well drained soil in full sun. 60cm.

CENOLOPHIUM denudatum. Baltic parsley. An admirable umbellifer to create an interesting vertical in cool conditions. Forms a mound of finely cut leaves, above which stand tall, erect, branching stems, topped with flat heads of tiny green flowers . Lovely above astrantias. 1m.

CENTAUREA cheiranthifolia. Similar to *C. montana*, the mountain knapweed, but with large, soft creamy-yellow cornflower blooms. For open sunny situation. 45cm.
hypoleuca 'John Coutts'. This fine knapweed is seldom out of flower from early midsummer until autumn. Deep rose flowers are held on stiff stems above deeply-cut grey-green leaves. 60cm.
macrocephala. A bold plant. Stiff stems carry large, shining buds of brown papery scales from which burst a mass of golden thread-like petals in late summer. When the flowers fade the knobbly, scaled head dries well. 1.2m.
montana 'Alba'. Mountain cornflower, usually grown in its blue form, associates well with old favourites like lupins and catmint. This white flowered form is especially lovely, flowering first in early summer, intermittently till autumn. 45cm.
montana carnea. The mauvish-pink form of mountain knapweed, flowering early summer on 45cm stems.
nigra subsp. rivularis. A very free-flowering hard-headed cornflower. Dark brown buds add to the effect among myriads of thistle-like flowers in light and dark rose-purple. Loved by bees. Makes low bushy shape of branching stems. Midsummer. 75cm.
pulcherrima. From very handsome silver-grey, cut leaves rise stiff stems bearing large cyclamen-pink flowers emerging from straw-coloured papery buds. Midsummer. 90cm.

CENTRANTHUS lecoqii. A Mediteranean valerian thriving in warm, dry conditions. Mauve-pink umbels of small tubular flowers attractive to insects. Will benefit from regular deadheading to prolong flowering and reduce seeding. 60cm.
ruber 'Albus'. Old cottage garden plant ideally seen on crumbling walls or stony banks. Fleshy grey-green leaves set off tall-stemmed clustered heads of tiny white tubular flowers in midsummer. 75cm.

ruber 'Atrococcineus'. Commonly called Red valerian, but seldom seen is this striking form with long heads of brilliant red starry flowers, marvellous in early summer with acid greens of euphorbia. 75cm.

CEPHALARIA alpina. From a base of dark green pinnate leaves rise tall, upright stands of branching stems, crowded with large pale sulphur-yellow, scabious-like flowers, a truly glorious sight in midsummer. 1.5m.
dipsacoides. Elegant from top to toe, a tall airy bouquet high above surrounding plants on 2m stalks with hundreds of small greenish-yellow scabious-like flowers carried on many branching stems standing above a base of dark green, deeply divided leaves. Would be lovely in a meadow garden, in retentive soil. Still attractive in October when each branched head carries round scaly seed cases, making good profiles in autumn or winter sunlight.
gigantea. From a woody rootstock comes a basal clump of large divided leaves. Strong branched stems are flung well above. They carry primrose-coloured scabious flowers with greenish centres, intermittently all summer. 2m.

CERASTIUM tomentosum var. columnae. A dwarf and delectable form of that rampant invader, *C. tomentosum*. Its striking white foliage is irresistible, and its manners are far more refined. The white flowers, in early summer, are good too. 7cm.

CERATOSTIGMA plumbaginoides. A valuable autumn plant, forms creeping clumps of wiry stems which carry clusters of blue flowers, intermingled with the crimson-red of changing foliage. 25cm.
willmottianum. A delightful small flowering bush covered all autumn with startling blue flowers. The winter seedheads are a nice bonus. We cut ours back to the ground in spring. 60cm.

CESTRUM parqui. Tall, willowy stems carry narrow green leaves topped with large, loose heads of small, yellow tubular flowers, scented at night. Forms a shrub in mild districts, but best cut to ground in spring when it produces better flower stems. Stands out among grey-foliaged plants. Is hardy below ground. Late summer-autumn. 1.5m.

CHAEROPHYLLUM hirsutum 'Roseum'. This lovely Cow parsley is one of the joys of early summer. Over a base of feathery leaves stand branching stems, each holding a flat-topped head of lilac-mauve tiny flowers. Likes sun or part shade in good soil. 75cm.

CHAMAEMELUM nobile 'Flore Pleno'. Double form of Lawn camomile. Exquisite creamy-white pom-poms over flat, ferny mats. Midsummer. 10cm.
nobile 'Treneague'. The Lawn camomile, a non-flowering perennial. Rosettes of finely cut bright green leaves form a dense, aromatic carpet. 2-3cm.

CHAMAENERION angustifolium var. album. The white-flowered Rose bay willow herb. Tall stems carry slender spires of pure-white flowers, enhanced by star-shaped green sepals which show between spaced, tissue-paper petals. From the centre of each extends a curly, four pronged, pale green pistil. Spires of unopened buds above open flowers, with rows of pale sterile seed pods below, maintain interesting form and colour for weeks, in late summer. Slowly invasive, not troublesome. A restful plant for retentive soil and sun. 1.5m.

CHELONE glabra. Has upright spikes of white gaping 'mouths' held in whorls around the top of the pale-green leafy stems. 60cm.

obliqua. Forms a clump of stiff, leafy stems bearing heads of curiously-shaped rich pink flowers like gaping mouths, hence the common name Turtle head. Very useful, flowering late summer to early autumn. 75cm.

CHELONOPSIS moschata. Narrow tubular pink flowers held in leaf axils on many slender stems. Oval leaves, red flushed. For cool damp shade. 25cm.

CHIASTOPHYLLUM oppositifolium. Creeping rosettes of succulent round green leaves, small yellow flowers, in June, on drooping red stems, reminiscent of catkins. Prefers cool position. 25cm.

oppositifolium 'Jim's Pride'. Attractive fleshy, rounded pale green and cream variegated leaves, with wavy edges. Arching stems of bell-shaped, deep yellow flowers. 50cm.

CHRYSANTHEMUM - MAY CAUSE SKIN ALLERGY.

The following forms of garden chrysanthemums add fresh colour to the garden in autumn and give much pleasure in the house, in mixed bowls.

'Clara Curtis'. One of the best late summer flowering plants, forming domes of blossom composed of single, clear-pink daisy flowers. Divide it in spring every few years and plant in full sun, in fertile well-drained soil. 75cm.

'Emperor of China'. This old hybrid has beautifully quilled petals, deep crimson in the centre but fading to silvery-pink as the layers of petals unroll. By flowering time, in November, the foliage becomes suffused and veined with rich crimson. 1m.

'Mary Stoker'. Strong stems, sprays of single flowers, 7cm across, soft maize yellow with bronze flush. Lovely late in autumn. 90cm.

CHRYSOGONUM virginianum. A modest plant seldom seen, but deserving more attention since it flowers from June to September. Bright yellow star-shaped flowers are set in every stem joint of the low sprawling plant, ideal for border edge or sunny spot in the rock garden. 20cm.

CHRYSOSPLENIUM davidianum. At first glance looks like a bright carpet of euphorbia heads. Round flat heads, 5cm across, on 5cm stems, consist of small cup-shaped, bright yellow saxifrage flowers surrounded by round, scallop-edged bracts. Hairy reddish stems carry soft furry leaves spreading horizontally to form low carpeting plants. Best in part shade and moist soil. March-April.

CICHORIUM intybus f. album. Stiff leafy stems support wide candelabra-like heads, studded with tassel-shaped semi-double white flowers. Early-midsummer. 1.2m.

intybus 'Roseum'. For weeks in midsummer this pink chicory sends up tall branching stems set with rose-pink flowers just like little pink dandelions. They close after lunch. 90cm.

CIRSIUM rivulare 'Atropurpureum'. Not prickly. This handsome thistle-like plant carries glowing ruby-red flowers on tall branching stems, a much-admired vertical, in summer and again in autumn. 1.2m.

CISTUS × **argenteus 'Peggy Sammons'.** Soft grey-green downy leaves are attractive all the year round and as a setting in June-July for flowers with crumpled petals in wild-rose pink. Forms a medium-sized shrub up to 1.4m.

× **hybridus.** syn. *C.* × *corbariensis*. Forms a medium-sized bush of light green crinkled foliage. Flower buds pink opening to white cups. 1.2m.

ladanifer. The dark green, slightly sticky foliage makes an excellent background all the year in the dry garden, but in midsummer, covered with huge white flowers splotched with purple, it commands admiration. 1.5m.

populifolius. Makes a dense bush of very attractive foliage, pointed, fresh-green aromatic leaves have deeply ruffled edges. In spring every tip shoot carries a handsome cluster of large round buds enclosed in red sepals, as attractive as the chalk-white flowers which open in May. 1.2m.

× **pulverulentus.** A small bush, with crinkled grey-green foliage, and striking magenta-pink flowers. 1.2m.

× **purpureus.** Fresh green foliage all year, slightly crinkled, smothered in summer with large rich pink flowers, each with a purple splash. 1.2m.

All cistus flower from July to August, and require well drained soil in sun. Pruning is best done after flowering.

CODONOPSIS clematidea. From long tangling, prostrate stems hang palest blue bells; tip them up to see the surprising vivid design inside. Midsummer. 45cm.

COLCHICUM – CAUTION: TOXIC IF EATEN.
Autumn crocus. Also called 'Naked ladies' because they appear in autumn without leaves. These emerge in spring when there is little else, when I enjoy the contrast of their large shining green clusters appearing through ground covering vincas, and *Geranium macrorrhizum* which protect the flowers from mud splash in autumn. Do not cut them down until they begin to wither or you will starve the bulbs. These are high mountain meadow plants, so do not belong to a woodland association of plants, but where there is ample light, along a path in an open glade, they flourish and bring a wash of welcome colour in early autumn.

agrippinum. Distinctly different from the goblet-shaped forms, the flowers open almost flat, with broad, pointed petals, which are pinkish-lilac heavily chequered in darker tones. Narrow, wavy-edged leaves appear after flowering. This bulb increases well in composted soil, in an open, sunny site. 10cm.

'Antares'. On taller greenish-cream stems, large, cup-shaped flowers, pale lilac-mauve outside, white inside, with petal edges stained lilac. 20cm.

bivonae. A large flower, chequered rich mauve with bold white throat, clumps up well.

bowlesianum. The earliest form we have and always surprises us with a large pointed, chequered flowers against Augusts hot gravel. 20cm.

'Glory of Heemstede'. Narrowish 'petals' create an upright chalice shape, rich mauve with faint chequering, on pale stems. 15cm.

'Lilac Wonder'. Deeper shade than *C. parnassicum*. Short white stems, faintly chequered narrow petals open to star shape. 10cm.

parnassicum. Smallish on short white stems, narrow uniformly pale lilac mauve 'petals' open to produce a star-shaped effect. 10cm.

'Rosy Dawn'. This extra fine form has large bold rosy-mauve flowers which open 10cm across in the sun, showing a deep white throat. Strong stems stand up well to wind and wet. Increases freely. 15cm.

speciosum 'Album'. Superb white flowers, rounded, like large wine goblets on pale green stems, to be treasured. 15cm.

speciosum 'Atrorubens'. A rarely offered wine-purple form, with purple stained stems. Later flowering than most. A gift from Chris Brickell. 15cm.

COMMELINA tuberosa Coelestis Group. Intense greenish-blue three petalled flowers fall from green hoods. One of the joys of autumn. Needs a warm spot. 45cm.

CONVALLARIA majalis. When conditions are right in humus-rich soil, among shrubs perhaps, where there is room for wandering rhizomes, why not plant a bed of Lily-of-the-valley to scent the air in late spring and perhaps have handfuls to pick for the house. 15cm.

majalis 'Albostriata'. We have tried several forms of variegated Lily-of-the-valley. Most have reverted to plain green in a disappointingly short time. This form has persisted for several years now, most leaves show attractive cream stripes, worth a try. 15cm.

majalis 'Hardwick Hall'. This fine form of Lily-of-the-valley has large, pointed oval leaves outlined with an irregular yellow edge, and large flowers. 30cm.

majalis 'Rosea'. Pink Lily-of-the-valley. A tough, creeping perennial with dark green foliage and stems of strongly scented, waxy mauve-pink, bell-shaped flowers. 25cm.

CONVOLVULUS cneorum. A treasure for a warm site in well-drained soil. Glistening small leaves, silky to touch, form a small neat shrub. Each tip holds clusters of long, narrow rose-coloured buds furled like umbrellas, which open fluted ivory-white yellow-eyed flowers for weeks in midsummer and again, a few in autumn. This plant must be given winter protection if required to be sent with an autumn order. 50cm.

sabatius. The exquisite blue cousin of bindweed, but never a menace. Needs well-drained soil, preferably draped over a raised bed. Top growth killed by prolonged frost, but shoots from below like fuchsias. Keep a few cuttings in the greenhouse. Flowers late summer until frosts. 15cm.

COREOPSIS verticillata. Quantities of upright stems delicately clothed in fine-cut foliage are topped for weeks in late summer with bright yellow daisy-like flowers, perfect contrast with *Calamintha nepeta* and *Anaphalis triplinervis*. 60cm.

verticillata 'Moonbeam'. Outstanding, with pale, creamy-yellow daisy-like flowers creating a display for months from midsummer to autumn. 45cm.

CORNUS canadensis. Exquisite ground-cover if you have a moist acid soil (not waterlogged) and part shade. Four petalled flowers, opening green, maturing to cream nestle in a bold ruff of deeply veined leaves. 15cm.

CORYDALIS cheilanthifolia. Fine-cut, fern-like leaves form a handsome base for a long succession in early summer, of greenish-yellow spurred flowers. Good in part shade with small ajugas, mitellas, or yellow Creeping Jenny, *Lysimachia nummularia* 'Aurea'. 30cm.

flexuosa 'China Blue'. This extraordinary plant has shown fresh flowers from spring until late July, when it still is three parts covered with clusters of glacier-blue flowers, looking like shoals of little fishes swimming through a sea of finely-cut blue-grey leaves. For humus-rich, loose soil and part shade. 30cm.

flexuosa 'Père David'. Low mounds of light green divided leaves, clusters of sky-blue tubular flowers for weeks in early spring. 30cm.

flexuosa 'Purple Leaf'. Immediately appealing. Low mounds of finely-cut leaves, stained and stroked with patches of reddish-tan, are smothered for weeks in spring and early summer, with clusters of tiny blue tubular flowers warmed with a red tone. Needs friable soil full of humus in cool conditions. 25cm.
solida subsp. solida 'Beth Evans'. A charming selection with fern like foliage and the showiest sugar-pink flowers in March and April. Best in sun or part shade. 20cm.

COTULA lineariloba. From South Africa. Slowly spreading rhizomes carry short silky tufts of finely shredded leaves forming a silver-grey carpet on poor gravel soil, dotted, in early summer, with yellow button-flowers on wiry stems, resembling hat pins. 10cm.

CRAMBE cordifolia. From a mound of huge green leaves, bare branching stems soar skywards, carrying wide clouds of starry white flowers in July, like a giant gypsophila. Midsummer. 2m.
maritima. Our native Sea kale adds style and grandeur to the filigree grey and silver plants. Waving, sea-blue and waxen, the leaves alone can dominate the border edge, while the short stout stems carry generous heads of creamy-white flowers in early summer. The stems are delicious, blanched in early spring, served as a vegetable. 75cm.
orientalis. This is a gem. From a base of acanthus-shaped (but much smaller) leaves rise much divided stems carrying thousands of tiny white flowers creating a lace-like effect. Needs to be on an edge, or in a void, where you can appreciate the effect from top to toe. 1m.

CREPIS aurea. From the European Alps this attractive little dandelion has burnt-orange flowers on short stems. Not a tiresome seeder. 15cm.
incana. This unusual dandelion is enchanting in late summer. Over tight rosettes of grey-green, deeply cut leaves stand sprays of many-petalled soft rose-pink flowers. 30cm.

CRINUM × powellii. A leafy bulbous plant. From the top of stout purplish stems tumble large trumpet-shaped rose-pink flowers for several weeks in late summer. Usually grown against warm wall, flourishes here in open ground, well-drained, well-fed, and well-mulched in winter. Good in tubs. 1.2m.
× powellii 'Album'. Large, beautifully shaped, pure-white trumpets. Both these crinums are deliciously scented. 1.2m.

CROCOSMIA 'Emberglow'. Above fans of pleated leaves stand tall branching, dark-stained stems carrying quantities of glowing red flowers, the colour deepened by dark calyxes. Spectacular in August. 1.2m.
latifolia 'Castle Ward Late'. Above broad ribbed leaves tall dark stems arch over to show dark buds opening star-shaped with bright scarlet faces. Elegant. August. 90cm.
'Limpopo'. Unusual colour form with flowers a shade of orange-apricot. Like all crocosmia it prefers a good soil in full sun. 80cm.
'Lucifer'. This imposing plant has stiff, pleated, blade-shaped leaves topped with large heads of brilliant flame-red flowers, from June-July. 1.2m.
masoniorum. Superior in every way to montbretia which it resembles. Large fiery flowers in shades of orange and scarlet in late summer. Our selected form. 75cm.
masoniorum 'Dixter Flame'. Wide-spread branching heads carry vivid scarlet flowers in July. 75cm.
'Severn Sunrise'. A new colour tone. Warm peachy-pink flowers on dark bare stems open wide to great effect. Goes well with *Kniphofia* 'Apricot Sensation'. 75cm.

'**Spitfire**'. Produces quantities of the most densely packed heads of rich orange-scarlet flowers heightened with pale throats. One of Alan Bloom's introductions. July-August. 1m.

× crocosmiiflora '**Carmine Brillant**'. Dark stems enhance loose sprays of flowers, warm red outside, paler in the throat. An unusual shade. August. 75cm.

× crocosmiiflora '**Coleton Fishacre**'. An improved version of *C.* 'Solfatare', being more vigorous, with copper-brown leaves and apricot flowers. 60cm.

× crocosmiiflora '**Citronella**'. Above sheaves of pale green leaves sprays of clear yellow flowers are produced in abundance. 60cm.

× crocosmiiflora '**Emily McKenzie**'. This hardy vigorous plant produces branching stems of rich orange flowers splashed with wallflower red. Each flower is large, the petals opening wide, create a flat star-shape instead of the small, lily-shaped flowers of common montbretia. August. 60cm.

× crocosmiiflora '**James Coey**'. Rich green leaves support showers of dark purple-tinted stems carrying heads of fiery-red flowers with yellow centres, very free-flowering, makes a remarkable show, as do also the handsome seedheads. 90cm.

× crocosmiiflora '**Norwich Canary**'. Above pale green foliage stand wide sprays of soft orange flowers opening to show pale insides. 75cm.

× crocosmiiflora '**Queen Alexandra**'. Above narrow light green leaves, slender stems carry wide-spaced burnt orange buds, opening flat-faced flowers, creamy-orange inside with dark maroon hearts, and red-stained backs. 75cm.

× crocosmiiflora '**Solfatare**'. Pale apricot flowers contrast with smoky-bronze foliage. Choice plant for warm situation but not too dry. 45cm.

× crocosmiiflora '**Star of the East**'. Large wide-opening flowers 7cm across in shades of orange, with burnt orange buds and backs, paler within. Flowers held well above leaves. 75cm.

CROCUS kotschyanus var. leucopharynx. Standing on ghostly pale stems, pale lilac petals, finely veined, open wide to show a white heart filled with white stamens and stigma. autumn flowering. 13cm.

medius. Soft violet petals with silvery sheen on backs, have yellow stamens and orange-scarlet stigma. September flowering. Makes up well. 10cm.

CRYPTOTAENIA japonica f. atropurpurea. Makes a handsome foliage plant. Trifoliate leaves with pointed leaflets are purple as the leaves of beetroot. Tip sprays of tiny flowers are insignificant. 45cm.

CYCLAMEN coum. Late winter flowering and so welcome intermingled with snowdrops. Shades of pink to white flowers with rounded green foliage often splashed silver. 8cm.

hederifolium. The earliest and showiest cyclamen for naturalising under trees. Established tubers produce rose pink flowers in autumn followed by clusters of overlapping leaves, beautifully marbled silver on sombre green. 10cm.

CYNARA cardunculus. Cardoon. A magnificent feature plant. Great arching silver-grey leaves, boldly cut, form a great mound above which stout stems carry large, luminous-blue thistle-shaped heads. These make good drieds. 2m.

cardunculus Scolymus Group 'Gros Vert de Lâon'. A good selected form of edible French artichoke. Makes large flavoursome heads. Established plants flower in early summer. Offsets planted out in April provide a late crop in early autumn. 1.2m.

hystrix. Smaller, more refined than *C. cardunculus,* flowers more important than foliage. Draws flower arrangers with its carved shape and overall pink effect of the flowers. Overlapping calyxes enfolding the central boss of blue stamens turn back as amethyst-pink spiky petals. Dries well, including some in bud, retaining excellent colour. From Morocco, needs well drained soil and a warm position. Flowers best in hot summers. 1m.

 DACTYLORHIZA × braunii. One of the most handsome terrestrial orchids for sun or semi-shade and good leaf-mould soil. Slender stems, clothed in handsomely spotted pointed green leaves carry pyramidal shaped heads, 25cm long, of crimson-purple flowers. Early summer. This and the following form were given me by Graham S. Thomas. 60cm.

× braunii. Dark form. Is similar in every way but has darker flowers, flowering slightly later. 60cm.

foliosa. The Madeiran orchid, where it grows in damp woodland glades is a hardy, easy and spectacular orchid soon repaying its initial price with heart warming clumps of fresh green foliage from which develop spikes of magenta-pink flowers. Best in a humus rich soil in part shade. 60cm.

DARMERA peltata. In early spring tall, naked stems appear from thick, flattish rhizomes, carrying flat heads of pale pink flowers. Scallop-edged, parasol-shaped leaves, up to 50cm across follow to make a mound of eye-catching splendour. For damp soil. 1m.

peltata 'Nana'. More suitable for smaller areas, it has shorter stems. Makes attractive carpet effect with round scallop-edged, bronze-tinted leaves whose colour intensifies to reddish autumn tints in full sun and retentive soil. 30cm.

DATISCA cannabina. Stout stems, clothed in attractive pinnate foliage, arch over at the tips, weighted by long strings of tiny green flowers forming graceful fringes in late summer. An elegant foliage plant to be used as a feature plant in retentive soil, or rising above low ground cover. 2m.

DELPHINIUM – HARMFUL IF EATEN

'Alice Artindale'. Tall spires of closely set flowers, well formed blue rosettes tipped with green. Amazing in the garden or cut. I particularly value its flowers in pot-pourri, individually dried they are exquisite. 1.5m.

(Belladonna Group) 'Atlantis'. Rich indigo-blue, velvety flowers, well-spaced on graceful branching spires. Has second flowering in late summer if early heads are removed before seeding. June-August. 90cm.

(Belladonna Group) 'Piccolo'. Clear, gentian-blue, long spurred flowers, well-spaced on slender branching stems with long flowering period. Needs no staking. Mid-late summer. 1m.

DEUTZIA pulchra 'Variegata'. An unusual variegated deciduous shrub; it appears palest cream from a distance; its arching habit shows off to perfection overlapping sprays of small pointed leaves faintly stippled green on a cream background. 1.5m.

DIANELLA caerulea. For lime-free soil in warm gardens. This fascinating plant came originally from Australia. From fan-shaped tufts of dark green leathery leaves spring sprays of small white flowers, which develop into shining, royal-blue berries, large as grapes! Quite sensational, but it does wander underground. Try it in pots, on a patio, or buried, to restrain it, and protect over winter in cold gardens. 50cm.

DIANTHUS. The following pinks are all valued as good cover in dry soil, making tidy close plants. Most flower midsummer, occasional flowers in autumn.

× **arvernensis.** Single pink flowers pressed against neat rounded clumps of grey leaves. Midsummer. 8cm.

'Badenia'. Neat low growing pink with tight grey leaves. Covered with single magenta flowers, with crimson centres. Highly scented. 8cm.

'Brympton Red'. Large single, velvety-crimson-red, shadow flecked flowers on 30cm stems.

deltoides. The Maiden Pink. Abundant little starry flowers of carmine for weeks stand over solid mats of dark green foliage. Lovely with thymes. 20cm.

deltoides 'Albus'. The white form. 20cm.

Highland Hybrid 'White Barn'. Our selected form makes low tidy cushions of blue-grey leaves which become buried beneath single rose-pink flowers, dark eyed. 13cm.

'Mrs Sinkins'. The heavily scented old favourite pink used for edging cottage garden paths, has fully double blooms of creamy-white. Midsummer. 25cm.

'Musgrave's Pink'. A very choice pink. Close tidy clumps produce quantities of sweetly scented white single flowers each with a green eye. 20cm.

'Pink Jewel'. Forms a low tight mound of foliage, studded with rose-pink semi-double flowers in midsummer. 5cm.

'Pink Mrs Sinkins'. The soft-rose-pink form is very attractive. 25cm.

'Sops-in-wine'. The single wine-red flowers have a white patch on each petal. 15cm.

DIASCIA. All diascias need well drained soil and warm situations such as base of south or west wall.

barberae 'Blackthorn Apricot'. There are now colour tones of diascia from mauve, through shades of rose-pink to this form which is a lovely creamy-apricot. I have it growing between *Sedum populifolium* and the yellow-leafed *Origanum vulgare* 'Thumble's Variety'. 20cm.

barberae 'Ruby Field'. This good form floats sprays of salmon-pink, nemesia-like flowers over neat flat mats of small green leaves. Enchanting, mid to late summer. 15cm.

integerrima. Begins the season with erect stiff stems clothed in very narrow grey leaves, but the weight of tapering heads crowded with richest salmon pink flowers spreads the plant apart making way for a display of stems fresh from the base. Lovely with blue saucers of *Convolvulus sabatius*. June-September. 45cm.

rigescens. This plant produces taller, stiffer stems of rose-pink flowers than *D.* 'Ruby Field', in flower from June-October. Said to be hardy, but overwintered cuttings under shelter would be a worthwhile precaution. 45cm.

vigilis. Produces a softer effect than many of the diascias. Flowers prolifically for weeks, midsummer to autumn. Pale, shrimp-pink flowers with dark eyes on more openly spaced spires than *D. rigescens*. 45cm.

DICENTRA 'Bacchanal'. Similar in habit to other forms of *D. formosa*, selected for its clustered heads of glowing wine-red flowers above pale-green, finely-cut leaves. 35cm.

formosa. Forms soft ferny hummocks of deeply divided leaves on juicy pink-tinted stems from which dangle, in spring and early summer, little mauvish-pink lockets. Easily grown in cool conditions. Beautiful contrast with hostas and tiarellas. 45cm.

formosa f. alba. Has much paler green leaves on glassy-green stems with fragile white flowers appearing for weeks in spring and early summer. 30cm.

formosa 'Langtrees'. Small cream and pink flowers are followed by new basal leaves of an outstanding colour, almost blue, finely cut. For cool soil. 30cm.

formosa 'Spring Gold'. Discovered as a seedling here. Young spring foliage is yellow, setting off pink flowers. 30cm.

macrantha. A rare treasure for those who can suit it. Branching stems set with finely-cut bronzed-green leaves carry pale greenish-yellow flowers, long and narrow about 7.5cm, dangling like elegant earrings. Needs cool, damp shady conditions, protected form drying wind and early frosts. 45cm.

Dicentra spectabilis see **Lamprocapnos.**

DICTAMNUS – CAUTION: SKIN IRRITANT IN SUNLIGHT

albus. An arresting sight when a mature plant carries many stems topped with spires of white, lily-like flowers, clothed in green divided leaves, smelling deliciously of lemons. 75cm.

albus var. purpureus. Erect stems clothed in aromatic leaves carry heads of lily-shaped flowers, soft mauve, veined purple. Curious, star-shaped seed-pods on both forms are a bonus for 'dried' flower arrangers. 75cm.

DIERAMA dracomontanum. Quickly forms a clump of narrow, grass-like leaves. Smaller and more open flowers than the following. A subdued shade of pink. 60cm.

pulcherrimum. Angel's Fishing Rod. A good name. The tall wiry rod emerges in August from stiff grassy foliage, the tip weighted gracefully with silvery-pink bells, which develop into bead-like clusters of seed. 1.2m.

pulcherrimum pale pink flowered. Seed raised plants from pale pink parents, shades will vary slightly. Full sun and a well drained yet retentive soil 1.2m.

Dieramas grow wild in South Africa, in grassland. They take 2-3 years to settle down and make good clumps of grassy leaves before they send up a sheaths of flowering stems.

pulcherrimum var. album. Strong 1.2m wands are tipped with long drooping chains of pale green buds emerging from papery bracts to open pure white slender bells. Exquisite in mid-late summer.

DIGITALIS – CAUTION: TOXIC IF EATEN

ferruginea. A gem. Sends up tall flower-stems bearing close-set rounded buds which open to smallish short trumpets of coppery-yellow, veined brown. 90cm.

grandiflora. From velvety-green foliage come branching stems of soft yellow foxgloves. Sound perennial. 60cm.

lutea. A vigorous plant, sending up tall spikes set with delicate narrow yellow flowers. Flowers small in relation to plant but useful for cutting. 90cm.

× **mertonensis.** (*D. purpurea* × *D. grandiflora*). Large flowers in lovely shades of deep old-rose with a hint of copper. Fairly perennial if divided after flowering. Comes true from seed. Likes part shade. 60cm.

parviflora. Close-packed, cylindrical heads of narrow bronze-brown flowers on stiff upright stems, most intriguing in July. Bold clumps of narrow dark green leaves. 60cm.

purpurea f. albiflora. Although a biennial we offer pot-grown plants of this lovely cream form of our native foxglove. Let them seed. Most seedlings come true but if any have purple leaf stalks they will have purple flowers. Remove these to keep strain pure. 1.4m.

purpurea 'Sutton's Apricot'. Again biennial with hairy, dark green leaves. One sided spikes of soft apricot flowers. 1.2m.

DIPHYLLEIA cymosa. The Umbrella leaf. An eye-catching foliage plant for cool shade and retentive soil. Large rounded leaves, deeply cut, almost divided in half, present a flat table top, red stained when young, maturing rich green. Above them, in early summer, appear clusters of small white flowers succeeded by sloe-coloured berries attached to brilliant red enamelled stalks. 60cm.

DIPLARRHENA moraea. From low clusters of strap-shaped leaves come orchid-like flowers. Three white sepals surround three smaller, narrow petals tipped with dark velvety purple and yellow, leading into a white veined throat. Early summer. 30cm.

DIPSACUS inermis. A perennial teazle. A plant of coarse character in late summer for the back of the border or the wild meadow garden. Strong branched stems carry small pincushion shaped heads crammed with tiny cream tubular flowers, visited by moths. By late autumn there are still a few pale lemon pincushions low down on fresh shoots, while earlier flowers have become dome-shaped seedheads, green when fresh, drying brown, making attractive skeletons. Needs retentive soil. 1.4m.

DISPORUM sessile 'Variegatum'. Like a small but daintier Solomon's seal. From a wandering starfish-shaped rootstock rise slender stems bearing pretty leaves, fresh green, broadly striped cream. Creamy-white bell-shaped flowers dangle beneath the leaves in spring. 40cm.

DODECATHEON meadia. Forms a basal clump of smooth broad-bladed leaves, rather like primrose leaves. Heads of down-turned dart-like flowers with reflexed petals, are poised on bare stems. In shades of pinky-mauve, they need damp soil laced with humus, preferably in part shade. 30cm.
meadia f. album. White scented petals flare backwards from the dart-like pointed centre, gold and purple ringed, held on bare stems above smooth cowslip-like leaves. Needs damp, humus rich soil. 30cm.

DOELLINGERIA umbellata. syn. *Aster umbellatus.* Upright, non-spreading perennial known as the Flat-topped aster. Stiff stems massed with heads of tiny white flowers over a long period. Foliage turns clear yellow in autumn. Totally mildew free and a good cut flower. August-September. Any good soil. Sun or light shade. 1.5m.

DORONICUM pardalianches. The Great leopard's bane. Although its tuberous roots are somewhat invasive I admire this plant's ability to thrive in thin woodland, even in grass. It will look well in the border and is easily restrained. In my wood garden the effect of a glade of yellow daisies on branching stems is a delight where they fill the space taken earlier by snowdrops and daffodils. 1.2m.

DRABA aizoides. An easy, early flowering alpine. Small bright green rosettes of stiff, bristly leaves make neat clusters, topped with short stems of yellow flowers, very cheering at the end of winter. 8cm.

ECHINACEA purpurea. An imposing plant with fine dark foliage carried on stiff branching stems which need no staking. Large, broad-petalled flowers of rich mauve-crimson are enhanced by the central cones which glisten orange-brown. Long flowering period, late summer-autumn. 90cm.
purpurea 'Rubinstern'. Amongst the multitude of new varieties this one stands out as a distinct and reliable form. Although it is a seed strain developed to produce uniform, deeper coloured flowers than the type, it reliably produces large deep carmine-red flowers, a real butterfly magnet Best in a good rich soil and full sun. 90cm.
purpurea 'White Lustre'. Bold daisy flowers. Greenish-white petals fall back from large central cones which look like tarnished brass as yellow stamens open and fade. Lovely effect beside *Miscanthus sinensis* 'Strictus'. August-September. 75cm.

ECHINOPS 'Nivalis'. Handsome effect where there is room to display this huge Globe thistle. Stout stems up to 1.8m tall, clothed in deep-cut prickly leaves, are topped with clusters of silvery-green buds opening white, nectar-rich flower heads. Mid-late summer.
ritro. Makes a statuesque plant in poorest soil. Handsome prickly foliage, green and silver. Tall grey stems carry prickly knobbly heads, steel-blue in bud and flower during late summer. 1.2m.
ritro. 'Veitch's Blue'. Silvered branching stems, up to 1m tall clothed in dark green, deeply cut leaves with white backs. Indigo-blue buds open into balls of starry-blue flowers, the colour intensified by dark calyxes. Loved by bumble bees in July-August.
sphaerocephalus. Stout stems clothed in deeply-cut tough green leaves, with silver undersides, carry branching heads of ball-shaped silvery pointed buds opening spidery white flowers. Effective mid-back of border. Loved by bees. 1.2m.
sphaerocephalus 'Arctic Glow'. Remarkable for strong branching stems which appear to be rich brown, but are actually green, heavily felted with maroon hairs, making good contrast with white, starry flowers densely packed in globular heads. 1.5m.

ELSHOLTZIA stauntonii. Forms a tall upward-branching plant bearing mint-like scented leaves topped with dense spikes of tiny mauve flowers. A good vertical in autumn among late flowering grasses or the final flowers of Japanese anemones. 1.2m.

EPIMEDIUM. Barrenwort. Always a surprise to learn for the first time that it is in the same family as berberis. Most valued and beautiful foliage plants which will put up with dry shade, but make superb ground cover more quickly in rich damp leafmould. Best cut down in early March to reveal the delicate sprays of tiny columbine-like flowers.
davidii. Above small pointed leathery leaves, stained bronze in spring stand wire-thin dark stems carrying flights of lemon-yellow, long-spurred flowers, backed with dark red calyxes. 30cm.
'Enchantress'. Hybrid from Elizabeth Strangman. Forms low mounds of long, leathery, pointed leaves, purple-stained in winter, bright green in spring, when it has sprays of pale pink flowers. 25cm.
grandiflorum 'Crimson Beauty'. Deep rose flowers, long calyxes and spurred petals in deep rose-pink create a semi-double flower effect. 30cm.
grandiflorum subsp. koreanum. Sprays of creamy-yellow columbine-like flowers with long shimmering spurs dangle among the clumps of emerging leaf stems, leaves light green, tinted bronze in spring. 40cm.

grandiflorum 'Lilafee'. Has narrow, oval leaves, softly bronzed when young. From dark purple buds open long sprays of light purple flowers fading to white-tipped spurs. Both this and *E.* 'Merlin' are very effective, differing enough to be equally desirable. 25cm.

grandiflorum 'Rose Queen'. Presents wide sprays of long spurred ivory flowers concealed in conspicuous deep-rose calyxes. Young leaves are flushed bronze. 30cm.

grandiflorum 'White Queen'. Has clustered heads of long spurred white flowers, faintly tinted lilac. 30cm.

× **perralchicum 'Fröhnleiten'.** This excellent plant forms neat clumps of evergreen foliage beautifully marbled with warm reds and bronze in spring, and colours again in autumn. Sprays of bright yellow flowers are held above the foliage. 40cm.

perralderianum. The toughest weed smother for awkward, rooty places, beneath or between shrubs. It forms formidable carpets of glossy, heart-shaped, evergreen leaves with spiny edges. Remove them by late February to make way for spires of little yellow flowers in spring. 30cm.

pubigerum. Handsome foliage with many small creamy flowers on tall stems, up to 40cm.

× **rubrum.** A splendid ground-cover in shade and among shrubs. Elegant heart-shaped leaves on wiry stems, they emerge in soft tints of bronze-red, fading to light green, but assuming vivid coral red shades in autumn. Old leaves remain on the plant until spring. Rose flowers in spring. 25cm.

setosum. Narrow, pointed, heart-shaped leaves in bright pea-green carry flights of creamy-white flowers on thread-thin stems. Enchanting. 30cm.

× **versicolor 'Discolor'.** Exquisite in early spring. Above overlapping layers of pea-green leaves, marbled reddish-bronze stand showers of stems smothered in curiously beautiful colour scheme. Tight ruby buds open faded pink petalled flowers with yellow mouths. Overall effect is soft bronzy-orange. Indescribable! 30cm.

× **versicolor 'Sulphureum'.** More vigorous than *E.* × *rubrum*. The leaves combine delicate shades of bronze in early spring, ideal for picking. The delicate sulphur yellow flowers are borne on wiry stems, half buried among the leaves for protection. In autumn the green summer foliage again becomes marbled with bronze, remaining all winter. 30cm.

× **warleyense.** Equally beautiful foliage with unusual orange shaded flowers. 25cm.

× **youngianum 'Merlin'.** Above the new spring foliage suffused with shades of brown, wiry stems carry spur-less chubby flowers opening soft purple and white from wine-purple pointed buds. 30cm.

× **youngianum 'Niveum'.** Neat clumps of smaller foliage in soft shades of milk-chocolate in spring, over which float clouds of pure white starry flowers. A gem. 25cm.

EPIPACTIS gigantea. Marsh helleborine from North America. Rather misleading name, but none the less attractive for a cool damp place. Many stiff stems clothed in simple pointed upturned leaves carry spires of small green and copper-coloured orchid flowers. Midsummer. 30cm.

ERIGERON 'Dimity'. Tidy clumps of evergreen leaves produce a succession of pinky-mauve daisies with orange eyes and buds-lovely combination, throughout June and July. 30cm.

'Gaiety'. A handsome cultivar. Many stems carry clusters of large, light-purple daisy flowers. Many fine-rayed petals surround a large central disc. Late summer. 60cm.

glaucus 'Roseus'. Crowds of light, mauve-pink daisies with greenish-yellow eyes stand on short stems above neat leaf rosettes. Good for edges in late summer. August. 15cm.

karvinskianus. Daintiest of daisies on branching, wire-thin stalks, opening white, fading to rose. Seeds itself admirably into cracks and crevices of walls or steps. 30cm.

'Schneewittchen'. I love this. Produces in high summer sheaves of lax branching stems smothered in fine-rayed white daisy flowers, fresh and appealing, propped among neighbours. 60cm.

'Sommerneuschnee'. Although flopping about a bit, this old-fashioned looking plant has many admirers. Almost white, lilac-tinted flowers, 5cm across with finely shredded petals, like eyelashes surrounding greenish-yellow eyes, are held in loosely branched heads. Flowers profusely in midsummer with a few in autumn. Lasts well in water. 60cm.

ERIOGONUM umbellatum. Exciting and unusual. Thin woody stems underpin a sprawling mat of tough, grey-green leaves held in open rosettes on wire-thin reddish stalks. From the centre of each appear umbels of yellow-green buds, opening acid lemon-yellow flowers, most attractive in early summer. Needs well drained soil. 15cm.

ERIOPHYLLUM lanatum. Very useful ground-cover in sun-parched soil, quickly making large patches of silvery-white finely divided leaves, with a show of orange-yellow daisies. Late spring to early summer. 30cm.

ERODIUM chrysanthum. Valued for its foliage effect alone. Makes neat rosettes of silvery-grey finely divided leaves, almost white in dry weather, above which float branching heads of creamy-yellow flowers in early summer on 25cm stems.

chrysanthum pink. Produces a succession of palest shell-pink flowers above a soft mound of ferny-grey-green leaves throughout summer till autumn frosts. 25cm.

'County Park'. Above finely dissected grey-green leaves stand clusters of lilac-pink flowers, held on 25cm stems, providing colour for weeks, from summer well into autumn. A great edging plant.

ERYNGIUM agavifolium. Makes a spectacular foliage plant. Forms large rosettes of broad, light-green strap-shaped leaves, sharply toothed, from which rise branched stems carrying cylindrical greenish-white heads. 1.5m.

alpinum. Has the largest of blue flowers, its finely cut lace-like ruff of exquisite metallic blue is soft to touch. Needs good deep soil. 75cm.

amethystinum. One of the best blues with flowers and stems stained deep-blue. Flowers later than most. 60cm.

bourgatii. Individual basal leaves shown off against dry bare soil are deeply divided, crisply curled and prickle-edged with broad, silvered veins and scattered spots like tiny sequins. Heads of blue-green flowers crown a plant which is distinctive all summer. 60cm.

eburneum. Forms striking rosettes of narrow finely toothed leaves, very reminiscent of the leaves on top of a pineapple. Tall stems carry branching heads tipped with thimble-shaped clusters of white flowers. Handsome all autumn. 1.2m.

giganteum. Miss Willmott's ghost. Widely branching heads of metallic silvery-green cones of flower are surrounded by spiny silver bracts. Dries well. Seeds freely. Biennial. Decorative from July to the frosts. 75cm.

maritimum. Shakespeare's Eryngo, the candied roots were used as a sweetmeat. Waxy blue-grey leaves, blue head and stems, total effect grey-blue. Dries well. This is our native Sea holly and despite my efforts will it ever look as fine as it does just a few miles away? 50cm.

× **oliverianum.** Forms slowly expanding clumps of boldly cut green leaves, with stems of several bracted cone flowers, the whole of strong blue and soft to touch. 90cm.

planum. Slender stems carry a large head of many thimble-sized cones each surrounded by a spiny ruff. Stems and flowers dark blue during late summer. 90cm.

✕ **tripartitum.** Wiry, wide-spreading branching stems carry many cone-shaped heads surrounded by deeper blue spiny bracts. The mass effect of dark, metallic blue is very good in midsummer. 60cm.

variifolium. Forms a flat handsome rosette of green richly marbled leaves, heads of small metallic-blue spiky flowers in late summer. 60cm.

✕ **zabelii.** This name covers hybrids between *E. alpinum* and *E. bourgatii*. They all have beautiful large blue flowers, enhanced by dark stained stems. 75cm.

✕ **zabelii 'Donard Variety'.** Has large soft finely cut ruffs of silvery-blue surrounding dark green central core. Leaves on upper stems have silver veins. Average soil. Sun. Midsummer. 60cm.

✕ **zabelii 'Violetta'.** A distinct colour variety displaying fine, large thistle-like flowers of violet-blue. Long lived perennial for full sun. 75cm.

ERYSIMUM 'Bowles Mauve'. Makes the boldest, most handsome bush of dark blue-green foliage topped with spikes of rich mauve flowers for months. Plants can become too woody and need replacing every three seasons or so. Cuttings are easy. 75cm.

cheiri 'Harpur Crewe'. Believed to be Elizabethan, retained by cuttings throughout the centuries. In well-drained soil makes a long-lived, neat bushy plant smothered in spring with spires of fully double, scented yellow flowers. 60cm.

'Jacob's Jacket'. Forms a low sprawling bush of dark green foliage with sort stemed, compact flower heads in more russet tones of lilac pink, brick red and peachy orange. 40cm.

'Orange Flame'. Prostrate carpets of fresh evergreen foliage and luminous orange flowers in midsummer. Useful cover in a poor soil in full sun. 20cm.

pulchellum. Above a prostrate woody framework clothed in narrow green leaves stand short stems 15-25cm of vivid lemon-yellow wallflowers, a delight for weeks in early summer. It spreads slowly, seeds too, weaving its way between border iris and origanum yet to come, at the dry sunny border edge.

'Ruston Royal'. A perennial wallflower forming an evergreen bush bearing spikes of pleasing light and dark mauve flowers. For full sun and a well drained soil. 70cm.

scoparium. Forms a woody bush carrying long stems of parti-coloured flowers. Dark purple buds open creamy-yellow flowers feathered with mauve, each flower becoming entirely mauve with age. Flowers for months, spring into summer. 70cm.

ERYTHRONIUM. All erythroniums do best in rich leafy soil, in part shade.

californicum 'White Beauty'. Pale cream, lily-shaped flowers reflex to show cream stamens with a ring of reddish stain at their base. Leaves strongly mottled with brown. April. 25cm.

dens-canis. Dog's tooth violet. Matt, chocolate-blotched, oval leaves, as attractive as the delicate, rosy-mauve flowers whose petals reflex like cyclamen in spring sunshine. Forms bundles of ivory-white pointed corms, in leaf mould soil. 15cm.

dens-canis 'Snowflake'. Selected form of Dog's tooth violet with almost white flowers, faintly touched with mauve. 15cm.

'Pagoda'. Taller than *E.* 'White Beauty' with several butter-yellow flowers on each tinted stem. Broad, wavy, shining leaves, slightly marbled. April. 30cm.

'Sundisc'. Huge tongue-shaped leaves 12cm across, 25cm long, boldly marbled with brown, looking like snakeskin. Well above, on bare stems dangle bright-lemon, lily-flowers with recurved petals. Tip them up to see the reddish-brown disc surrounding stamens and ovary. 40cm.

EUCOMIS comosa 'Sparkling Burgundy'. Pineapple flower. A bulbous perennial with purple strap-shaped leaves. A striking plant when in flower, with stems of pale pink flowers. Hardy in a sheltered site or grow in a pot. 50cm.

EUONYMUS fortunei 'Emerald 'n' Gold' - HARMFUL IF EATEN.
One of the best variegated small shrubs. Yellow, green, and in winter, pink-tinged leaves remain a fresh feature all the year round. I use bergenias at its base for contrast. 75cm.

EUPATORIUM cannabinum 'Flore Pleno'. Rarely offered, this beautiful form of Hemp agrimony enhances the autumn border for weeks in late summer and autumn. Tall leafy plants carry branching stems topped with dense clusters of tiny rose-coloured flowers, lovely in autumn flower arrangements. Up to 1.5m.
purpureum. A sensational plant for the wild garden or waterside. Stout stems carry huge domed heads of cinnamon-pink fluffy flowers from September to November. 2.5m.
purpureum subsp. maculatum 'Atropurpureum'. Has darker stems and brighter rose-purple flowers on slightly shorter stems. 1.5m.
purpureum 'Purple Bush'. For smaller spaces, wide flat heads of fluffy mauve flowers, on purple stems. August onwards. 1.2m.
All these herbaceous plants look superb by large ponds, or in big borders on retentive soil with giant grasses like miscanthus, spartina or cortaderia.

EUPHORBIA - HARMFUL IF EATEN/SKIN & EYE IRRITANT.
The Spurge Family. Invaluable in the garden and for flower arranging. Most euphorbias need an open sunny situation, the following two do well in shade or part shade.
amygdaloides 'Purpurea'. A superb form of the native Wood-spurge. Maroon stems carry dark evergreen leaves, while the new spring shoots are vividly tinted beetroot- red, followed by bright yellow-green flower bracts. 75cm.
amygdaloides var. robbiae. Handsome tall, rosettes of dark evergreen foliage. Sends up showy heads of yellow-green flowers which remain most of the summer. Excellent in shade where it will run to form useful ground-cover. 60cm.
characias 'Glacier Blue'. Differs from most of the recent variegated forms in that it retains the smoky grey-blue foliage, each leaf narrowly but strongly edged in creamy-white. The flower heads are variegated too with the individual flowers a pale lime-yellow. Full sun and a well drained soil. Also a good winter container plant. 75cm.
characias 'Portuguese Velvet'. Forms a large bulky plant, similar in size to *E. characias* subsp. *wulfenii,* but has leaves densely covered with minute silver hairs, strokable, like velvet. Large heads of green frog spawn-like flowers. Needs a warm sheltered position in cold districts. 90cm.
characias subsp. wulfenii. Makes a dramatic feature plant in the dry garden. Long stiff stems clothed in blue-grey foliage form a great clump, handsome all the year round. All March-April and into May each stem carries a huge head of lime-green flowers. Likes shelter from wind. 1.2m.
characias subsp. wulfenii 'John Tomlinson'. Glowing yellow-green, bell-shaped flowers packed into large cylindrical heads. Starts early. Difficult to root from cuttings, which is the only means of propagation. Originally from Kew Gardens. 1.2m.
corallioides. Daintily branching stems, lighter in habit than Euphorbia epithymoides also flowering throughout the summer. 45cm.

cornigera. Handsome for weeks in midsummer. Begins with a close-packed small head of vivid yellow-green flowers set off by conspicuously white-veined leaves. Side branches appear and more flowers until a large loose head is formed. Several stems arise from one rootstock. 90cm.

cyparissias. Very attractive ground-cover. Short running stems, narrow foliage, and heads of lime-green flowers. Charming to pick. Early summer. 30cm.

cyparissias 'Fens Ruby'. Remarkable foliage effect like colonies of small conifer seedlings, or bottlebrushes, its many stems clothed in dark blue/grey leaves, the top tufts stained maroon. Has the normal lime-green flower heads. The soft-yellow or apricot flowers, with red eyes of *Potentilla* × *tonguei*, planted nearby, look good sprawling through it. Foliage good all summer. Flowers spring-early summer. 30cm.

dulcis. Not remarkable until autumn when the entire plant becomes suffused with flaming reds and orange. 30cm.

dulcis 'Chameleon'. Soft oval leaves totally wine-purple all summer, turn to shades of orange, scarlet and plum in late autumn, a splendid contrast among silvers and greys, by the edge of the border. 30cm.

epithyomoides. syn. *E. polychroma*. One of the best. Tidy mounds of brassy-yellow heads all spring, the whole plant taking on coral tints in autumn. 40cm.

epithyomoides 'Candy'. Young foliage tinted bronze. If seedheads are removed after flowering, fresh growth makes attractive feature. 40cm.

epithyomoides 'Major'. A larger form of *E. epithyomoides*, but the foliage is more luxuriant and the second crop of autumn flowers is very welcome. 75cm.

griffithii 'Dixter'. A selected form. Very similar to *E.* 'Fireglow', but with stems and leaves shaded chestnut-tan. 90cm.

griffithii 'Fireglow'. From a running root-stock branching stems carry flat heads of small apricot-red flowers above light green foliage. June to August. 90cm.
Both flower for weeks in midsummer and prefer damper soils.

jacquemontii. From the west Himalayas. Branching stems clothed in pale-green leaves form a feature plant, carrying loose heads of yellowy-green flowers for weeks in midsummer. For sun or part shade. 1m.

× **martini.** An impresive plant. Forms compact mounds of evergreen rosettes. In spring, flower stems carry handsome crests of red-stained leaves followed by heads of lime-green flowers. Long decorative season. 60cm.

mellifera. A beautiful feature plant, but rarely seen because it will not stand prolonged or severe frost, but can be grown in southern counties, in well-drained soil against a warm west or south wall. Forms a large, shrub-like plant with smooth green stems, topped with whorls of long narrow, acid-green leaves, each striped with a central white vein. By late spring these carry round heads of curious knobbly brown flowers, heavily scented like honey. 1.5m.

myrsinites. From a central point radiate prostrate stems clothed in waxed blue leaves, each terminating in a large head of lime-green flowers. A delight in early spring. 15cm.

palustris. Needs deep retentive soil. Makes a large plant, spectacular all summer with great heads of gold-green bracts. 1.2m.

palustris 'Walenburg's Glorie'. Produces on upper half of erect branched stems, heads of bright yellowy-green flowers, similar to *E. palustris*, but with warmer yellow tones. Narrow, pale green leaves have a white central vein. 1m.

pithyusa. L'Euphorbe sophinette or Little fir spurge as it is called in France where it grows along the Mediterranean coast in rocky places. Its chief attraction lies in its vivid foliage effect, each dome-shaped plant is made up of closely-packed upright stems clothed in whorls of tiny blue pointed leaves. Compact heads of small green flowers last for weeks throughout summer. Not totally hardy but self-seeds. Ideal in hot, dry gravelly soil in warmer counties. 45cm.

sarawschanica. This spurge makes tall, upright stems clothed in willow-like, narrow sage-green leaves, topped with large heads of lime-yellow flowers from mid-late summer. Fertile soil in sun or light shade. 1.2m.

seguieriana. True form. This superb plant dominates the scene for months from June to November. Many polished mahogany-red stems carry heads of tiny lime-green flowers, still attractive in low autumn sunlight. 76-90cm.

sikkimensis. Ruby-red leaf rosettes and stems are one of the joys of early spring. By midsummer willowy stems carry light green leaves creating a very fresh effect topped with flat heads of yellow-green flowers. By August blue-green seed pods contrast with vivid lime collars. 1.2m.

EURYBIA divaricata. syn. *Aster divaricatus.* Found in open woodlands and thickets. Standing drier conditions than many other asters, this plant comes from southern Canada and the eastern United States. It has taken me some time and several plantings to appreciate this, one of the first Michaelmas daisy-like plants to flower. It produces quantities of very thin, rather floppy branching stems which are almost black and make good contrast with clouds of tiny, white star-like flowers. But initially the flowers look just too small to be effective. However, gradually they expand a little more, and as they age they flush lilac-mauve, starting at their pointed tips until they are suffused to their central darkened hearts. I learnt from Gertrude Jekyll to group them among bergenias which they soften with pretty disarray, from mid August and into September. 60cm.

x herveyi. syn. *Aster* × *macrophyllus.* 'Twilight'. Above healthy-looking basal foliage, mildew-free, stand self-supporting, branching stems, carrying a profusion of light-blue daisy flowers, 5cm across, each smaller than *Aster* × *frikartii* 'Mönch' which are 7.5cm across. Early flowering. August. 75cm.

 FAGOPYRUM dibotrys. Exciting in September, combining great height with breathtaking delicacy. Branched stems soar skywards bearing flat lacy panicles of tiny white flowers, floating above bold companions like *Helianthus* 'Lemon Queen' or *Eupatorium cannabinum* 'Flore Pleno'. Slowly invasive, so best in the large border or wild garden, in retentive soil and an open situation. 1.5m.

FERULA communis. A noble fennel, unscented. From a huge mound of dark-green, finely-cut foliage rises the vast flower-stalk, thick as a broomstick, purple tinted, topped with yellow umbellifer flowers. Wonderful against a blue summer sky. 3m.

tingitana 'Cedric Morris'. This form was collected by Cedric Morris. It makes a handsome mound of glossy-green, small-lobed leaves topped with large umbels of yellowy-green flowers. 1m.

FICARIA verna var. aurantiacus. syn. *Ranunculus ficaria.* A single celandine with orange flowers. March-April. 7cm.

verna 'Brazen Hussy'. Discovered in his wood by Christopher Lloyd. Has yellow celandine flowers set off by dark brown polished leaves. March-April. 7cm.

verna subsp. chrysocephalus. The largest of the celandines, often in flower in January continuing for weeks. Above large, round, burnished leaves stand glistening yellow bowl-shaped flowers. For sun or part shade in a soil which does not dry out. 20cm.

verna 'Coppernob'. Dark brown leaves, similar to 'Brazen Hussy' are set off by shining orange flowers. 7cm.

verna Flore Pleno Group. This is a double celandine, very attractive with tightly packed petals of glistening yellow, green-centred when young in April. 10cm.

FILIPENDULA palmata. Strong clumps of graceful stems bearing elegant foliage and large flat heads of tiny, softest pink, fluffy flowers. Midsummer. 1.2m.

purpurea 'Elegans'. This lovely meadowsweet has deep rose-pink flowers which imperceptibly change into bronze-red seedheads, making a feature for weeks in the late summer and autumn months in good moist soil. 90cm.

rubra 'Venusta'. A stately plant. Tall stems, large flat heads of deep rose flowers and vine-like leaves. Midsummer. 2m.

ulmaria 'Aurea'. Most beautiful golden-yellow foliage when well grown in moist soil and shade. Scorches badly when exposed to too much sun. Flowers best removed, then it makes new fresh foliage for autumn. 45cm.

ulmaria 'Variegata'. A meadow-sweet with very attractive foliage, its dark green leaves lit up with a central patch of bright gold. Needs a good damp soil. 45cm.

vulgaris 'Multiplex'. Basal rosettes of fine ferny foliage look attractive against the soil. Drooping panicles of double, cream-coloured flowers open from bronze buds held on bare slender stems in midsummer. 60cm.

FOENICULUM vulgare. Fennel. Forms clumps of tall lush green stems covered with thread-like, aromatic foliage. A lovely sight, useful to cut with its heads of yellow cow parsley-like flowers in late summer. 1.5m.

vulgare 'Purpureum'. Bronze fennel. As above, but with foliage a cloud of bronzy-brown. Both are handsome throughout summer to autumn. 1.5m.

vulgare 'Smokey'. This selected form has smoky-bronze foliage. It retains this colour, making effective contrast to the lacy heads of yellow flowers. Seeds true. 1.5m.

FRAGARIA chiloensis 'Chaval'. Although its pink leaf stalks are 15cm long, this plant appears to hug the soil, forming close-knit, wide-spreading carpets of small polished evergreen leaves. Makes quick and handsome ground cover beneath trees and shrubs (in sun too), ideal to set off bulbs, from snowdrops to late summer lilies. 2cm.

vesca 'Golden Alexandra'. A new seed strain reliably producing attractive yellow foliaged plants. Will slowly spread by runners to form an evergreen cover. 10cm.

FREESIA laxa. Above fans of light green blade-shaped leaves are held sprays of six-petalled coral-red starry flowers. Large bead-like seed pods are attractive too. Dainty plant for rock garden or gravel bed with raoulias, sempervivums etc. June-July. 25cm.

FRITILLARIA camschatcensis. Several open bells, unbelievably black, smooth outside, heavily corrugated inside, dangle from the top of fleshy stems clothed in whorls of green glossy leaves. Needs rich leaf-mould soil in sun or part shade. Flowers end of May. 50cm.

meleagris. The well-known Snakeshead fritillary. Slender stems bearing narrow, grey-green leaves carry large, bell-shaped flowers with square 'shoulders', varying in colour from white through pink to dark brooding purple, marked with distinctive chequering. 30cm.

persica. From the Middle East, growing on rocky slopes, in scrub and the edge of cornfields. Stout stems up to 1m tall in good soil, are clothed half way up with twisting grey-green leaves while the top half carries a spire of dusky purple bells.

× **tuntasia 'Chatto'.** Almost black thimble-shaped flowers coated with metallic brown are the result of chance hybridization between, we believe, *F. tuntasia* and *F. messanensis*. Several flowers carried on 40cm stems, clothed in linear grey leaves during late April.

verticillata. From a bulb, ascends a tall thin stalk set with very narrow grey-green leaves, which become curling tendrils towards the top, where several nodding open bell-shaped flowers hang, pale green with brown chequered pencilling inside. The seedheads are lovely too. Needs well fed, well drained soil in sun. Flowers in April. 60cm.

FUCHSIA. Fuchsias make ideal garden plants, providing both flower and leaf colour from June to the frosts. The following are hardy. If not cut by winter frosts it is better to cut to the ground in spring. Then new branches will spring up with great vigour. For some years now my fuchsias have had their flower buds attacked and destroyed by some pest, resulting in no flowers but abundant, if damaged growth. (It might be Capsid Bug.) It is necessary to spray early in the season to prevent this, and with fuchsias to keep watch and continue spraying an insecticide of some kind as new growth is produced late in the season. In well-fed retentive soil the following will make large shrubby plants of over 1m but can be pruned hard in spring where space is limited.

'Genii'. Valued for its beautiful golden foliage set off by red stems, and red and purple flowers. Mulch well first winter, cut back top growth each spring. 60cm.

'Hawkshead'. This enchanting form of *F. magellanica* has long, narrow ivory-white flowers. The tip of each pointed petal is stained green, like elegant painted finger nails. Will make a shrub 1m plus, depending on conditions, prefers cool site, retentive soil. 90cm.

magellanica gracilis 'Variegata'. Not quite so vigorous as the others. A dainty plant, leaves strongly variegated grey, rose and cream. 60cm.

magellanica var. gracilis 'Versicolor'. One of the most beautiful foliage plants. Tall arching stems bearing dainty foliage, a symphony of colour, suffused grey, rose and cream. Long succession of slim cherry coloured flowers with violet petticoats. 1.2m.

magellanica var. molinae 'Sharpitor'. A very pretty neat shrub. Small oval leaves on green stems are brightly variegated cream and green, setting off long slender flowers in palest pink and lilac. Gives a fresh effect among darker shrubs from midsummer to autumn frosts. 75cm.

'Mrs Popple'. An old favourite, reliably hardy and a joy in late summer-autumn when it is bowed with quantities of bold scarlet and purple flowers. 75cm.

'Pumila'. Makes a compact bushy plant clothed in green, small pointed leaves, with arching branches fringed with dark red buds which open long slender scarlet flowers revealing purple 'petticoats' and tassels of long stamens. 40cm.

riccartonii. Often seen at its best in seaside gardens. Forms a tall, spreading shrub, bearing small dark green leaves, smothered in small richly coloured flowers, crimson and purple, followed by purple seed pods. 1m.

'Whiteknights Pearl'. Is decked with slender, uniformly rose-pink flowers for weeks in late summer - early autumn, an irresistible sight. 90cm.

GALANTHUS. We offer the following good garden forms of snowdrop. Although traditionally sent 'in the green', we will also send in autumn, bulbs which have been freshly dug and which you should plant immediately on receipt. We divide clumps after flowering, every 3-4 years:

'Bill Bishop'. An enormous snowdrop of the 'Mighty Atom' clan, characterised by its long outer segments and a bold inverted V-shaped mark on the inner. Early flowering and for us the easiest of this group. 25cm.

'Brenda Troyle'. A large, elegant snowdrop. When open wide the petals measure 5cm across, held well on 30cm stalks. It is similar, but a little longer, than *G.* 'S. Arnott'.

elwesii 'Cedric's Prolific'. From stock originally grown in Cedric Morris's garden, we have selected this exceptional snowdrop. Large single flowers are held on stems up to 40 long supported by broad grey-green leaves 2.5cm across. A vigorous grower, quickly making generous clumps of bulbs, outstanding for effect. 30cm.

elwesii 'Comet'. Large heavily weighted flowers, nodding on long pedicels. The inner segments are marked with a broad V at the tips. Sometimes the outer segments are marked with fine short green lines. The grey-green leaves, up to 2.5cm across are an effective feature. 25cm.

elwesii 'Galadriel'. Chance seedling discovered in our woodland garden and named after Tolkien's Lady of the Wood. Late flowering, often with a second scape extending the season. Broad grey pointed leaves, stiff scapes hold the large globular flowers with a distinct Y marking on the inner segments. Much admired. 30cm.

elwesii var. monostictus 'Hiemalis'. This form opens its first flowers in November, always some for Christmas, emerging from enfolding grey leaves. 20cm.

elwesii 'Mrs McNamara'. Puts on a fine show early in the New Year, a tall upright plant with well developed narrow glaucous foliage at flowering time. Slender flowers held well clear of the foliage. Small rather slim V marking on the inner segment. The plant originated from Dylan Thomas's mother in-law, Mrs McNamara. 30cm.

elwesii 'Three Leaves'. Mature bulbs have three leaves instead of the usual two, which are broad and bluish-grey. 20cm.

elwesii 'Washfield Colesbourne'. A very distinctive snowdrop. Above broad, grey-green, ribbon-like leaves, tall stems carry large flowers with long petals suspended from a conspicuous dark green ovary, while the inner segments are entirely green, edged with white. 35cm.

'Galatea'. Although considered not to be James Allen's original form the modern stock of *G.* 'Galatea' is a fine robust plant. Similar to the well known *G.* 'Maget' but different in the perfect right angle of the inner marking and earlier flowering. Increases well. 25cm.

'Headbourne'. A fine early snowdrop originally from the garden of Lewis Palmer, Headbourne more often associated with agapanthus. Distinct narrower blue-grey foliage splayed out forms attractive clumps for the pristine white flowers with quite subtle markings on the inner segments. A good addition to a collection. 20cm.

'Hippolyta'. One of the last to appear, but one of the best, beautifully formed, rounded bells, filled with green edged 'petticoats'. One of the Greatorex doubles. When established makes two flowers per bulb. 20cm.

'James Backhouse'. This is the aberrant form often sold as *G.* 'Atkinsii' A wonderfully vigorous and easy mid January to mid February snowdrop with large, distinctive elongated flowers, often slightly deformed which in no way distracts from its effectiveness, along with the true *G.* 'Atkinsii', as the best early snowdrop. 30cm.

'Lady Beatrix Stanley'. Has large well-shaped double flowers. Long narrow pointed sepals enclose many layered neat white petticoats, faintly edged green. Early flowering, this snowdrop increases well, making bold garden effect. 20cm.

'Magnet'. Another indispensable snowdrop, the flowers of which have a charming habit of shaking in the slightest breeze on their long thin pedicels. Nicely proportioned flowers make this one of the best cultivars. 25cm.

'Mrs Thompson'. A remarkable snowdrop, distinguished by long wire-thin pedicels from which sway large buds opening 3, 4, and sometimes 5 large, cupped outer segments. 25cm.

nivalis 'Flore Pleno'. Has been in cultivation since at least the 1730s. It has six long, individually curved outer 'petals' embracing loosely gathered layers of light green and white-striped inner segments. The nodding heads, almost 5cm across, generously produced make some of the best 'snow patches' in the garden. 20cm.

nivalis 'Viridapice'. Has strong green tips to each of the outer segments. A fine strong-growing snowdrop. 30cm.

'Ophelia'. A fine early Greatorex double with rounded flowers held well above the foliage. Often has slightly aberrant inner segments and the green U-shaped marking fades down towards the base. Has a singular habit of producing pointed flower buds that fail to develop. 25cm.

plicatus 'Washfield Warham'. Makes vigorous clumps of broad grey leaves above, which dangle quantities of large, well-shaped, rounded snowdrops. I prize it because it is the latest to flower, well into March, creating a late "snowfall" effect. It produces 2 flowers per bulb and increases well. 20cm.

'Robin Hood'. A tall upright and narrow snowdrop in all its parts with a nicely marked flower held on a short pedicel. The distinct inner marking heavily shaded green, broad open and scissor like. G 'Robin Hood' was originally a James Allen selection in the 19th Century but it is unlikely this is the plant now grown today. 20cm.

'S. Arnott'. Much admired cultivar. Winter sun flares wide-open large cupped sepals, 5cm across, to show the strong green arch at the top of the inner petals. Increases well and is scented. 25cm.

'Straffan'. Good vigorous Irish snowdrop, possibly a hybrid between *G. nivalis* × *G. plicatus* originating in the Crimea and one of the oldest cultivars known. 1858. A late flowering snowdrop prolonged by the production of two flowering scapes. The marking on the inner segment is often likened to a Chinese bridge. 25cm.

'Wisley Magnet'. Another large snowdrop. The outer 'petals' are 3.5cm long, while the central segments have an extra broad V, very effective seen swaying from the long, thread-like pedicels. Stock given to me by Chris Brickell. 20cm.

GALIUM aristatum. Stands 60cm tall, making showers of tiny starry, sweetly scented white flowers on leafy stems, creating a delicate effect among ferns, hellebore leaves, and dark-toned heucheras in part shade. Midsummer.

odoratum. Sweet woodruff. Whorls of tiny, fresh-green leaves are topped in spring with starry white flowers. Makes spreading ground-cover in root-infested soil between shrubs. 20cm.

GALTONIA candicans. An elegant plant, lovely to cut. Tall stems carry large wax-white bells, like a huge hyacinth. Plant the bulbs in spring. Flowers July-September. 1.2m.

princeps. Handsome, broad grey-green, strap-shaped leaves. Erect stems carry green waxy bells, earlier than *G. candicans*. 60cm.

viridiflora. Flowers much later than the other two with heads of wide open pale green bells, remarkable in the garden or picked. September-October. 90cm.

GAURA lindheimeri. Flowers from midsummer through autumn when there is nothing else like it. White flowers, pink flushed, float for weeks among graceful branches set with small willow-like leaves. Needs full sun and well-drained soil. Up to 1.2m.
lindheimeri 'Corrie's Gold'. This introduction and the next were spotted here by one of my propagators, Debbie Allcock. The overall effect of pale, yellow-edged leaves below showers of pinkish-white flowers is very refreshing from midsummer until autumn, an endless display. 75cm.
lindheimeri 'Jo Adela'. Another of Debbie's finds. This time the foliage effect is of two tone green with paler edges surrounding each leaf. Equally as long flowering as the species. 75cm.
lindheimeri 'Siskiyou Pink'. Wire-thin, branching stems are bowed with spires of four-petalled flowers, almost white at the edges, deepening to rose in the centre. The massed effect of hovering rose-pink butterflies is a joy for weeks from midsummer to late autumn. 45cm.

GERANIUM – Border Forms
The hardy geraniums or cranesbills are invaluable garden plants bettered by none for attractive and weed-proof ground-cover. Especially valuable beneath shrubs and roses. Their parasol-shaped foliage, more or less deeply cut, is always beautiful and often scented. Their flowers are jewel-like in intensity of colour, and produced over a long period in great profusion. They are all easy to grow, most of them in ordinary soil and sun or light shade.
'Ann Folkard'. Young leaves are a delicious lemon-yellow, contrasting with the darker green of mature leaves. Scattered overall are rich magenta flowers, accented with dark eyes. Long extending stems trail a succession of leaves and flowers over neighbouring plants without harm. Trails 1m plus in good soil.
'Brookside'. A fine hybrid of *G. pratense* with handsome cut foliage and a profusion of pale-eyed mid-blue flowers throughout summer. 45cm.
× **cantabrigiense 'Biokovo'.** Forms low spreading cushions of smooth, green, divided leaves smothered in midsummer with white flowers tinted with pale-pink veins. Very good autumn colour. 30cm.
× **cantabrigiense 'Cambridge'.** Irresistible in flower, good ground-cover rest of year. In midsummer luminous soft-mauve flowers smother low cushions of neat, parasol-shaped leaves. Very good autumn colour. 40cm.
clarkei 'Kashmir Pink'. An attractive form of *G. c.* 'Kashmir White'. See below. 60cm.
clarkei 'Kashmir White'. From Nepal comes this lovely plant. Over spreading carpets of finely cut leaves stand sheaves of saucer-shaped white flowers veined with lilac, early to midsummer. 60cm.
endressii. Rose-pink flowers summer to autumn over pretty pale green foliage. Excellent spreading ground-cover, in sun or part shade. 40cm.
himalayense. From north east Afghanistan to Nepal. Above finely cut parasol shaped leaves float quantities of large blue flowers, finely pencilled with crimson veins which join to make a deep pink ring around the small white eye. One of the loveliest hardy geraniums, forming beautiful ground cover beneath roses where it spreads by underground roots, tolerating some drought or part shade. 40cm.
himalayense 'Plenum'. Beautiful double flowers in shades of rose, purple and blue. Lovely beneath old roses. Midsummer. 25cm.

'Johnson's Blue'. Abundant, luminous blue flowers with no inner shading for long period in midsummer. 40cm.

macrorrhizum. This group includes some of the best ground-cover plants for sun or shade and especially suitable for dry shade. They spread by rooting stems, making weed-proof carpets of scallop-edged, aromatic leaves, partially evergreen. Some develop warm autumn colour. There are several forms, all flower May-June.

macrorrhizum 'Album'. Perhaps my favourite, it has in fact palest shell-pink flowers which contrast well with deep coral-coloured calyxes and long protruding anthers and pistil. 40cm.

macrorrhizum 'Bevan's Variety'. Has somewhat taller stems of vivid magenta-pink flowers. 40cm.

macrorrhizum 'Ingwersen's Variety'. Colonises the ground with rooting stems making dense cover in cool conditions, green fragrant foliage, soft lilac-pink flowers, some autumn colour. 40cm.

macrorrhizum 'Variegatum'. The slightly felted leaves are splashed with cream, primrose-yellow and a dash of red around the scalloped edges. Magenta pink flowers are held just above the leaves. 30cm.

maculatum. It is neither blue nor pink, but an in-between shade of cool lilac with paler centres which bleach into the edge of the petals as the flowers fade creating a very delicate effect. Lovely with *Aquilegia* 'Adelaide Addison'. 60cm.

maculatum 'Chatto'. Relatively new to us, and we would love to know who named it! Appears more clump forming than *G. maculatum.* Carries fine heads of pale, lilac-pink outward facing flowers on 70cm stems.

× **magnificum.** Strong clumps of handsome dark green foliage, which colours well in autumn. The flowers are rich violet-blue, heavily veined on 60cm stalks in midsummer.

'Nimbus'. (*G. clarkei* 'Kashmir Purple' × *G. collinum*). Originally from Axletree Nursery. Forms a lacy mound 75cm across of finely-cut leaves smothered in high summer with starry bluish-purple flowers. Effective singly or grouped for bold effect in sun or part-shade. 60cm.

nodosum. Produces myriads of light purple flowers whose pale centres are enlivened by thin crimson veins and pale blue stamens, all fluttering on thin dark stems above smooth, maple-shaped leaves. Good in shade or sun. 40cm.

'Orion'. A new hybrid with exceptionally large blue flowers and a long flowering season from June onwards. Best cut down when flowering is over. 70cm.

× **oxonianum 'Claridge Druce'.** An excellent ground-cover for large scale planting with lovely foliage and long succession of rich rose-pink flowers. For sun or part shade. 45cm.

× **oxonianum 'Katherine Adele'.** Grown as much for its attractively marked foliage soon forming sprawly clumps of rusty brown centred leaves. Flowers are pale pink. Good ground cover in shady areas. 40cm.

× **oxonianum 'Rebecca Moss'.** Near white flowers that deepen to a darker pink as they age. A reliable, easy and long flowering hardy cranesbill that provides excellent ground cover. 50cm.

× **oxonianum 'Wargrave Pink'.** Similar to *G. endressi* but with flowers of salmon-pink. 40cm.

'Patricia'. A *G. psilostemon* hybrid with similar magenta-pink flowers but neither as tall or as floppy. 75cm.

phaeum. The Mourning widow or Dusky cranesbill. Strong grower in shade, small flowers of sombre purple, silk-textured. Early summer. 75cm.

phaeum 'Album'. Creates contrast and light, delicate effect in dim places. 60cm.

phaeum 'Lilacina'. Forms an upright sheaf of stems clothed in fresh-green, parasol-cut leaves topped with heads of deep lilac-blue flowers. Long season, spring-summer. 75cm.

phaeum 'Misty Samobor'. Spotted in the garden by Sally Anne Turner. A welcome colour break with creamy flowers subtlety stained pink and mauve, fading as they age. Probably best planted in a sizeable group for best effect. Foliage as *G. phaeum* 'Samobor'. 75cm.

phaeum 'Samobor'. I value this for its large leaves, handsome throughout growing season. They are strikingly marked with a central brown blotch, making an interesting addition to the floor of the Wood Garden. 75cm.

pratense 'Striatum'. A large weed-smothering plant with handsome cut-parasol leaves, and masses of single clear blue flowers striped white. Midsummer. 60cm.

procurrens. Prostrate stems, well branched, covered with pretty cut leaves, quickly cover yards, ideal ground-cover in the right place. Small purple flowers look entrancing trailing over Cistus bushes in late autumn. 20cm.

psilostemon. Superb foliage plant, forms a great clump of deeply cut leaves odd ones having brilliant autumn colour. Crowded in June with the brightest magenta-pink flowers, each with an indigo eye. Marvellous among shrubs or old roses. 90cm.

renardii. A particularly attractive plant. Forms low mounds of round sage green leaves, scallop-edged and quilted. The almost white flowers have a network of delicate purple veins in early summer. 25cm.

renardii 'Tschelda'. Possesses the same foliage quality as *G. renardii*, but has pale-blue flowers, heavily veined. 30cm.

× **riversleaianum 'Russell Prichard'.** Forms a central clump of grey-green leaves from which all summer and autumn it flings long streamers of light magenta-pink flowers. Very showy among silver plants. 20cm.

ROZANNE = 'Gerwat'. This unlovely name is the registered cultivar name of a dazzling new hardy geranium. It is better known as Rozanne's cranesbill, so I prefer to write *Geranium* 'Rozanne', named after Rozanne Waterer, who, with her husband, spotted it in their garden. It is a hybrid of *G. himalayense* and *G. wallichianum* 'Buxton's Variety', producing large (5cm across) intense violet-blue flowers lit with large white centres. In flower from May onwards, it takes a rest in late summer, but a trim then will check its sprawling habit and induce a fresh crop of blooms well into November. Planted at the border edge, in sun or part shade, it stops every passer-by. 50cm.

sanguineum. Over a neat hummock of finely cut leaves there is a constant succession from early summer to December of vivid magenta pink flowers. 30cm.

sanguineum 'Album'. Pure white flowers on taller plants. 45cm.

sanguineum 'Cedric Morris'. Is similar to *G. sanguineum,* but with a more upright habit and taller. 40cm.

sanguineum var. striatum. Exquisitely pretty with pale pink flowers veined crimson. Sun, ordinary soil. 25cm.

'Sirak'. From Hans Simon in Germany. Produces quantities of large, lilac-pink flowers held above neat clumps of foliage, creating a gay effect in a sunny border, or light shade. 60cm.

'Spinners'. Over finely cut leaves this plant produces a shower of exquisite flowers, a luminous light-purple paling towards the centre created by translucent red veins threading through a blue base, a colour which glows under thunderous skies. Midsummer. 60cm.

sylvaticum 'Album'. Forms large mounds of soft divided leaves above which stand much branched stems carrying pure white flowers in spring. 60cm.

sylvaticum 'Mayflower'. Creates a vivid effect of massed colour. Foliage is hidden by quantities of flowers opening light purple and fading to violet-blue. The combination of shades is very effective. Lovely among cool yellows. May-June. 60cm.

wallichianum 'Buxton's Variety'. From a central cluster of small dark, prettily mottled leaves are flung lax stems bearing a succession of rich blue flowers, white eyed and appealing, to trail over a wall or embroider the border edge from July to November. 30cm.

GERANIUM – Rock-garden Forms
cinereum 'Ballerina'. A charming small cranesbill, covering the ground with rounded, cut greyish foliage and large lilac flowers, heavily veined purple, for weeks throughout summer. 10cm.
dalmaticum. Small leaves, makes spreading mats, delightful soft rose-pink flowers. Midsummer. 15cm.
malviflorum. Disappears like *G. tuberosum* after flowering, but the large rich blue flowers, red-veined, are very lovely in May. 30cm.
× **sessiliflorum subsp. novae-zelandiae 'Nigricans'.** Low rosettes of small soft brown round leaves, highlighted by the occasional bright orange leaf. Tiny white flowers, seeds true. 5cm.
tuberosum. The finely cut low foliage is up all winter, excellent for marking bulbs. In spring it is an airy mass of tiny floating pink and white flowers, all disappeared by summer. 30cm.

GEUM 'Borisii'. Makes slowly spreading clumps of rich green, roundish, hairy leaves. The single flowers are an unusual shade of rich orange-red, very vivid against the bold foliage. Early, and sometimes late summer. 30cm.
'Coppertone'. A seedling which occurred here. Over tidy clumps of fresh green foliage sprays of almost translucent pale apricot flowers. Midsummer. 30cm.
'Lemon Drops'. One of our chance seedlings, this makes a healthy clump of rich green foliage, the better to set off drooping heads of greenish-yellow single flowers clasped in green and red calyxes, filled with orange stamens. 40cm.
rivale 'Album'. Nodding heads of white flowers in green calyxes in early summer. A modest plant, charming for a cool spot. 30cm.
rivale 'Leonard's Variety'. Above rounded, deeply cut basal leaves stand mahogany tinted branching stems holding old rose bell-shaped flowers held in maroon calyxes. For retentive soil, lovely with *Deschampsia flexuosa* 'Tatra Gold'. 30cm.
rivale 'Pink Frills'. Has petals deeply and narrowly divided creating a frilled effect. 30cm.

GILLENIA trifoliata. A graceful plant for semi-shade or full sun in cool retentive soil. Slender russet-coloured stems, set with small trifoliate leaves carry sprays of narrow-petalled, white flowers which float like moths at dusk in June. When the flowers have gone, reddish-brown calyxes remain, quietly attractive for weeks. 90cm.

GLADIOLUS communis subsp. byzantinus. Native of Spain and North Africa. Remarkable for magenta-crimson flowers making vivid vertical accents among grey-silver plants. Thrives in light soil, full sun. 60cm.
papilio. Strangely seductive in late summer and autumn. Above narrow, grey-green blade-shaped leaves stand tall stems carrying downcast heads. The slender buds and backs of petals are bruise-shades of green, cream and slate-purple. Inside creamy hearts shelter blue anthers while the lower lip petal is feathered and marked with an 'eye' in purple and greenish-yellow, like the wing of a butterfly. It increases freely. Needs warm well-drained soil. 90cm.
tristis. Exquisite flowers, 2 or 3 per slender stem, cream with bronze-green shadows, strongly perfumed in the evenings. Narrow, rush-like leaves are damaged in hard winters. Best in well-drained soil and warm site, or under light cover, in plastic tunnel in pots or in cool greenhouse. May not be hardy in cold areas. 75cm.

GLAUCIUM flavum. Our native Horn poppy, still seen on east coast shingle beaches. Handsome rosettes of blue-grey deeply ruffled leaves, branching heads of lemon-yellow poppies. 50cm.

flavum f. fulvum. Large rosettes of grey-blue heavily cut leaves, flowers burnt-orange, all late summer and autumn are followed by long horn-like pods. 60cm.

GRASSES. See page 156.
Do not miss the introductory paragraph to our list of ornamental grasses. A whole new concept of gardening might be opened up for you.

GRINDELIA chiloensis. Branching stems set with narrow, curving, evergreen, tooth-edged leaves are lightly silvered with white dots. Large yellow daisies stand well above foliage on long bare stems the centre of each opening bud glazed with sticky white, like soft icing sugar. For sheltered spots in well-drained soil, good with greys, flowers late summer. 60cm.

GUNNERA – Low-growing Ground-Covering Forms.
hamiltonii. So different from the giant forms you would not imagine the following three plants could be gunneras. For a moist place. Creates a dense carpet of fleshy rosettes, composed of heart-shaped, tooth-edged leathery leaves overlaid with a bronze tint. Runs but easily dislodged. May not be hardy in cold areas. 5cm.

magellanica. Forms a dense mosaic of small, crinkle-edged leaves about 6cm across which completely hides the tangle of prostrate branching stems. Useful and attractive ground-cover in heavy damp soil. Reputedly not evergreen except in mild districts but has survived very hard winters here. 8cm.

prorepens. Similar, more warmly bronzed but makes irregular clusters rather than the well-formed rosettes of *G. hamiltonii*. By late August studded with upstanding 5cm spikes, looking like sticks of sealing wax, made with closely-set, tiny red round fruitlets.

GUNNERA – Giant Border Forms. **CAUTION – SKIN IRRITANT.**
manicata. The grandest foliage plant for damp or boggy soil, giving a tropical air to temperate gardens. You may shelter beneath huge parasol-like leaves. 1.5m across held on wrist-thick, bristly stalks. Curious flower spikes hide beneath. Apply farmyard manure lavishly. Protect coconut-sized resting buds in winter with own foliage bent over, plus bracken or herbaceous remains. 2.5m.

tinctoria. Differs from *G. manicata* in having more rounded, deeply lobed leaves, while the leaf stalks are not so tall. A more obvious difference is in the seedhead. In *G. tinctoria* the primaeval-looking seedhead resembles a densely knobby club, while the fruiting spike of *G. manicata* has long, narrow side shoots, separated, like fingers. 2m.

GYPSOPHILA paniculata 'Bristol Fairy'. This is an old garden favourite, traditionally grown to put with sweet peas and carnations. I prefer to plant it near something blue, like agapanthus. It produces a huge tangle of interweaving stems, creating a cloud-like effect in midsummer when smothered in tiny white flowers. If this plant and *G*. 'Flamingo', the pale pink variety, are trimmed half-way back after flowering, they will produce the show all over again throughout autumn. 1.2m.

paniculata 'Flamingo'. Inter-tangling branching stems support a cloud-like mass of tiny double pink flowers, with minimal grey-green leaves. Good to pick or hovering like a cloud above lower plants, i.e. *Euphorbia seguieriana* or *Origanum laevigatum* 'Herrenhausen'. 90cm.

repens 'Dubia'. Ground-hugging mats of pewter-tinted foliage on dark red stems, smothered with white flowers flushed pink. Lovely for a crevice, or trailing from a ledge. May-June. 8cm.
repens 'Rosa Schönheit'. Rich rose-pink flowers smother low cushions of grey-green leaves, flowering non-stop from spring until autumn. A gem. 20cm.
'Rosenschleier'. Forms a low cumulus cloud of palest-pink tiny double flowers, on the border edge, for weeks, mid to late summer. 30cm spread.

HACQUETIA epipactis. An endearing little plant, not least because it appears in January before most snowdrops and aconites have made a start. The flowers open, almost at ground-level, clusters of tiny, yellow fertile flowers surrounded by conspicuous olive-green, petal-like bracts, a bit like an astrantia to which it is related. A succession of these cheering little faces appears well into spring. They need moist soil in shade during the growing season, will tolerate drier conditions later in the year. 15cm.
epipactis 'Thor'. Unusual and cheerful form of this early flowering woodlander. Domed yellow centres to variegated bracts show up well against the bare soil. Best in a humus rich soil that does not dry out. 15cm.

✕ **HALIMIOCISTUS sahucii.** A wide spreading low bush, whose twiggy branches are covered with neat dark evergreen leaves, smothered in medium-sized white flowers throughout June and July. Needs a well-drained warm site. 75cm.

HAPLOPAPPUS glutinosus. Forms a cushion of dark evergreen finely cut foliage studded with sun-loving orange daisy-flowers, from August till frosts. Looks beautiful hanging over low wall or steps. 20cm.

HEBE cupressoides 'Boughton Dome'. Easily mistaken for a conifer, my 15-year-old plant (1m x 1m) sits like a large strokable boulder among small alpines. Close packed stems divide and subdivide to create a dense head of soft olive-green tips.
macrantha. Very choice small shrub with a stiff, compact habit. Fresh green leaves topped with surprisingly large white flowers, midsummer. 60cm.
recurva. Makes a neat tidy rounded shape with blue-grey leaves. In late summer it carries racemes of nutmeg-tinted buds which open white. 60cm.

HEDERA - HARMFUL IF EATEN/SKIN ALLERGEN.
Most valuable plants, not used as effectively as they might be. Invaluable for covering unsightly walls or fences, the variegated forms provide bright contrast, especially in winter. Perfect ground-cover in dark places, most long suffering as a house plant, and what variations!
colchica 'Sulphur Heart'. Large, floppy dark green leave shave a vivid central zone of butter yellow, softening to palest green at the edges which merges into the strong irregular border of holly-green.
helix 'Ivalace'. Small in-curved leaves, dark green with pale green veins. Interesting and attractive.
helix 'Lutzii'. Small leaves prettily mottled cream, green and primrose.
helix 'Melanie'. A selected form of *H. helix* 'Cristata' which occurred here on the nursery, and named after a member of staff. Every round and crimped leaf is bordered with plum-red, very unusual, and much admired.

helix f. poetarum 'Poetica Arborea'. Poets ivy. Another rarely seen ivy, this is a mature fruiting form which slowly makes a dome-shaped bush and is covered throughout the winter with clusters of fruit which, by spring, have become not black, but orange. 1.2m.

HEDYCHIUM densiflorum. Ginger lily from east Himalayas. Many strong stems handsomely dressed in long tapered leaves topped with bottle-like spikes of small apricot flowers, a grand feature plant to tower above *Hosta* 'Gold Standard', *Rudbeckia fulgida* var. *deamii*, surrounded by a yellow carpet of Creeping Jenny, *Lysimachia nummularia* 'Aurea'. Open situation, retentive soil. 1.4m.

HELENIUM. Some of these can be gawky in habit and brassy in colour, especially if mixed with other strident colours, like purple phlox or crimson monarda. Among cool companions they add fresh gaiety to autumn, and are a joy to pick for several weeks. They perform better if divided occasionally.
'Moerheim Beauty'. An old favourite. Makes compact, self-supporting bushy plants, much branched, crowded with autumnal-coloured flowers; brown velvety central knobs are surrounded with rich orange-red petals when fresh, fading to amber, effective over many weeks. August-October. 75cm.
'Sahin's Early Flowerer'. Produces a medley of shades, with streaked orange petals opening from bronze-red buds, finally maturing to yellow, a joyful and endless display from June to October. 1m.
'Sonnenwunder'. 1.2m tall stems need no staking. Are topped with large branching heads of clear yellow daisies. This and the following fill my vases for several weeks during late summer.
'Zimbelstern'. Stout stems carry bouquets of yellow, upward-facing daisy flowers enhanced with velvety-brown, cushion-like centres. 1.2m.

HELIANTHEMUM. Related to cistus, the Rock Roses make invaluable ground-cover in dry sunny situations. They quickly form low, tidy shrubs, evergreen or ever-grey. A good trim after flowering keeps them compact. We grow the following: 'Ben Nevis', 'Cerise Queen', 'Cheviot', 'Firedragon', 'Henfield Brilliant', 'Regenbogen', 'Rhodanthe Carnea', 'Schnee', 'Sudbury Gem', 'The Bride', 'Tomato Red', 'Wisley Primrose', 'Wisley White'. In flower for weeks in midsummer. 30-45cm.

HELIANTHUS 'Capenoch Star'. This specially fine sunflower has medium sized flowers, its large dome-shaped yellow centres surrounded by broad yellow petals. Impressive in the garden or picked. Forms large, leafy self-supporting plants for mid-border. Late summer-autumn. Needs retentive soil. Mid to back border. 1.8m.
'Lemon Queen'. Stout stems support wide branching heads carrying myriads of pale lemon daisy flowers. Superb for back of border in retentive soil, flowering for weeks from late August. 2m.
microcephalus. This and H. 'Lemon Queen' are similar, both make huge, bushy much-branched plants, so are both tall and wide. *H.* 'Lemon Queen' has light lemon-yellow, opening over many weeks in late summer-autumn. *H. microcephalus* has purple-brown stained stems, somewhat smaller golden yellow daisy flowers. Both these create a grand landscape effect. 1.8m.
salicifolius. Stout stems clothed from top to bottom with narrow willow-like leaves form a fine architectural feature all summer, back of border, or wild garden, topped in autumn with heads of daisy flowers. 2m.

HELICHRYSUM italicum. Commonly called the Curry plant, because of its strongly aromatic scent. A small tidy bush of mid-grey leaves carrying crowded heads of small yellow flowers. Midsummer. 60cm.

'Schweffellicht'. A splendid plant for the edge of a sun-baked well-drained border. It makes slowly spreading clumps of narrow leaves covered with white felt. Felted stems carry felted buds opening into clusters of tiny sulphur yellow daisies which retain their colour when hung up to dry. Flowers late summer. 45cm.

stoechas 'White Barn'. This natural cross produces larger leaves and shoots than the type, making a bush similar to a lavender, with very white felted leaves, and shining buds opening to small pale sulphur-yellow flowers, in midsummer. 60cm.

HELIOPSIS helianthoides 'Hohlspiegel'. Leafy stems carry a profusion of yellow daisies accented with brown cone-shaped centres. August onwards. 1m.

HELLEBORUS - HARMFUL IF EATEN. Plants of long-lasting beauty, having handsome evergreen foliage, many making bold ground-cover and bearing flowers of sculptured form. Easily grown when drainage is good and humus abundant.

argutifolius. One of my favourite plants. In spring it sends up weed-resistant clumps. Many stiff stems bear handsome claw-like foliage of cool jade-green. In winter these tend to fall out like the spokes of a wheel to make way for the new shoots. By January every stem is topped by clusters of apple-green cups. Flowers from January to June. 60cm.

× ericsmithii. A cross between the Christmas rose *H. niger* and *H. × sternii*. This cross has been made several times, giving some variation in flower and leaf. Each plant produces several stout stems clothed in dark green leaves netted with pale veins above, which are poised clustered heads of large, saucer-shaped flowers, cream in February, maturing to green, flushed with bronze, and still attractive in May when setting seed. 40cm.

foetidus. The native Stinking hellebore. Neater and smaller clumps of holly-green, divided fan-shaped leaves, from which fall clusters of palest green bells, thimble-sized, edged with maroon. A true winter flower. 60cm.

× hybridus. Strong, flowering-sized plants grown from seeds, of good parentage, varying in colour from white to deep plum, spotted, speckled or plain, shadowed with green. All desirable! Fine evergreen foliage makes a feature all summer. We cut our leaves off in winter before the flowers appear, to prevent the spread of botrytis which sometimes damages the flowering stems. Flowers February-April. 45cm.

× hybridus guttatus pink. Nodding deep pink flowers heavily spotted inside and shadowed green. 40cm.

× hybridus Kochii Group. Many leafy branching stems carry quantities of pale, nodding buds opening shallow saucers of primrose-yellow, very effective in the winter garden. Flowers at the same time as *H. niger*. January-March. 30cm.

× hybridus 'Limelight'. Another shade to lighten the heart on dull days. Large, nodding, cup-shaped flowers with pointed petal tips, in palest lime-green. 40cm.

× hybridus 'Plum Stippled'. Hangs its head. Plum shaped and coloured like a half ripe plum, inside heavily spotted all over. 40cm.

× hybridus purple. Well shaped, rich plum shades, lovely near the pale pink flowers and dark leaves of *Primula* 'Guinevere' or yellow leafed *Valeriana phu* 'Aurea' for contrast. 30cm.

× hybridus white. Much easier to grow than the true Christmas rose, these exquisite large white flowers hang their heads from 40cm stems, each delicately shaded green. Buds in January, flowers till April.

niger. The well known Christmas rose. Just above dark green, leathery leaves stand white, wide-open blooms, sometimes tinged pink. They need retentive but well-drained soil, in sun or part shade, top dressed with old manure or compost. 25cm.

× **nigercors.** A cross between the Christmas rose and the Corsican hellebore. Large, open faced flowers, cream shadowed green in February, maturing to green tinged bronze as they age and still attractive in May. 40cm.

× **sternii 'Boughton Beauty'.** (*H argutifolius* × *lividis*). Stout maroon stems clothed in dark green leathery leaves, sometimes laced with silver, carry branched heads of old rose buds opening pale green centres, filled with cream stamens, overall an exciting combination. Needs shelter from icy winds. Flowers January-April. 75cm.

viridis. An established clump of fresh leafy stems, crowded with buds and shallow apple-green saucers filled with cream stamens is a pleasure for weeks, form early February until late spring. 30cm.

HEMEROCALLIS. Daylilies are easy plants in any soil except the very dry. They thrive in sun or part shade. Their bright, light green foliage is valued in early spring. Later these grassy clumps make good ground-cover. Among those we grow I recommend the following:

HEMEROCALLIS Species. I am particularly drawn to the smaller flowering species who tend to carry their flowers well above the foliage.

dumortieri. The first daylily to make a fine show in early spring. Slender stems carry a wealth of perfumed flowers whose rich yellow petals are accented by dark reddish buds. 60cm.

lilioasphodelus. This lovely old species has been grown since the 16th century. Perfect lily-shaped flowers of clear light yellow are very sweetly scented, lovely in early summer among blue or pink cranesbills (geraniums). 75cm.

thunbergii. Tall stems carry branched heads of narrow lemon-yellow flowers well above basal foliage making an effective vertical in July. 1.2m.

HEMEROCALLIS Hybrids. All flowering July-August.

'Ali Sheldon'. Above short green tussocks of foliage stand elegant stems of wide-faced greenish flowers with ruffled edges to their petals. Mid-late summer. 60cm.

'Anzac'. Large open-faced trumpets in rich guardsman's red with orange throats. Sumptuous. 75cm.

'Baroni'. Above narrow grassy leaves stand stems of long-trumpeted, narrow-petalled, greenish-yellow flowers. 1m.

'Berlin Red'. Similar to *H.* 'Anzac'. Rich fiery-red, opening many buds per stem, each petal has pale central vein leading to vivid yellow throat. 90cm.

'Corky'. Similar to *H.* 'Golden Chimes' but cooler. A small dainty plant whose slender branching stems carry a long succession of pale yellow flowers with bronze reverse. June.-August. 60cm.

fulva 'Green Kwanso'. Four layers of burnt orange petals, diminishing in size as they reach the centre, produce a strangely handsome effect as the outer petals carry a dark red V, the original bee guide. Flowers last a bit longer being double. Bold foliage. Midsummer. 90cm.

'Eenie Weenie Non-stop'. Another border-edge type. Forms neat low clumps of narrow green leaves. Flowers have lemon-yellow slightly ruffled petals. 40cm.

'Gentle Shepherd'. A smaller plant than *H.* 'Light the Way' with smaller flowers, the three outer petals a deeper shade of cream, the inner 3 petals a paler shade of cream, leading into a green heart. 40cm.

'George Cunningham'. Lovely colour, mango mixed with orange, with slightly ruffled petals. July-Aug. 75cm.

'Golden Chimes'. A popular hybrid which has lost none of the charm and elegance of the species. On branching stems, light reddish-brown buds open well-shaped rich-yellow flowers over a long period. June-August. 75cm.

'Happy Returns'. Small prettily shaped flowers, slightly ruffled petals of clear yellow. Continues to produce new flowering stems well into autumn. 30cm.

'Hyperion'. Above narrow grassy leaves stand stems of narrow trumpet-shaped flowers with curved-back tops to clear yellow petals, a variation perhaps on 'Baroni'. Both are attractive in natural plantings. 90cm.

'Lemon Bells'. My preferred style of daylily. Sheaves of stems holding well above the foliage open branched heads of medium-sized clear yellow lily-like flowers with bronze backs, fresh and elegant. Mid-high summer. 1m.

'Light The Way'. From low clumps of leaves rise strong stems each holding a cluster of long, lily-shaped, pale-cream flowers filled with pale yellow stamens springing from a green heart. Exceptionally lovely. 60cm.

'Mauna Loa'. A daylily the colour of which grows on you. Best described as a coppery-orange with amber hues petal edges are slightly ruffled. Prolific in flower, forming fine clumps in most soils given full sun. 90cm.

'Oom-pa-pa'. The name is acceptable when you see the clustered heads of large cream trumpet-shaped flowers, produced for weeks, through mid to late summer. 50cm.

'Orchid Beauty'. Since it hadn't a name I have chosen this for a stunning flower, of indescribable colour. Ruffled petals form wide-faced flowers whose colour resembles cream stirred into plum juice with dark-shadowed bee guides leading into an orange heart. Overall a delicate pastel effect, immediately desirable. Stout in all its parts. Mid-high summer. 90cm.

'Pardon Me'. A smaller growing daylily with cranberry red flowers and a bright yellow-green throat. Late season variety which will repeat flower. 75cm.

'Pink Charm'. Narrow pointed petals, rich salmon-pink with pale central vein creates a star-like effect, standing on slender stems above neat foliage. 60cm.

'Pink Damask'. A soft reddish-orange sauce blended with cream creates this glowing colour, with flowers held well above neat leafy clumps. 60cm.

'Pink Sundae'. Softly ruffled pale apricot petals with a paler zone along the centre of each petal. Good impact on landscape. July-August. 90cm.

'Raspberry Wine'. Rich raspberry-red petals with slightly ruffled edges, and pale bee-guides leading to red anthers. Loved by bumble-bees. Midsummer. 50cm.

'Satin Glow'. Cream petals washed with green towards the centre stand well above short neat foliage. 75cm.

'Scarlet Flame'. A brilliant clear jewel-like red with pale narrow bee guides disappearing into the pale orange centre. Free-flowering above neat tussocks of leaves. Mid-late summer. 60cm.

'Sleepy'. Produces quantities of medium sized soft apricot-orange flowers with dark centres. 90cm.

'Stella de Oro'. Low growing neat bushy foliage. Just above clustered heads of smallish trumpet-shaped pale orange flowers produced over many weeks. Mid-late summer. 40cm.

'Summer Wine'. Free-flowering, makes warm effect with large ruffled petals, light maroon marked with fine dark veins leading into orange-yellow throat. July. 60cm.

'Susie Wong'. Medium sized clear yellow, scented flowers open from clustered head of buds over long period. Midsummer. 75cm.

'**Thumbelina**'. Many small flowers of deep even orange with bronze tinted backs. 60cm.
'**Whichford**'. Slightly curled, slim green buds open sharp lemon-yellow flowers on 1m stems.
'**Winsome Lady**'. Beautifully formed wide lily-shaped flowers. Pale plum-washed creamy flowers create a lovely effect, held well above short neat foliage. Mid-late summer. 75cm.

HEPATICA nobilis 'Rubra Plena'. The desirable-on-sight double pink form of this collectable woodlander. Alas, division is slow. Needs damp leaf-mould soil in part shade. 10cm.
transsilvanica. I am uncertain of the name for this fine form I found in an old garden. In early spring many petals of rich blue make flowers the size of a 10p piece, smothering the over-wintered leaves. New ones continue to make handsome ground-cover for the rest of the year. 10cm.
transsilvanica 'Elison Spence'. A treasure from Mrs Molly Sanderson in Ireland, via Elizabeth Strangman. Powder-blue flowers have a neat cushion of extra petals in the centre. 15cm.
transsilvanica 'Lilacina'. Has pale lilac flowers, almost as large as the type, freely produced, early spring. Part shade. 10cm.

HESPERANTHA coccinea f. alba. Syn. *Schizostylis.* Pale-green, pointed buds open starry, pure white flowers. Free-flowering in autumn. Smaller than the following. 40cm.
coccinea 'Major'. Makes spreading patches of grassy-leafed shoots which send up slender spires of slim buds. Throughout autumn and mild days in winter they open glistening shallow cups, jewel-like and cherry-red. They need moisture all summer but also warmth to encourage early flowering. 60cm.
coccinea 'Jennifer'. A lovely mid pink to compliment our range of Kaffir lilies, flowering as they all so usefully do in late summer. An extra mulch for those in cold districts is a wise precaution. Best in direct sun and a moist soil. 60cm.
coccinea 'Pallida'. Large, well-formed flowers in pale shell-pink. 60cm.
coccinea 'Sunrise'. Another good selection from Eric Smith, large salmon-pink flowers open in October and continue into December. 60cm.
coccinea 'Zeal Salmon'. A softer shade of red than *H.* 'Major'. 75cm.

HESPERIS matronalis. Dame's violet or Sweet rocket. Makes a large bushy plant full of highly scented violet blue flowers. Short lived but will seed about in all but the driest of soils. 90cm.

HEUCHERA. Do not like to be scorched or dried out, so a cool situation, partial shade suits them best. Also they need to be replanted in fresh soil every few years.
Stunning as the myriad of new cultivars are, I am finding many of them difficult to use in the garden and recent problems with rust disease leads me to choose with caution.
americana. Mounds of rounded, ivy-shaped leaves with silky top-sides appear in spring in soft shades of tan, finally becoming dark green. New leaves continue to appear, if conditions are good, maintaining interesting colour effect. Thin, bare stems carry broad spires of tiny brown and green flowers in early-midsummer. 45cm.
americana 'Dale's Strain'. In immature leaves the pattern of veins is picked out with an attractive brown tinge which turns dark green as the leaf matures to pale green, thus retaining the marbled effect. 45cm.
'**Beauty Colour**'. Coral Flower. A clump of large dark maroon leaves edged with a pink-orange rim Panicles of large, pale pink flowers in early summer. 40cm.
'**Chocolate Ruffles**'. Produces a succession of leaves variously flushed in shades of tan and bronze on the surface, light beetroot purple on the reverse, while the deeply cut edges curl and ruffle to produce an attractive textured effect. 40cm.

cylindrica 'Greenfinch'. Lovely for picking. Tall well-formed spikes of olive-green bells. Midsummer. 75cm.

'Huntsman'. Scallop-edged leaves have soft gleams like burnished pewter with dark hints of bronze in the shadowed veins, a perfect setting for sprays of salmon-pink, bell-shaped flowers. Given to me by Dennis Davidson of Thropton, Northumberland. 45cm.

'Persian Carpet'. One of the best dark-leafed heucheras, flat smooth leaves show off a sumptuous marbled effect, intricate veining over a dark purple background slowly fading to silvery-pewter with plum-purple reverse. 45cm.

'Plum Pudding'. Rounded, deeply scalloped leaves richly marbled with silver over a dark purple base. 45cm.

'Ruffles'. From a base of fresh green ruffle-edged leaves come tall stems holding tiers of palest green 'bobbles', made up of tiny bead-like buds poking out minute stamens and stigmas. Lovely airy effect, picked or growing. 60cm.

villosa. Much admired. Above a mound of fresh green maple-shaped leaves stand long-lasting spires of tiny greenish-white flowers. Creates a fresh spring-like effect on edge of sunny, but not too dry border for weeks. Mid-late summer. 60cm.

villosa 'Palace Purple'. Overlapping heart-shaped leaves with irregularly cut edges are dark bronze-red on the surface, light magenta-pink on reverse. Faint puckering between the veins accentuates the glistening texture. The flowers are equally beguiling. Masses of dark wiry stems carry feathery heads of tiny white flowers which expand into rosy-bronze seed pods, all stages to be seen for months, from summer to autumn. 45cm.

villosa 'Royal Red'. Our own name for this seedling. A striking foliage plant, low mounds of maple-shaped leaves, dark mahogany-brown. 45cm.

× **HEUCHERELLA alba 'Bridget Bloom'.** Interesting marbled foliage all year round, massed with spikes of light pink flowers, late spring-early summer. Likes a little shade and humus-fed light soil. 45cm.

alba 'Rosalie'. Fluffy heads of shrimp-pink flowers stand above light-green lobed leaves, prettily marbled tan. April-May. 45cm.

'Stoplight'. This variety has striking yellow-green leaves with skeletal burgundy centres and spires of white flowers in spring. A mound forming perennial that provides a colourful patch for a shady corner. 20cm.

HOSTA. A family of aristocratic plants. Although they will survive almost anywhere they look best, and do better, in partial shade, in cool well-fed soil, where, once established, many will produce immense leaves, totally weed proof. Strategically placed nothing can create such a bold or lush effect. Trumpet-shaped flowers add interest from late summer-autumn. Most yellow-leafed forms need shade or part shade.

'Blue Heart'. A smaller sieboldiana type with mounds of overlapping blue leaves and masses of lavender flowers, one of the most abundant in fact. 50cm.

'Blue Mouse Ears'. An award winning miniature hosta soon making mounds of overlapping blue-grey leaves. Short scaped lavender blue flowers are perfectly to scale. Remarkably slug resistant and ideal for containers. 15cm.

fortunei var. albopicta. Large leaves, each one magnificently marbled in shades of bright yellow, primrose, soft green and olive, turning green by midsummer. 45cm.

fortunei var. albopicta f. aurea. In spring the young leaves are totally soft buttercup-yellow slowly ageing to green. 40cm.

fortunei var. albopicta f. aurea. Eric Smith's Form. In May-June much larger broad, pointed, pale-yellow leaves, 'stitched' with fine green veins, create a quilted effect. Matures to light green by midsummer. 60cm.

fortunei var. aureomarginata. A good name for this fine plant. Rich green leaves have broad creamy-yellow borders, retaining the colour well into autumn. 75cm.

fortunei 'Marginata Alba'. Large sage-green leaves, grey beneath, are broadly edged with white. Some, buried beneath the top layers, may be half white. Needs time to establish, and shade, to produce best variegation, when it is one of the best white edged kinds. 75cm.

'Frances Williams'. I suspect there are several variations sold under this name. Mine was bred originally by Eric Smith, and seems larger, more handsome than some! Broad, heavily quilted waxed blue leaves have wide, irregular butter-yellow margins all summer. Sumptuous in part shade. 75cm.

'Ginko Craig'. Has narrow green leaves edged white. Similar to *H.* 'Louisa' but smaller, very effective in a group. Where the leaves are thoroughly shaded they are more white than green, sometimes entirely white. 30cm.

'Gold Standard'. Desirable on sight whether in a border or in a flower arrangement. Medium-sized leaves strongly veined, are a lovely shade of yellow, thinly rimmed with green. The colour becomes rich-yellow as the leaves mature. Pale lavender flowers in midsummer. 60cm.

'Guacamole'. Much admired, this recent hybrid creates a strong growing mound of subtle gold centered, green margined leaves. If this wasn't enough the flowers are large, long lasting and exceptionally fragrant. 80cm.

'Halcyon'. Raised by Eric Smith, possibly the best blue-leafed hosta on offer at present. Heart-shaped leaves are so coated with a fine wax film they appear blue. Fine heads of lilac-blue flowers on purplish stems in late summer. 30cm.

'Honeybells'. Good fresh green leaves and a fine show of fragrant lilac flowers in late summer. 90cm.

'Krossa Regal'. Another large, grey leafed hosta. Handsome glaucous leaves on tall stems are lightly corrugated with parallel veins. Because each tip is tilted upwards the wavy edges show a glimpse of pale grey-blue bloom on the underside. Spires of lilac flowers, mid to late summer. 1.2m.

lancifolia. Beautiful shining dark green leaves, narrow and pointed make attractive ground covering clumps. Tall slender stems, freely produced in late summer carry a long display of deep lilac flowers. 60cm.

'Louisa'. Forms attractive clumps of overlapping leaves, edged with white, complemented by spires of white flowers. Lovely for border edge. 45cm.

'Orange Marmalade'. Sport of the highly-rated *H.* 'Paul's Glory.' It is unique in that it is brightly variegated all season long. The leaf centre emerges a glowing yellow-gold, later turning a golden-orange. As summer approaches, the leaf centre turns yellow best kept out of direct bright sun to keep it more orange. Pale lavender flowers from mid-July into early August. 60cm.

'Patriot'. I was immediately taken with this hosta. Puckered grey-green leaves, boldly and brightly edged with creamy-white. Lavender blue flowers during summer. 60cm.

plantaginea var. japonica. This rare hosta provides the clearest fresh-green foliage in late summer and autumn, when many of the others are beginning to look tired. If planted in a sheltered position in rich soil, there is further delight in late autumn to find heads of long pure white trumpet-flowers, deliciously scented. 45cm.

'Praying Hands'. 2011 hosta of the year. Makes a tight clump of long stemmed, folded waxy leaves with a cream edge giving a very upright fluted appearance. 35cm.

'Royal Standard'. This lovely hosta has the good looks of one of its parents, *H. plantaginea*, but is more robust and flowers much more generously. The broad heart-shaped foliage is light green, above which stand tall strong stems of flowers which are a joy in late summer, being large, pure white and scented. 75cm.

sieboldiana. Another spectacular plant. Crisp, robust leaves, of a marvellous bluish-grey, each heavily wrinkled and veined, making a huge overlapping mound, impossible to pass by. The palest lilac flowers command admiration too, and finally the seed-pods, which, having burst and scattered their black seeds, split into tiny straw-coloured segments like starry flowers. 75cm.

sieboldiana var. elegans. Breathtaking when well established in deep rich soil in a cool situation. Superb large leaves are more deeply veined and quilted than *H. sieboldiana* so colour appears a deeper shade of blue-grey. 75cm.

The autumn colouring of all hostas is good but these two forms of *H. sieboldiana* are spectacular. Almost overnight blue-grey changes to glowing shades of honey and amber before the great piles of large leaves slowly disintegrate.

sieboldii. A charming small hosta. Narrow green leaves are boldly edged with white, overlapping to create small, eye-catching clumps. Above them stand slender stems of rich violet flowers in midsummer. 45cm.

'Snowden'. Another raised by Eric Smith makes an impressive mound of long, pointed, grey-green leaves. In late summer, ice-white flowers lift the scene. 1.2m.

'Spinners'. Makes large robust clumps of overlapping sage-green leaves boldly edged with cream. They remain fresh, creating a strong focal point all summer. 60cm.

'Tallboy'. Makes an impressive clump of rich green, heart-shaped, long pointed leaves. Large, rounded, violet-mauve flowers dangle from tall stems over a long period in midsummer. 1.2m.

'Thumb Nail'. Standing only 15-20cm tall, in full flower, this tiny hosta is well named, making dense clusters of pointed, oval leaves scarcely 5cm long, yet freely produces dainty spires of lilac flowers. Looks well on shady raised bed with dwarf ferns and mossy saxifrages.

undulata. Not such large and elegant leaves as *H.* 'Marginata Alba' but so easy and robust, it is perhaps the most effective of cream-edged hostas. It produces throughout the growing season, new fresh-green leaves with broad creamy margins. Because of their smooth upper surfaces these leaves are not disfigured by sediment from dripping trees. Tall stems of lilac trumpet-shaped flowers freely produced early-midsummer. 60cm.

undulata var. univittata. Medium sized, spirally twisted leaves of rich shining green are boldly striped with creamy-white, the central zone often totally white. Fresh leaves produced throughout summer. 45cm.

ventricosa 'Aureomarginata'. Retains fresh bright variegation until late autumn. Young leaves radiate light colour, with irregular borders of cream and primrose slashing into rich green centres. Deep violet flowers make a strong contrast in late summer. 75cm.

'Yellow Splash'. General effect of soft olive-green and cream, with glossy ribbed leaves well presented in overlapping layers. The irregular cream border fades to white, so the variegated effect is retained all summer. Length of leaf and stem up to 45cm, but overall height of laid back leaves is about 30cm.

HOUTTUYNIA cordata 'Chameleon'. Vivid as a Turkish carpet with low-growing, heart-shaped leaves brilliantly variegated in green, yellow, amber and red. It appears to flourish in most soils and situations except the very dry. Not evergreen. 25cm.

cordata 'Flore Pleno'. A distinctive plant for cool moist soil or pond-side. Elegant heart-shaped leaves shaded with purple are strongly scented of orange, while the pure white double flowers are borne in cone-like clusters. Midsummer. 40cm.

HUMULUS lupulus 'Aureus'. The most attractive yellow-leafed hop. It colours best in full sun on not too dry soil. Rapid cover for walls, fences, old stumps.

HYPERICUM androsaemum. Will grow in shade or sun. The fresh green leaves often have a reddish tinge, while the heads of fluffy yellow flowers sit in green collars, turning into bronze-red berries, which finally are black. All these colours and stages on one bush. Handsome all summer and autumn. About 60cm.
coris. Distinctive dwarf shrublet of wiry reddish stems clothed in tiny evergreen leaves smothered with golden flowers in midsummer followed by nut-brown seedheads. 15cm.
x hidcotense 'Hidcote'. A most beautiful semi-evergreen shrub with large saucer-shaped golden-yellow flowers, generously borne throughout summer and autumn. 1.2m.
x indorum 'Ysella'. I would not be without this shrubby St. Johns wort, even though it can be disfigured with rust by midsummer. Young foliage is a delight, lemony-green. Best if pruned to a framework in spring. Part shade, but not gloomy. 75cm.
olympicum. Erect stems covered with tiny leaves are showered with surprisingly large golden yellow flowers massed with stamens in midsummer. A very showy plant. 25cm.
olympicum f. uniflorum 'Citrinum'. The delightful lemon-yellow form, lovely with blue-green leaves. Midsummer. 25cm.
reptans. We have had this confirmed as the true form by Dr. Norman Robson of the Natural History Museum. Soft prostrate stems will hang like a curtain down a wall or rock face. Quite large rounded golden flowers are set off by buds and tiny leaves tinted bronze-red. Late summer. 2.5cm.

HYSSOPUS officinalis. Should be planted more often in sunny well-drained gardens as relief among silver-grey leaves. Forms small dense bushes covered with tiny dark green aromatic leaves, topped for ages in midsummer with spikes of deep violet-blue flowers. 45cm.
officinalis f. albus. Spikes of close-set white flowers. 45cm.
officinalis 'Roseus'. Has spikes of rose-pink flowers. 45cm.

 IBERIS sempervirens 'Weisser Zwerg'. Draws attention in spring when its prostrate dark green mats are smothered with chalk-white candytuft flowers. Lovely to spill over a low wall. 10cm.

INCARVILLEA delavayi. An exotic looking plant. From divided foliage come stout stems bearing great flaring trumpets of a rich rosy-pink. Needs a warm position in rich, well-drained soil. Early summer. 40cm.

INULA hookeri. Useful filler plant for good damp soil. Spreading clumps send up leafy stems topped with very attractive furry buds like little birds nests which open to yellow, fine-rayed daisies in late summer. Adored by butterflies. 75cm.
magnifica. Truly magnificent where there is room to show it off from top to bottom and where it will not be tattered by strong winds. Rough textured leaves, not unlike dock leaves but far larger, arching and wavy edged, make a handsome pile. They ascend stout stems in diminishing size to wide branching heads of flower, large, fine-rayed yellow daisies. Splendid in rough grass in retentive soil, or by the waterside. August-September. 2m.

IPHEION uniflorum. Upward-facing star-shaped flowers of palest blue held on bare stems 15cm appear over many weeks from early spring onwards above soft clumps of pale-green grassy leaves. Increases freely in well-drained soil. Leaves die down in summer.
uniflorum 'Album'. Lovely strong-growing white form. Silky white pointed petals have strong central veins picked out in dark brown, lightly shadowed green. 15cm.
uniflorum 'Charlotte Bishop'. An exciting new colour break, this pink-flowered form has a strong constitution and free-flowering habit. 15cm.
uniflorum 'Wisley Blue'. Has deep violet-blue flowers with dark central veins. 15cm.

IRIS – Bearded Iris. **HARMFUL IF EATEN**
We offer the following exceptional forms of well-known Bearded iris, for dry sunny positions.
'Benton Nigel'. A Cedric Morris iris. c.1956. Blue-purple bicolour with blue standards and the inky purple falls, paler towards the edge. Full sun and a well drained soil. 90cm.
'Benton Sheila'. Given to us by the late Sir Cedric Morris from his garden Benton End, in Suffolk. This is a pale version of *I.* 'Kent Pride'. 90cm
'Black Swan'. Upright silk-textured standards of translucent purple contrast with broad, black velvet falls. Sumptuous among grey and silver plants. 75cm.
'Blue Shimmer'. This free flowering, heavily scented iris has light, lavender-blue flowers with conspicuous white blotches on the falls, flowering in May-June. 75cm
'Florentina'. Held above handsome fans of broad grey-green leaves are palest grey-blue buds opening almost white flowers enhanced with faintly pencilled green veins and pale yellow 'beard'. In summer I put cut-up pieces of rhizome to dry in the airing cupboard. When crisp I pulverise them to use as a fixative in pot-pourri. 60cm.
'Green Spot'. A superb dwarf iris. Absolutely flat ivory falls, each marked with a green 'thumb-print'. May. 25cm.
'Jane Phillips'. Deservedly popular. This bearded iris has well-shaped standards, softly ruffled falls, in clear azure-blue with white beard. Lovely among cool greys. To 1m.
'Lemon Ice'. Creamy-yellow standards, falls same at edge, merging to a white center. Yellow beard. 60cm.
pallida 'Argentea-Variegata'. A good clump of this superbly variegated iris, the leaves boldy striped blue-green and white, is more eye-catching than most flowers. It highlights a well drained sunny border for six months, then dies down in winter. 45cm.
pallida subsp. pallida. Worth growing for its beautiful foliage alone. Fans of broad-bladed grey leaves make a good accent all summer and well into autumn. Scented flowers with silk-textured crinkly petals in pale lavender-blue are a bonus in early summer. 75cm.
pallida 'Variegata'. The richly golden variegated form, rarely offered. 45cm.
'Pearly Dawn'. Translucent chiffon-textured petals in palest creamy-pink tones, deepening towards centre. Free flowering. Enchanting. May-June. 75cm.

IRIS – Other Forms. **HARMFUL IF EATEN**
chrysographes 'Black Knight'. Remarkable for its velvety flowers of deepest indigo-blue, almost black. For a cool soil. 60cm.
ensata 'Alba'. A specially lovely pure white form of this Japanese iris. Flowers midsummer. 45cm.
ensata 'Moonlight Waves'. Large, flat-faced flowers, 14cm across, large smooth rounded petals, pure white, accented with green bee guides leading into the centre on 60cm stalks. Retentive soil. Midsummer.

ensata 'Rose Queen'. Is a hybrid with *I. laevigata* but needs a less soggy soil. Tall branching stems carry beautiful flowers with broad drooping falls in soft brownish-rose in midsummer. 75cm.

ensata 'Variegata'. The young, white-striped foliage in spring is very striking. Purple flowers in midsummer. Cool soil. 60cm.

foetidissima 'Citrina'. Strong shining clumps of rich evergreen leaves, which alone are invaluable as a garden feature or for decoration. The flowers, small for the size of the plant, are of soft ochre-yellow, delicately pencilled with brown. Followed in late autumn by great bursting seed pods, packed with vivid orange seeds. Does suffer from rust. Flowers June and July. 60cm.

foetidissima 'Variegata'. Lovely foliage, variegated all the year round in shade. 45cm.

graminea. A charming small iris, in rich shades of rosy-purple and violet mixed. But the scent! Shut your eyes and smell; it is exactly like a sun-ripened greengage. June. 40cm.

innominata hybrids. From large clumps of narrow, dark, evergreen leaves, the flowers, like delicate orchids on thin stems, come in all shades: white, yellow, mauve, violet, or all combined in May-June. Beautiful curving seed-pods. 30cm.

japonica 'Ledger's Variety'. Has creeping ground-level stems which send up short fans of shining green leaves. Above them thin branching stems carry orchid-like small flowers, white, flat and frilled, touched with blue and orange. Needs a warm, sunny site to flower well. Early summer. 45cm.

japonica 'Variegata'. Leaves boldly variegated with creamy-white, remaining a feature most winters. 30cm.

'Katherine Hodgkin'. A small bulbous iris with delicately patterned flowers of palest blue with yellow and blue marks on the falls from late winter to early spring. Unlike many of these bulbous iris this will reliably flower and increase each year. 15cm.

laevigata. Handsome by the waterside, not objecting to its feet in the water. Clumps of broad soft green leaves make a lovely setting for the lavender-blue flowers. June. 60cm.

laevigata 'Alba'. One of the loveliest of water-irises. Cool white flowers remarkable for their large, softly drooping falls. Perfect companion for the lavender-blue version, both thrive at water's edge. Up to 75cm.

laevigata 'Variegata'. The best of variegated plants for the waterside, or in a few inches of water. Leaves sharply striped in green and ivory-white, keep their bright colour throughout the growing season. Light blue flowers. 45cm.

ochroleuca × spuria hybrids. For heavy or damp soil.

'Ben Hasel'. Very clear yellow. Good impact. 1m.

'Marilyn Holloway'. Ruffled lilac standards, wide falls of greenish-lilac, bordered lilac ruffle. 1m.

'Sahara Sands'. Coppery brown buds open large warm-yellow flowers veined brown. A sensation. 1.2m.

pseudacorus var. bastardii. Is valued in early summer for its pale creamy-yellow flowers. Makes a bold clump of sword-like leaves, handsome in large damp gardens. 1.2m.

pseudacorus 'Variegata'. This is a handsome form of our native yellow Flag iris which grows in marshy ground or shallow water. It will also grow in rich, retentive soil. In early spring the newly emerging fans of leaves are pale butter-yellow. This remains for several weeks, deepening as the leaves mature, until by June they are green. Yellow flowers have distinct brown markings. 1m.

x **robusta 'Gerald Darby'.** Valued for the purple-stained base to leaves and purple flower stems which carry blue flowers in midsummer. Will grow in shallow water or heavy, retentive soil. 90cm.

'Sibirica Alba'. This graceful iris will thrive by the waterside or in ordinary good soil. Branching stems of pure white flowers, narrow foliage. June-July. 75cm.

sibirica Alan Rogers form. Tight cream buds open palest grey-blue translucent falls, faintly pencilled with blue, pure white standards. 75cm.

sibirica 'Blue Burgee'. Lovely to look down into dark blue, velvety depths on short stems. Early flowering. 60cm.

sibirica 'Butter and Sugar'. Small and appealing in colour and form. Butter-yellow falls contrast with translucent standards of palest cream. 60cm.

sibirica 'Dear Dianne'. Opens later. Its rich blue rounded falls have wavy edges rimmed faintly with white. Inner standards are waved and curled, attractive and unusual. 75cm.

sibirica 'Dreaming Yellow'. Eye-catching creamy-white petals lit with conspicuous olive-green bee guides. Midsummer. 75cm.

sibirica 'Ego'. Well-shaped flowers rich blue. 75cm.

sibirica 'Harpswell Happiness'. Tightly rolled primrose-yellow buds open broad cream falls faintly veined pale green, centred with frilly-edged standards, paler than *I.* 'Dreaming Yellow'. 75cm.

sibirica 'Harpswell Haze'. Delightful free flowering form of Siberian iris. Pleasing mid blue flowers on tall slender stems. A picture with lemon globe flowers (trollius) in a damp soil. 90cm.

sibirica 'Royal Blue'. One of our seedlings. Good form and rich colour. Royal blue falls with purple standards and central heart richly veined purple over green and yellow base. 90cm.

sibirica 'Savoir Faire'. Dark purplish-blue flowers which have the short central standards of *I. ensata.* 60cm.

sibirica 'Sky Wings'. Light blue flowers, yellow throat. 75cm.

sibirica 'Teal Velvet'. Presents well its broad, purple-blue falls, showing white/purple veined bee guides beneath light-purple standards. 75cm.

sibirica 'Vi Luihn'. Wide-opening falls and standards present heart-stopping shades of dark blue faintly marked with pale netted bee guides. 75cm.

sibirica 'White Swirl'. Ivory-white falls lead into a yellow and green veined heart, partially obscured with transparent standards. The flowers combine size, substance and elegance. 90cm.

tuberosus. The Widow iris. Slowly creeping clumps of long, thin four-angled leaves among which show the extraordinary flowers of glass-like green with black velvet falls, sweetly scented. March-April. 30cm.

unguicularis 'Alba'. White pointed 'petals', narrower than the blue forms, have vivid yellow bee guides sliding into a green throat. All these Algerian iris require a warm spot at the foot of a wall or fence. 25cm.

unguicularis 'Mary Barnard'. Large soft flowers of rich purple, lovely companion for the following form. 30cm.

unguicularis 'Walter Butt'. Plant this lovely version of the Algerian iris against a warm wall and you will be enchanted with large flowers of palest icy-blue in early spring, primrose scented. Very free flowering. 30cm.

versicolor 'Kermesina'. Handsome and easy in damp soil or shallow water. Grey-green foliage sets off rich claret-purple flowers highlighted with white veining. July. 75cm.

JASIONE laevis 'Blaulicht'. A pretty edging or rock garden plant. Narrow-leafed rosettes make low cushions crowded with thin stalks holding bobbly heads of dark blue, ribbon-petalled flowers. Midsummer-autumn. 30cm.

JASMINUM officinale 'Argenteovariegatum'. This elegant climber produces long, twining stems of finely cut leaves beautifully variegated in green, pink and cream. Try it on a wrought-iron garden staircase or cover a west wall. Will reach in full sun. 5m.

KALIMERIS incisa 'Blue Star'. This deserves to be better known, being very easy and adaptable plant. Single, 2.5cm soft blue daisy-like flowers over a compact mound of green are a delight from mid to late summer, longer if dead-headed. 40cm.

integrifolia. Forms a self-supporting mass of branching stems smothered with white Michaelmas daisy-like flowers, fading to lilac. Starting in May it lasts for weeks and well deserves its place in a sunny border but not too dry. 75cm.

mongolica. Tall graceful stems carry wide branching heads of lilac-blue daisy flowers, a most attractive introduction for late summer. Lasts well when picked. 1m.

yomena 'Shogun'. Compact bushy plants make a feature covered with fresh-looking variegated leaves. Crowds of small, pale lilac daisy-flowers throughout autumn. Needs fertile soil and sun. 50cm.

KIRENGESHOMA palmata. Needs humus-fed, lime-free soil in semi-shade among ferns and hostas. From late summer to autumn, heavy clusters of fat swelling buds open shuttlecock-shaped flowers about 5cm long, pale butter-yellow, of thick waxen texture. Irregularly cut maple-like leaves clothe dark purple stems which bow under the weight of flowers. Needs shelter from wind. 90cm.

palmata Koreana Group. Some gardeners may find this slightly shorter, more upright plant more convenient than *K. palmata*. It has the same drooping clusters of pale butter-yellow, shuttlecock-shaped flowers in autumn. 75cm.

KNAUTIA macedonica. Pity it cannot remain a scabious (was *Scabiosa rumelica*) because you would recognise it on sight. Very free flowering over a long period, dainty curving stems and branches full of crimson pin-cushions. Late summer to autumn. 60cm.

KNIPHOFIA. Kniphofias make valuable vertical accents in the garden whether among shrubs, herbaceous plants or grasses. They vary in colour from cream through many shades of orange, salmon and red. They can also be found in tempting shades of green, we offer *K.* 'Green Jade'.

Some kniphofia are spectacular and made for large settings, but we tend to select seedlings with well-shaped slender flower heads, and with less rushy foliage to flop about on other plants. You do need to make some allowance, particularly with the larger forms, for their tumbled sheaves, but when well placed no other plant can create the same dramatic effect from midsummer onwards.

Kniphofias grow wild on the edge of river banks which dry up during the very hot season in South Africa, so they need some care in cultivation. Well-drained soil enriched with compost suits them best, but almost any soil excepting water-logged will do. In very cold areas some protection of the crowns is advisable using the cut-down remains of the plants as a mulch. Some people advise tying the foliage up like a wigwam. This keeps moisture away from the crowns.

KNIPHOFIA – Species
caulescens. Short herbaceous form. Makes good feature plant in poor, well-drained soil. From woody underground stocks arise several clusters of grey, almost yucca-like leaves. Flowers in midsummer, orange-red buds opening silvery yellow. Foliage affected by severe cold but plants have survived here many years. Collected in South Africa by Brian Halliwell, Kew Gardens. 45cm.
caulescens B.H. 5020. Collected in the wild by Brian Halliwell. From a woody base spring several crowns, or clusters of long arching blue grey strap shaped leaves, making a remarkable feature by themselves. Above them, in September-October rise stout stems carrying densely packed heads of tubular flowers. Opening from the bottom upwards, they are pale luminous yellow packed with protruding stamens loaded with pollen, a feast for foraging bees. Unopened buds, topping the flower spikes are a warm rusty orange. 1m.
rooperi. An impressive landscape plant. Strong stems carry large, chunky-heads, opening brilliant orange and lemon flowers above broad arching foliage. From late summer into autumn. 1.2m.
thompsonii var. thompsonii. A slightly tender red-hot poker from Uganda, needs well drained soil, probably best in southern counties. Slender stems carry elegant and unusual looking heads of widely spaced, curving flowers in shades of coral, from dark to light. August-November. 90cm.

KNIPHOFIA – Hybrids
'Apricot Sensation'. Beth Chatto seedling. Outstanding in colour, form and wealth of flowers produced. Long tapering spikes densely set with coral buds shading to salmon and finally cream give a two tone effect. Produces flowers over long period. Looks well with *Crocosmia* 'Severn Sunrise' planted nearby. 1m.
'Bees' Lemon'. Large well-shaped heads, opening lemon-yellow from acid-green buds on 1.5m stems. August.
'Bees' Sunset'. syn. *K.* 'Shining Sceptre'. Fine introduction from Blooms, of medium size, with well-shaped flower heads in lovely shades of amber and cream. 1m.
'Brimstone'. A small scaled plant with narrow grassy leaves, and slender heads of soft yellow flowers. July-August. 75cm.
'Bressingham Comet'. Has small neat heads opening pale yellow flowers from orange buds. Late summer-autumn. 45cm.
'Burnt Orange'. Beth Chatto seedling. Useful hybrid, sending up elegant slender pokers shaded brown in bud, opening to warm orange. 75cm.
'Drummore Apricot'. For large borders or landscape. Well shaped, large heads of apricot buds maturing to yellow, from late summer to autumn. 1m.
'Flaming Torch'. Beth Chatto seedling. Of medium stature, makes good impact in landscape, opening pale yellow from flame buds, free-flowering. August-Sept. 1.2m.
'Green Jade'. Beth Chatto seedling. Forms a medium sized plant with flowers of delicate jade-green. Late summer into autumn. 1.2m.
'Green Sherbet'. Impressive, later than *K.* 'Bees Sunset'. Well-shaped densely set heads open pale-green from acid-green buds. August-September. Medium to large. 1.2m.
'Ice Queen'. One of the palest hybrids, green tipped buds opening palest creamy-yellow. There will probably never be a pure white poker but this is probably the closest so far. 80cm.
'Light of the World'. A small poker with long, neat heads of translucent orange flowers above grassy leaves. Late summer-autumn. 60cm.

'**Little Maid**'. Beth Chatto seedling. Originally listed as 'Small Maid'. Has neat narrow foliage topped by slender stems closely set with narrow tubular flowers extending more than halfway down the stem. Green in bud, the flowers open ivory- white. New flowers produced for weeks in autumn. 60cm.

'**Limeade**'. Early June-July. Smaller than *K.* 'Green Jade'. 1m.

'**Lord Roberts**'. An old variety, but still one of the best. Tawny-brown slender buds, slightly out curved, form a long tapered head of warm red flowers. Lovely, well into late autumn. 1.2m.

'**Nancy's Red**'. Dense, slender heads of brick-red buds open sealing-wax red, superb, above its clump of grassy foliage. 75cm.

'**Nobilis**'. Closely allied to the well-known Red hot poker. Despite its height seldom needs staking. Flower heads are fiery red, large, long and imposing. Magnificent as a feature plant. Late summer-early autumn. 2m.

'**Orange Sorbet**'. Beth Chatto seedling. Similar in form to *K.* 'Nancy's Red', but brighter orange. August 1.2m

'**Peaches and Cream**'. Beth Chatto seedling. Well-shaped, narrow cylindrical heads open cream flowers from peach buds. Midsummer, second crop in early autumn. 1m.

'**Percy's Pride**'. Stout stems carry large heads of cream flowers opening from pale green buds, cool and beautiful, in colour and form. July-August. 1.2m.

'**Strawberries and Cream**'. Beth Chatto seedling. Another small, slender-headed poker. Unopened buds at top of spike are flushed red, below them flowers open cream. This poker originated here as a selected seedling. Early autumn. 75cm.

'**Sunningdale Yellow**'. A small early poker, well-formed slender flower heads of warm yellow. 90cm.

'**Tawny King**'. Burnt-orange buds open creamy-yellow flowers to form bold, well-shaped heads on dark olive stems. Good impact, single or grouped. Mid-late summer. 1.2m.

'**Toasted Corn**'. Another of our seedlings. Long narrow heads of closely-set, brownish-red buds, open maize-yellow, retaining a red tip to each flower. Long season, standing out like slender torches among ballotas, santolinas and flowering grasses. 1m.

'**Yellow Hammer**'. From acid-green buds open clear yellow flowers in large well-formed heads. Fine large feature plant over several weeks, late summer-autumn. 1.2m.

 LAMIUM galeobdolon subsp. montanum 'Florentinum'. Ideal for smothering untidy hedge bottoms or as ground-cover in shady places. Long trailing stems are clothed in dark nettle-like leaves, brilliantly frosted with white. Yellow flowers. 30cm.

galeobdolon 'Silberteppich'. Not invasive, very attractive, forming clusters of silver leaves netted with green veins. Pretty sprays of yellow nettle flowers in spring. 25cm.

maculatum 'Album'. Less rampant, green leaves with a central silvering. Pure white flowers. 20cm.

maculatum 'Aureum'. Has smaller leaves than *L. maculatum* 'Cannon's Gold' which become a strong yellow-ochre as they mature, marked with a narrow white zone down the centre of each leaf. 15cm.

maculatum 'Beacon Silver'. Originated in a customer's garden and given to me to introduce in 1976. Makes very good cover in cool soil, part shade, leaves totally silvered apart from narrow green edging. 10cm.

maculatum 'Cannon's Gold'. Has larger bolder leaves than *L. maculatum.* 'Aureum' of a uniform yellowish-green tone, with lilac-pink lipped flowers tucked between the leaves. 20cm.

maculatum 'Golden Anniversary'. Loose rosettes of small green-centred leaves with wide yellow margins creating light effect overall. 18cm.

maculatum 'Pink Pewter'. Totally silvered leaves with crinkly green margins, make a setting for pale-pink flowers. 20cm.

maculatum 'White Nancy'. Another silver-leafed form which occurred in the garden of Mr. Phillip S. Levesley, and was kindly sent to me to introduce. Has ivory-white flowers in early summer. 20cm.

orvala. A handsome Dead nettle. Thick stems carry pairs of dark, pointed, strongly-veined leaves. Beneath each pair is a whorl of rich strawberry-pink lipped flowers.

orvala 'Alba'. As above, but with white flowers slightly tinted pink. 60cm.

Lamprocapnos spectabilis. Syn. *Dicentra spectabilis.* Bleeding heart, or Ladies' locket. Needs rich, deep soil to produce tall stems drooping with the delicate rose and white lockets. A most elegant plant. Flowers early summer. 60cm.

spectabilis 'Alba'. In my garden this grows stronger than *L. spectabilis.* Above delicately cut green leaves arch green stems bowed with beautiful ivory-white, heart-shaped lockets. A most lovely plant which flowers for weeks in late spring, early summer. 75cm.

LATHYRUS grandiflorus. A handsome perennial pea for scrambling into neighbouring shrubs. Large two-toned flowers, pink and maroon red make a display for weeks in midsummer. Unscented. Has spreading roots, do not plant among small treasures. Scrambling to 2m.

latifolius 'Rosa Perle'. Everlasting Pea. A climbing perennial with winged stems and blue-green leaves and rose-pink flowers from summer to early autumn. Alas no scent. 2m.

latifolius 'White Pearl'. A perennial pea producing sprays of pure white scentless but beautifully formed flowers. I let it scramble through old-fashioned roses and pick it for weeks in midsummer to put in little mixed bowls. Up to 1.2m.

vernus f. roseus. Forms a bushy little plant with many stems bearing neat divided leaves. In April it is covered with tiny rose-pink pea-flowers. For sun, or semi-shade, not too dry soil. 30cm.

LAVANDULA angustifolia 'Hidcote'. A neat compact lavender with the deepest violet-blue flowers. The best for a low edge. 45cm.

angustifolia 'Nana Alba'. Dwarf compact bushes with comparatively broad grey-green leaves, carry heads of white flowers in July. 30cm.

angustifolia 'Rosea'. Spikes of dusty-pink flowers in June-July, over compact bushes of narrow, grey-green leaves. 60cm.

lanata. Perhaps the loveliest of lavenders but it must have a warm well-drained site in full sun. The slightly broader than usual leaves are so felted they appear almost white, perfect to set off very dark purplish-blue flower spikes. Mid-late summer. A well rounded bush under a warm wall is a sight to treasure. 60cm.

pedunculata subsp. pedunculata. Is distinguished by much longer 'flags' or 'ears' of rose-pink. Has survived here severe winters in well-drained soil. 75cm.

pedunculata subsp. pedunculata 'James Compton'. Differs with much darker as well as longer 'flags' or 'ears' of a rich clover-pink. Has survived cold winters here in well-drained soil and full sun. 60cm.

stoechas. Is a compact little bush covered in late summer with curious knobbly flower heads which carry two kinds of flower. The fertile flowers arranged in vertical rows, are small, and very dark purple-blue. Above them, to entice pollinating insects, is a 'flag' of large wavy petals, of a lighter shade of purple. Mid-late summer. This plant needs very well-drained soil. 40cm.
stoechas f. leucantha. The attractive white-flowered form. 40cm.

LAVATERA × clementii 'Barnsley'. A spectacular shrubby mallow, which quickly makes a large, loosely-branched shrub clothed in soft, felted green leaves spangled throughout summer and autumn with large white flowers which fade to shell-pink, accented with red eyes. For a sunny well-drained site. 1.5m.
x clementii 'Bredon Springs'. Seems to be an extra good form of the popular shrubby mallow. Its strong branching stems are crowded with deep rose pink flowers. 1.5m.
olbia 'Lilac Lady'. A less coarse grower than *L. 'Rosea'*. Has more upright growth, clothed in grey-green maple-shaped leaves, with smaller flat-faced flowers, about
5cm across, held in spires. They are translucent, silk-textured pale lilac-blue, mid-late summer. 1.2m.
olbia 'Rosea'. Equally vigorous and free-flowering, forming a remarkable feature in its first year. This form opens large rose-pink flowers. 1.5m.
thuringiaca 'Ice Cool'. White flowered form of shrubby mallow. 1.2m.

LEPTINELLA potentillina. Similar to L. squalida, leaves slightly tinted pewter. These plants have been a blessing as ground-cover where little else was suitable, i.e. on root-starved soil under an acer, and hiding concrete edges round a small pool. 2.5cm.
squalida. Useful small carpeter or paving-crevice plant. Masses of tiny fern-like leaves press themselves into tight masses of green and bronze. 2.5cm.
squalida 'Platt's Black'. Chocolate brown really, anyway creates a pleasing gound hugging carpet in most soils given a sunny situation. 5cm.

LEUCANTHEMELLA serotina. A beautiful fresh feature for the end of the season, either in grass, among shrubs, or in a big border. Strong clumps of stiff leafy stems carry sprays of green-eyed, chalk-white daisies. They turn to face the sun, throughout October. Good to pick. 2m.

LEUCANTHEMUM × superbum. The Shasta daisy. Many forms have been introduced. Names have become confused. After advice from higher authority I now grow the following named varieties.
'Aglaia'. Outstanding among the Shasta daisies; flowering July-August, when most others are over. Produces quantities of upstanding stems holding flowers which appear fully double at first, slowly unfolding finely shredded petals to show a good yellow eye. Long season in garden. Lasts well in water. Very attractive. 1m.
'Beauté Nivelloise'. Large single uncomplicated white flowers with wide petals on good strong stems which do not need support. Very fine in the garden or picked. 90cm.
'Becky'. Yet another form of Shasta daisy but one I heartily recommend for its sturdy upright habit and abundance of flower, each consisting of a double row of flat chalk-white petals surrounding the large central yellow disc. Flowers later than most. 1.2m.
'Cobham Gold'. Has creamy-yellow double flowers on shorter stems. 60cm.
'Phyllis Smith'. Finely cut rayed petals, can be used effectively to lighten a summer arrangement. 75cm.

'**Snowcap**'. Irresistible, a dwarf Shasta daisy, very free flowering, no faults. 45cm.

'**Sonnenschein**'. Pale lemon-yellow form of Shasta daisy, very attractive. 75cm.

'**T. E. Killin**'. The slightly raised greenish-yellow centre is surrounded by a double layer of petals, perhaps the best for flower arranging. 75cm.

LEUCOJUM aestivum 'Gravetye Giant'. Above bold clumps of narrow strap-shaped leaves stand stout, upright stems carrying graceful heads of white, bell-shaped flowers. Although called Summer snowflake they flower with the late daffodils during April, in stiff, heavy soil often by the water's edge. 60cm.

vernum var. carpathicum. Each pointed petal has rich yellow tips. 20cm.

vernum var. vagneri. Spring snowflake. Makes strong clumps of daffodil-like bulbs, often mistaken for a snowdrop, since it flowers at much the same time, but it has lampshade-like bells, made up of six pointed petals held open wide, showing green tips. It carries two flowers per stem, above lush, strap-shaped leaves. 30cm.

LIATRIS spicata. Sturdily upright stems, clothed in whorls of fresh green narrow leaves carry flower buds in the top two thirds, opening from the top downwards bright mauve fluffy tassels. Midsummer. 75cm.

spicata 'Alba'. Does the same in white. Both succeed best in full sun. 75cm.

LIBERTIA grandiflora. Above strong clumps of narrow dark green grassy leaves stand many stiff stems carrying sprays of white saucer-shaped flowers in midsummer. Needs good drainage and sunny situation. 90cm.

ixioides. Forms arching clumps of rush-like leaves supporting airy bouquets of small, white 3-petalled flowers held in clusters on dark-stained slender stems. Needs well-drained and sunny situation. 75cm.

peregrinans. Individual fans form clumps of very narrow, stiff leaves with such wide central veins stained orange, the entire plant gives off an orange flow, especially in winter. Increases by running stolons, so babies may appear some way off. I enjoy mine coming through carpets of *Thymus pulegioides* 'Bertram Anderson'. 45cm.

LIGULARIA dentata 'Desdemona'. For moist soil, having large heart-shaped leaves, bronze-purple above with bright magenta backs, and with big branching heads of orange-rayed flowers in late summer. 1.2m.

dentata 'Sommergold'. Erect purple stems carry bunched heads of yellow, strap-petalled daisy flowers. July. 1.2m.

fischeri. A good vertical accent. Above mounds of large kidney-shaped leaves rise stiff spires of small orange-yellow daisy flowers. June. 1.6m.

'Gregynog Gold'. Most noble feature plant for damp soil or waterside. Forms mounds of large heart-shaped leaves above which tower great clustered spikes of rich yellow daisy-flowers. Mid to late summer. 2m.

japonica. Dramatic feature plant. Beautiful deeply-cut foliage. Sturdy stems support large branched heads of light orange daisy flowers. July. 1.6m.

'The Rocket'. Forms a fine mound of large round leaves with serrated edges. Tall, almost black stems standing well above the leaves carry long cylindrical spires of small, bright yellow flowers, making a distinguished vertical feature in damp soil, in late summer. 1.5m.

LILIUM candidum. The Madonna lily. Needs planting in good soil containing chalk or lime and then to be left undisturbed. 1m.

hansonii. A summer flowering bulb with stem roots. Long leaves in whorls are lance shaped. Stems hold 3-12 scented turk's cap flowers, orange-yellow in colour with dark purple-brown spots towards the base. 80cm.

martagon. The Turk's cap lily of the Swiss Alps. Forms tall slender stems carrying several pink or purplish flowers in June-July. Does best in light soil with added compost. 1m.

martagon var. album. This white-flowered form is especially lovely in semi-shade, its position marked out and protected by carpets of *Tellima grandiflora* or any of the tiarellas, but it does well in sun. 90cm.

regale. This white, heavily scented, trumpet shaped lily with golden throat and cinnamon stained back, needs full sun, good drainage and good feeding, plenty of compost. Susceptible to spring frosts, grow in pots till the frosts are passed to avoid this. Up to 1.2m.

speciosum var. rubrum. In this form the wavy-edged recurved petals are almost totally stained raspberry-red with pale rims. Stout stems carry numerous nodding flowers, a spectacular sight growing through forms of *Persicaria amplexicaulis,* both late season plants. August-September. 1.4m.

LIMONIUM bellidifolium. A neat little sea lavender for the rock garden. Beautifully formed evergreen rosettes of leaves carry branching sprays of mauve flowers, late summer. 15cm.

platyphyllum 'Violetta'. Both the wavy dark-green leaves and rich purple flowers, which dry well, make this sea lavender a useful cutting plant, late summer. 30cm.

LINARIA anticaria 'Antique Silver'. Very welcome in late summer, early autumn. Makes frothy trails of greyish-blue tiny snapdragon flowers where its wandering stems covered in narrow grey-green leaves push through stony soil, in full sun. 15cm.

dalmatica. Cool lemon-yellow snapdragon flowers on branching spires make attractive vertical accents above low-growing plants in poor gravelly soil in full sun. Has a wandering rootstock, but not troublesome. 90cm.

purpurea 'Canon Went'. A tall delicate toadflax, carrying spires of tiny, pale pink flowers throughout summer. 75cm.

purpurea 'Springside White'. Exactly like *L. purpurea* 'Canon Went' but with spires of tiny white snapdragons. 75cm.

triornithophora. This means 'bearing three birds'. Flowering all summer until the frosts, this enchanting plant has buds which look exactly like tiny budgerigars. The flowers are purple, sometimes pink. 90cm.

LINUM narbonense. Much admired in our dry garden. Reliably more perennial than *L. perenne.* In flower for weeks with vivid blue flowers. Sets little seed and not easy from cuttings, we never have enough. 60cm.

perenne. Blue flax. Many slender wands carry cascades of silken pale blue flowers. Midsummer. 45cm.

perenne 'Album'. A beautiful sight in midsummer when arching sprays are smothered with glistening white flowers. Flax do best in well-drained chalky or neutral soils in full sun. 45cm.

LIRIOPE muscari. A feature all the year are clumps of narrow, dark evergreen leaves. In late autumn curious spikes of violet-blue flowers appear which never really open, looking rather like grape-hyacinths. 40cm.

muscari 'Monroe White'. Has shorter spikes of white flowers opening from greenish-cream buds. 40cm.

muscari **'Samantha'.** Has spikes of lilac-pink flowers. 40cm.
In my experience all forms of Liriope muscari produce better flower spikes in shade or part shade and look healthier.

LITHODORA diffusa 'Heavenly Blue'. Trailing stems clothed in small bristly leaves are transformed by the long display of gentian blue flowers in mid-late summer, in lime-free soil, associating well with heather. 15cm.

LOBELIA – HARMFUL IF EATEN/SKIN & EYE IRRITANT.
cardinalis 'Queen Victoria'. A startling plant for damp soil. Beetroot-red leaves combine with brilliantly vivid scarlet flowers. 75cm.
x gerardii 'Vedrariensis'. Lovely plant for damp soil. Spikes of bright purple flowers in late summer on 75cm stems.
tupa. Long tapering spires of curious brownish-red tubular flowers carried on tall dark stems, contrast with light green tobacco-like leaves. A magnificent feature plant for sheltered gardens in full sun, and deep moist soil. 1m.

LONICERA nitida 'Baggescen's Gold'. This bright golden form of the usual hedging plant should be allowed to grow as a specimen shrub, when it makes a delicate filigree accent among darker green bushes. 1m.

LOTUS hirsutus. A delightful small shrub. Arched branches are covered with soft grey divided leaves, carrying clusters of small pink-white pea flowers in June, which develop into stars of chocolate-brown seed pods. 60cm.

LUNARIA biennis 'Variegata'. The variegated biennial honesty has very handsome green and white foliage. The seed-cases are variegated too. Comes true from seed. Vivid purple flowers in the spring. 45cm.
rediviva. This is a perennial honesty, deserving to be better known. In early spring, I value its heads of pale lilac-white sweetly scented flowers. The white paper seed-cases which follow in autumn are elliptical, not round as has the biennial honesty. 75cm.

LYCHNIS × arkwrightii. This hybrid campion is a dazzling combination of brownish-purple leaves topped with orange-scarlet flowers in mid to late summer. For well-drained soil, in sun. 40cm.
chalcedonica. Called Maltese cross, or Jerusalem cross, with cross-shaped flowers known since the Crusades. Small, brilliantly scarlet flowers arranged in dense flat heads on tall stiff stems, make sharp accent in midsummer. Needs full sun in retentive soil. 90cm.
chalcedonica var. albiflora. The less commonly seen dusky-white form. 90cm.
chalcedonica 'Flore Pleno'. Although I tend to prefer single flowers, I am impressed by the strong effect of this double form of Maltese cross. It is very handsome. Flowers again if cut down as soon as faded. 75cm.
coronaria. Handsome clumps of downy grey leaves send up wide branching stems bearing deep burgundy-velvet campion flowers. Midsummer. 75cm.
coronaria 'Alba'. The same, with pure white flowers. Both forms will self sow. 75cm.
flos-jovis. Above tight tufts of mouse-eared leaves stand heads of shocking pink campion flowers. Lovely next to *Aster tongolensis* 'Napsbury'. Early summer. 20cm.
viscaria. The Sticky catchfly. Has sticky patches on its stems, which carry bunched heads of bright pink flowers. Good to pick. Early summer. 30cm.

viscaria 'Alba'. Over narrow-leafed clumps of green leaves stand spikes of white flowers, subtly shaded with cool green. Lovely to pick. 30cm.

viscaria 'Splendens Plena'. Outstandingly good, flowers fewer and larger on taller stems, doubled and frilly of almost luminous magenta-pink. Early to midsummer. 40cm.

LYSICHITON americanus. This bog arum must have deep rich mud. Then in spring it delights with its thick yellow spathes unfolding first, followed by magnificent huge leaves, making an architectural feature throughout the summer. 1.2m.

camtschatcensis. From Siberia and Japan comes the pure white species of these two superb bog-garden plants. Foliage 90cm.

x hortensis. A cross between *L. americanus* and *L. camtschatcensis*, showing hybrid vigour, the flower spathes and foliage are much larger than in either parent. The creamy-white spathe can stand 60cm tall, up to 30cm across at its widest point. Inside the spathe is dimpled and making wondrous curves to support the emerging spadix. Vast clusters of paddle-shaped leaves, up to 1.5m tall, push up fast to finally make a grand architectural statement by the water's edge throughout the summer months.

LYSIMACHIA ciliata. Emerges through the soil in spring with clusters of soft milk-chocolate brown leaves whose colour is only slightly diluted green as the stems elongate to carry a spire of delicately hung yellow flowers which last for weeks in mid to late summer. Creeping root stock in rich damp soil. 75cm.

ciliata 'Firecracker'. Tall leafy stems clothed from top to toe with handsome pointed leaves, richly tinted dark coppery-brown, provide good contrast for heads of pale lemon flowers. Late summer. 1m.

clethroides. In rich soil this loosestrife forms running clumps of tall stems clothed with narrow green foliage and topped in late summer with shepherd-crook spikes of tiny white flowers. 90cm.

ephemerum. Plant of quiet dignity. Curiously grey narrow leaves ascend erect slender stems, topped with spires of close-set small white flowers, long lasting. Finally makes good seedhead of round brown capsules. July-September. 90cm.

nummularia 'Aurea'. Delightful ground-cover in cool soil, this form of Creeping Jenny has bright golden foliage. 5cm.

punctata. Can be seen anywhere, from ditch side to seemingly dry front gardens. Ideal for semi-wild planting in damp soil, where its spires of bright yellow can be most enjoyable and where its invasiveness would be welcome. Mid to late summer. 90cm.

punctata 'Alexander'. This variegated form brings a touch of glamour to a plant often unfairly dismissed, when seen in rubbishy situations where it thrives. New leaves have broad cream margins, suffused with pink, retaining cream and green in mature leaves. Has spires of yellow flowers in leaf axils in mid to late summer. If kept pruned retains fresh variegated effect. 75cm.

LYTHRUM salicaria 'Blush'. This most attractive form has slender spires of pale rose-pink flowers from summer to early autumn. For retentive soil and sun. 1.2m.

salicaria 'Robert'. Makes a fine feature plant, with branching spikes of small rose flowers. Will grow in any good soil, including the bog-garden. Late summer to autumn. 90cm.

virgatum 'Rose Queen'. Makes a smaller tapering, branched plant, ablaze in late summer with rosy-pink flowers which practically hide the small narrow leaves. Needs soil that does not dry out. 60cm.

MACLEAYA × kewensis 'Flamingo'. Plume poppy. A fine introduction. Strong stems carry large plumes of small cream and apricot pink flowers. Attractive grey-green lobed leaves. 1.8m.

microcarpa 'Kelway's Coral Plume'. A statuesque plant, either in isolation or in a bay among shrubs. A running rootstock throws up many tall strong stems which need no staking. Large, rounded, deeply indented leaves are grey-green above, grey-white beneath. Long branching plumes of small, pale apricot buds, open to rich-cream, fluffy flowers. Late summer-autumn. 2m.

MAINTHEMUM bifolium subsp. kamstschaticum. An attractive ground cover for cool shade. It spreads carpets of glossy heart-shaped leaves, above which stand thin spires of little white flowers in spring, followed by crimson, translucent berries if your soil remains moist. 40cm.

racemosum. Related to Solomon's seal, and very like it in its beautiful arching foliage, but instead of bells it has a tapering head of massed fluffy, creamy-white flowers sweetly scented. Late spring. Likes cool soil. 75cm.

stellata. Invasive but good in large shady areas with wild garlic, *Allium ursinum,* Lily of the Valley, where its colonies of short, leafy stems topped in spring with spires of starry white flowers make it effective ground cover. 40cm.

MALVA moschata. The Musk mallow is one of our most beautiful natives. In midsummer saucer-shaped rose-pink flowers crowd the branching stems which are lightly clothed in finely-cut leaves. Up to 60cm.

moschata f. alba. Covered in silky-white saucer-shaped flowers, this pretty mallow causes comment for weeks in summer. Seeds itself usefully. Up to 60cm.

sylvestris 'Primley Blue'. A well selected form of our roadside mallow with stiff, ground-hugging branches studded with wide-open flowers in soft grey-blue, lovely with blue-grey grasses and *Melianthus major.* 20cm x 1m across.

MARRUBIUM catariifolium. Makes a very effective foliage plant. Many thin, much branched, whitened stems form a cage-like structure covered in tiny pointed greyish-white leaves, with insignificant clusters of tiny white flowers in September. Good in poor, well drained soil and drought conditions. 75cm.

bourgaei var. bourgaei 'All Hallows Green'. We used to call this *Ballotta* 'Gold Leaf'. Makes a small neat foliage plant, attractive grouped on the edge of a sunny border, or isolated among alpines. Young summer foliage and stems are olive-green with a patina of gold. 30cm.

cylleneum. Sometimes confused with *Ballota.* Has similar growth habit, but its colour and texture are unique. It appears to have been cut from old Victorian velvet, and of the softest sage-green. 40cm.

libanoticum. Makes a low cushion plant composed of many branching upright stems crowded with rosettes of greenish-grey leaves. The leaves have heavily ridged surfaces densely covered with fine silky hairs, giving a velvety appearance. Inconspicuous flowers followed by attractive whorls of seedheads. 40cm.

MATTHIOLA incana alba. A perennial stock that has thrived in our hot dry gravel for several years. Originally given to us as seed from Great Dixter. Felty-grey foliage and pure white scented flowers. 50cm.

MELIANTHUS major. The most sumptuous foliage plant for the hot, dry garden. Comes from South Africa, so not reliably hardy in coldest counties. Has survived many years in my East Anglian garden, in well-drained soil, sprouting from its woody base after severe winters. A mulch of light material protects the underground shoots. Large grey-green leaves, deeply cut and tooth-edged are proudly presented on thick branching stems. If over-wintered a deep maroon flower spike may appear but adds little to the effect. Foliage usually about 1.2m by the end of the summer but can be much taller.

MELISSA officinalis 'All Gold'. Golden lemon balm. Has matt, rich yellow leaves from beginning of season to the very end. Partial shade prevents leaf scorch on this delicately lovely foliage plant. 45cm.
officinalis 'Variegata'. Gold and green variegated form of Lemon balm. Ideal for foliage arrangements. 60cm.

MENTHA × gracilis 'Variegata'. A vividly variegated mint, bright yellow and green. Beautiful ground-cover in cool places, charming to pick. 45cm.
x piperita. Peppermint. Dried for winter use it makes a comforting drink with honey in hot water. 45cm.
x piperita f. citrata. Eau de Cologne-scented mint. Ideal to fill a dark corner with this fragrant perfume. 45cm.
spicata var. crispa. Pairs of leaves set alternately up the stems have toothed edges and are crisply curled, an attractive foliage effect, plus an appetising flavour for mint sauce, drinks, etc. 40cm.
suaveolens 'Variegata'. Strongly scented, brilliantly variegated, in ivory-white and green, a lovely foliage plant to find in a damp dark corner but will also grow in sun in good soil. 25cm.

MENYANTHES trifoliata. Bog bean. Water-edge softening, horizontal stems of smooth grey-green leaves, not unlike a Broad Bean. Short stems of delicate white flowers, heavily fringed, in May. 45cm.

MIMULUS luteus. Monkey flower. From Chile. Soon forms dense patches in damp soil or shallow water. Yellow, sometimes spotted flowers during early summer. 30cm.
'Wisley Red'. A splendid introduction. Not scarlet but a rich, velvety blood-red, vigorous, but not overbearing in damp soil. 15cm.

MITELLA breweri. Rounded, scallop-edged dark green leaves, arranged in neat clumps. In spring, tiny forests of pale, leafless stems carry wands of minute green flowers with fringed edges. Charming on the edge of a shady path. 15cm.
caulescens. A delight in awkward shade. Thread-like stems run over the soil, forming carpets or edgings of pea-green heart-shaped leaves, with tiny, palest-green, frilly flowers in spring. 8cm.

MONARDA. Bergamot or Bee balm. Sun-loving plants with self-supporting square stems bearing aromatic pointed leaves. The upper half of the stems carry spaced clusters of hooded, tubular flowers surrounded by pointed bracts which often add to the colour scheme. The flower heads picked at their best and dried, add both scent and colour to pot-pourri. The following cultivars have occurred from two species, *M. fistulosa* which stands drier soil and *M. didyma* which needs moist, but in my experience all the following do best in humus enriched retentive soil. We struggle with them in the dry atmosphere here in summer.

'Beauty of Cobham'. Is remarkable for its pale pink flowers, contrasting with dark purplish calyxes. Late summer-autumn. 90cm.

'Croftway Pink'. The same thing in a good strong pink. 75cm.

'Prärienacht'. Strong growing plants produce a mass of rich violet-purple flowers from June-September. 1.2m.

'Schneewittchen'. Less robust, but flowers freely, with pure white flowers. 90cm.

'Shelley'. Originally obtained from Glen Chantry and named after a Suffolk village has impressed over many seasons. Unusual deep pink-red flowers. Has persisted when others have died out. 1.2m. Spreading habit.

'Squaw'. A very vigorous grower. Self-supporting leafy stems carry massed heads of guardsman-red flowers springing from brownish knobby centres. July-August. 1.2m.

MORINA longifolia. A most distinctive plant, forming rosettes of prickly aromatic foliage, from which rise tall stems bearing pagoda-like chalices, set at intervals. These are packed with jade green tubes from which spring white tubular flowers changing to crimson with age. After the flowers are finished the standing green stem with its fantastic outline is perhaps even more beautiful for green arrangements. Dries very well. Effective midsummer to winter. 75cm.

MORISIA monanthos 'Fred Hemingway'. Rosettes of narrow, saw edged leaves reminding me of starfish are held in tight hummocks. In spring they are buried beneath stemless clear yellow arabis-like flowers. Very pretty. Needs full sun and good drainage. From sandy beaches in Corsica. 5cm.

MUSCARI macrocarpum. A rarely seen delight. Dense heads of wax-textured yellow flowers open from purplish buds, wonderfully scented. Hardy against warm wall in well-drained soil. Fills the space with perfume in conservatory or cool greenhouse. Spring-flowering. 20cm.

MYOSOTIS scorpioides 'Mermaid'. This waterside forget-me-not will grow in a few inches of water or in the border edge which does not dry out. It forms spreading carpets of small shiny-green leaf rosettes. Clouds of tiny bright blue flowers are carried on 20cm branching stems.

scorpioides 'Ice Pearl'. White counterpart, charming mixed in with the blue form. 20cm. Spreading habit.

MYRRHIS odorata. Sweet cicely. I recognise this handsome feathery-leafed umbellifer by the occasional white splash on some of the leaves which are both sweet to taste and have the flavour of aniseed. Try adding them to a bowl of hot plums, or to salads, while the large crunchy seeds are edible too. Has attractive white cow parsley-like flowers. 1m. For herb or wild garden.

NARCISSUS – HARMFUL IF EATEN/SKIN IRRITANT

'Bowles Early Sulphur'. Similar to N. 'Cedric Morris', but flowers later in spring with slightly larger flowers. The pointed petals open more widely away from the trumpet, which pales from a very frilly lemon-yellow tip to the pale of the petals. 20cm.

The late Sir Cedric Morris, artist, was famous for his garden in Hadleigh, Suffolk, where he grew a vast collection of unusual plants and bulbs. He was my friend and inspiration for 35 years, and gave me the following forms of Narcissus.

'**Cedric Morris**'. This unique daffodil is usually in flower for Christmas Day, continuing to bloom through worst of weathers till March. Small, lemon-yellow perfectly formed daffodils with lightly frilled trumpets, a joy to pick with early snowdrops and leaves of *Arum italicum* 'Marmoratum'. Plant in shade to protect from Narcissus Fly, whose grubs eat the bulbs. 25cm.
'**Eystettensis**'. (Queen Anne's Double). Is a gem, with fully double flowers. Pale creamy-yellow petals are laid neatly back to form a rosette. About 20cm.
minor. Flowers early in spring, opening buds almost at ground level, stems lengthening to about 15cm. Has yellow trumpet, with paler yellow sepals. Makes low swirling clumps of narrow, grey-green leaves, flowers freely, most attractive for border edge, rock garden, or scattered in grass.
pallidiflorus. Also given to me by Cedric Morris. Has a curious characteristic. The unopened buds face skywards like beaks, gradually lowering as they open pale creamy-yellow perfectly shaped trumpet flowers. Early flowering. About 25cm.
'**Rijnveld's Early Sensation**'. Was given me many years ago by Graham S. Thomas. This old hybrid earns its place in open spaces in my Wood Garden by flowering precociously early, often in January and it continues to look well into March. It does not have the grace of the wild species, but I warm to such a sturdy, jolly looking flower so early in the year, with its confident dash of colour made with rich yellow trumpets and slightly paler 'petals'. I enjoy the dark green shading on their backs. 45cm.

NECTAROSCORDUM siculum subsp. bulgaricum syn. *Allium bulgaricum.* Curious and beautiful. On a thick stem, a pointed papery case splits to release creamy-green and faintly purple flushed bells. As they fade they turn upright to form fascinating seedheads. Will seed around if allowed. Early summer. 90cm.

NEPETA govaniana. This lovely, graceful plant should be seen more often. Makes an erect much-branched plant with soft-green, oval leaves, topped with long open spikes of pale creamy-yellow catmint-like flowers, produced for weeks in late summer-autumn. Likes cool retentive soil. 90cm.
grandiflora 'Dawn to Dusk'. Forms a wide bushy plant set with matt green scented leaves. Many branching stems set with whorls of pinky-brown tube-shaped calyxes, paler pink lipped flowers, overall effect enchanting, sturdy habit and delicate colour scheme. Mid-late summer. 75cm.
nervosa. Very appealing, makes underground running roots which end up many short stems clothed in narrow green leaves topped with thick spikes of blue and white lipped flowers. Watch for snails and slugs. Midsummer to autumn. 30cm.
nuda. Follows on from *Salvia pratensis* Haematodes Group where a delicate vertical is needed in late summer. Narrowly upstanding, it forms a candelabra of spires carrying small lilac flowers. Small grey-green leaves ascend partway up the stems. Easy in open sunny places. 1.2m.
nuda subsp. albiflora. A most effective vertical. Upright branching stems carry spires of aromatic tiny white flowers for weeks, from early to high summer. 1m.
racemosa 'Walkers Low'. Produces long flowering stems above crinkly grey-green leaves. Dark buds and stems add to rich effect of strong blue flowers. May-June. 75cm.
sibirica. Much valued in mixed sunny, well-drained borders where its wandering roots send up tall slender spires of rich blue flowers creating delicate accents for weeks in midsummer. 90cm.

'Six Hills Giant'. Although larger than the well-known catmint this form is equally useful and said to be hardier in cold districts. Large sprays of lavender-blue flowers in midsummer. 75cm.

subsessillis pink-flowered. Leafy stems, branched at the top carry clusters of lipped flowers opening from bundles of buds wrapped in dark calyxes in shades of lilac rather than pink, while the protruding lower lips are heavily spotted. Handsome. Midsummer. 60cm.

tuberosa. Unlike most catmints this is remarkable for providing a striking vertical, placed among lower plants. Stiff squared stems carry upright branching flower heads densely packed with tiers of mauve-tinted buds among which sparkle tiny blue-lipped flowers. Leaves, stems and buds are densely clothed in white wool, giving a pale silvery-grey effect. Colourful for weeks in midsummer, still providing good outline when drought drains colour. Has thick swollen roots like a dahlia, another adaptation to drought. Needs well drained soil in sun. 60cm.

NERINE bowdenii. Glorious pink trumpets in October. Winters well under a warm wall, or in very well drained soil. 45cm.

bowdenii 'Alba'. Not pure white as *N. flexuosa* 'Alba', but has large glistening flowers faintly washed with pink. Autumn. 40cm.

bowdenii 'Mark Fenwick'. Has large, deeper pink flowers on taller stems than *N. bowdenii*. 60cm.

sarniensis. Not hardy but superb in a frost-free greenhouse or conservatory (does not need high temperatures). I have large pots standing out all summer, overflowing with crowded bulbs, producing, in September, brilliant scarlet flowers flecked with gold glitter. 40cm.

undulata. Enchanting dainty flowers, paler than *N. bowdenii*, each petal slightly crimped, giving an almost orchid-like effect. 30cm.

undulata (Flexuosa Group) 'Alba'. Another gem. Forms a round head of lily-shaped flowers. Each has six chalk-white petals, crimped at the edges. Breath-taking perfection, flowering in gloomy November. Needs shelter of warm wall, or pot-grown in a cool greenhouse. 45cm.

NIEREMBERGIA caerulea. Small bushy plant, lightly set with small grey-green leaves, carries long display of large, shallow, bowl-shaped flowers, white, stained with blue veins leading to small yellow eye. A delight. June-September. 25cm.

OENOTHERA glabra. A choice plant, introduced by Clarence Elliott. Small basal rosettes of round, shining, mahogany leaves produce stiff stems set with enamelled-red pointed buds opening shallow, cup-shaped yellow flowers in July. 30cm.

macrocarpa. Large lemon-yellow evening primroses smother the foliage and sprawling, lax, crimson stems for weeks. Mid to late summer. Loves dry soil. 20cm.

speciosa 'Pink Petticoats'. Quantities of shallow cups, soft pink striped with faint red veins produced for weeks, from midsummer onwards, into September. For hot sunny situations. Well drained soil. Is invasive. 30cm.

OMPHALODES cappadocica. Forms dense clumps of oval, slightly crinkled green leaves over which float sprays of intense gentian-blue flowers, larger than forget-me-nots. Breathtaking in spring, a few nostalgic reminders in autumn. A very good ground-cover among shrubs. 25cm.

cappadocica 'Cherry Ingram'. Gentian-blue forget-me-not like flowers larger than the type, free-flowering, outstanding effect. 25cm.

cappadocica 'Starry Eyes'. A star of dark blue bars pinned to the centre of each flower, stands out against the base of the pale lilac petals. Overall effect, enchanting. 20cm.

verna. Blue-eyed Mary. Creeping mats of rich green, broadly oval leaves make good ground-cover in deep or part shade, embroidered with little forget-me-not like flowers in spring. 10cm.

verna 'Alba'. Has sprays of pure white starry flowers for weeks in spring. 10cm.

ONOPORDUM acanthium. Commonly and wrongly called the Scotch thistle. A splendid feature plant. In its first year forms a rosette of huge spiny leaves, copiously felted with white down. The towering flower stem is statuesque, carved out of stiff white felt, topped with pale lilac thistle flowers. A biennial, seed dropping freely. Midsummer to autumn. 2m.

ONOSMA alborosea. Good drought resister, stiff sprawling stems carry packed rosettes of narrow hairy leaves. Drooping head of white flowers, turning pink. May. 15cm.

OPHIOPOGON planiscapus. We grow the black leaved form below from seed. About 10% of these seedlings come up green, these are they. A patch of mature plants has slowly covered a dry shady area at the base of an oak tree. Fresh olive-green leaves are a pleasant contrast to the short white flower spikes. 25cm.

planiscapus 'Nigrescens'. Arching strap-shaped leaves make spidery clusters against soil, a feature all year round and remarkable because they are black. In summer, short sprays of tiny mauve bells appear, maturing as shiny black berries which last well into winter. Creeps slowly in well drained but retentive soil, in sun or part shade. 25cm.

ORIGANUM 'Bristol Cross'. Forms clusters of long narrow hop-like calyxes, green and rose-tinted, creating the main effect. The tiny paler pink flowers make highlights. Effective for weeks, late summer-autumn. Dries well. 30cm.

laevigatum 'Herrenhausen'. This strongly-growing form of marjoram makes a dense carpet of unscented leaves held in neat rosettes. By late summer-autumn stiff, wiry stems carry bunched heads of tiny purple flowers. Very effective as a border edging among blue grasses and other grey foliage plants. 30cm.

laevigatum 'Hopleys'. This pretty late-summer plant has small pointed leaves on wiry stems topped with daintier heads of tiny pink flowers held in scaly purple bracts. Both this and O. 'Herrenhausen' are handsome additions to edge the dry border with blue grass and thyme mats although O. 'Hopleys' is the prettiest to pick. 30cm.

'Norton Gold'. Forms a bright fringe of yellow foliage curving round a border edge in my Gravel Garden. Dense tuffets of thin wiry stems crowded with bright golden aromatic leaves, topped with leafy spires of pale pink flowers in early summer. Cut down after flowering it will replace itself for late summer-autumn display. Making contrast for the lavender spires of Russian sage. 45cm.

'Rosenkuppel'. Stiff stems of scented oval leaves are clothed all along the upper half with clusters of deep maroon buds opening rich wine coloured tiny flowers. Very effective beside pastel colours, good in drought. Mid-late summer. 60cm.

rotundifolium. Another plant with magnetic appeal. Lax short stems set with smooth blue-green leaves are topped with loose rosettes of palest apple-green, hop-like flowers. Dries well. Late summer to autumn. 25cm.

vulgare 'Aureum Crispum'. This form of sweet marjoram makes low spreading plants covered in bright yellow, rounded, crinkled leaves, contrasting with thymes, aubrieta, or calamints. Scorches in intense sunlight. Plant beneath a taller plant which forms a sunshade. 20cm.

vulgare 'Aureum' Long-leafed form. Long narrow pointed leaves create an almost ray-like effect as the lengthening shoots spread out to form a low buttery-yellow cushion. Best colour by midsummer. 30cm.

vulgare 'Compactum'. I am enchanted by this modest plant. It makes low dense cushions of small, aromatic leaves, smothered from midsummer to autumn with clusters of tiny, pale pink flowers, emphasised by dark maroon calyxes. Ideal as edging plant, or ground cover beneath roses. 15cm.

vulgare 'Thumble's Variety'. Forms good ground covering carpets of fresh yellow-green leaves, making bright contrast. Does not scorch in hot sun. 40cm.

ORNITHOGALUM nutans. Makes large clumps, like bluebells, of lax strap-shaped leaves, appearing in spring as snowdrops fade. Beneath leafless trees and shrubs is the setting for spires of wide open bells, each composed of 6 pointed petals, transparent in texture, a glistening silvery-white with green shadowed backs. 30cm.

pyrenaicum. Bath asparagus, introduced as an edible by the Romans. This bulbous plant produces long narrow heads of small green star-shaped flowers, a charming vertical to set among mat and cushion plants. 50cm.

OSTEOSPERMUM jucundum. There are a number of different forms of this drought-loving daisy from South Africa. This one makes large sprawling clumps of narrow aromatic leaves. On warm sunny days they erupt with deep pink flowers, freely produced throughout summer and autumn. In well-drained soil and in full sun, this plant has survived several winters here. 30cm.

jucundum 'Blackthorn Seedling'. Intense rose-magenta daisy flowers, making a fine display for weeks in mid-late summer. All osteospermums are best in well-drained soil, not overfed. 25cm.

'Lady Leitrim'. Has survived in my garden, in well-drained gravel for 25 years. Makes a sprawling tangle of stems, carrying narrow, evergreen, strongly aromatic leaves. Slim buds (tightly closed on dull days) show metallic blue-mauve backs to the petals which open to the sun, blushed-white daisies with navy-blue centres. Flowers deepen to pink with age. Blooms continuously on and off all summer. 30cm.

OTHONNA cheirifolia. Something different for the dry sunny border in well-drained soil. Lax stems carry paddle-shaped fleshy blue-grey leaves of waxy texture, topped in early summer with fresh yellow daisies. 45cm.

OXALIS sp. ex Mount Stewart. This handsome wood sorrel spreads beneath trees and shrubs weed proof carpets of rounded, handsome leaves with pale central veins. Large pale pink flowers. Attractive and valuable where space allows, interrupted with ferns, hostas and hellebores. 25cm.

PACHYPHRAGMA macrophyllum. To see under trees and shrubs an established carpet of these large round green leaves overlapping to make weed-free cover is very pleasant all summer. Veins and stems become purple tinted in winter. As snowdrops fade showy heads of white cress-like flowers appear early in March before new leaves emerge. 40cm.

PACHYSANDRA terminalis. Most valued rich green carpeter for covering bare earth beneath trees or shrubs. Evergreen rosettes of toothed glossy leaves, insignificant white flowers, scented in spring. 30cm.

terminalis 'Green Sheen'. Pachysandra make classic ground cover in shade, spreading by underground rhizomes in well-drained moist soil, which has plenty of organic matter added. This new variety is outstanding with the glossiest evergreen leaves, topped in early spring with short spikes of small white flowers. 20cm.

terminalis 'Variegata'. Leaves edged cream, not quite so vigorous. 25cm.

PACKERA aurea. Produces many yellow daisy flowers held on loosely branched stems arising from slowly spreading rootstock. Effective in groups, must have damp soil. Low growing. 45cm.

PAEONIA 'Avant Garde'. A sumptuous flower. Silk-textured petals are washed in shades of rose and cream forming flowers up to 15cm across. Each opens flat to show a striking eye formed by dark crimson filaments carrying a fringe of yellow anthers. Makes strong vigorous plants. 75cm.

lactiflora 'Evening World'. An outer bowl of rose-pink petals fading to white at the edges contains a centre filled with rows and rows of finely shredded petals stained pink at first, slowly turning cream securely pinned with five pale-green ovaries. Each flower 18cm across on 75cm stems; pretty as a ballerina's tutu. Lasts well when picked.

'Late Windflower'. Raised by Prof. Saunders of New York (*P. emodi* × *P. veitchii*). For many years I have supplied this plant erroneously as *P. emodi*. It is rare and exquisite. Finely-cut foliage, bronze-tinted when young, sets off branching stems of nodding white, sweetly-scented flowers. The inner circle of orange stamens surrounds a pale green ovary. Needs part shade and enriched soil. 75cm.

mascula. Wavy edged petals open into wide frilly shaped flowers revealing a boss of yellow stamens contrasting with shining magenta-pink petals. 75cm.

mascula subsp. arietina. A gem. Round fat buds open large bowl-shaped flowers sheltering the boss of yellow stamens. One established plant is a joy, a group of them with flowers floating above finely cut leaves like cherry-red balloons is enchanting. May-June. 75cm.

mlokosewitschii. Grows wild in the centre of the Caucasus, a plant of exceptional beauty. In early spring the buds and young leaves are a rich pinkish-bronze. As they turn to soft grey-green the buds gradually open to full beauty, perfect bowls of cool lemon-yellow, filled with golden stamens in May. 60cm. We do not sell these plants less than 5 years from sowing.

wittmanniana. This glorious plant from the Caucasus is breathtakingly beautiful. Above bold, deeply veined leaves appear, in late spring globular buds stained bronze pink which open large single flowers whose translucent petals are the colour of champagne; their centres enhanced by a quivering circle of fine purple filaments supporting butter-yellow anthers. 75cm.

All these paeonies need a cool situation, sheltered from wind. Being single each bloom is short lived, but so lovely they linger for ever in the mind.

PAPAVER 'Fireball'. Bright orange and double, with smaller heads, just right for the short stems. An unusual effect for the border edge. About 30cm.

orientale 'Aslahan'. Frilled champagne-tinted petals are flushed and edged with salmon pink, forming a large, exquisitely delicate flower. Purple-black blotches and quivering stamens fill the heart. 1m.

orientale 'Ballkleid'. While larger-flowered poppies are laid flat by wind and rain, this remains upright, freely producing a succession of semi-double flowers, a deeper shade than *P.* 'Halima', yet still a soft shrimp-pink above light green foliage. June. 60-70cm.

orientale 'Beauty Queen'. Earlier than most, medium-sized single flowers of pure clear orange with the faintest purple blotch, sometimes with none. 90cm.

orientale 'Beauty of Livermere'. Has large sumptuous flowers of rich crimson enriched by purple-black blotches around the central velvet knob. June-July. 90cm.

orientale 'Black and White'. Upright stems carry large pure white flowers with black central blotches. June-July. 60cm.

orientale 'Cedric Morris'. A seedling raised by Sir Cedric Morris. Huge poppies of greyish-pink with a purple-black blotch at the base of each frilled petal. Dramatic feature in the grey garden. June-July. 75cm.

orientale Goliath Group. A rich, ruby-red flower, large and well-shaped on strong stems. 90cm.

orientale 'Halima'. Remarkable for its dark, almost bluish-green finely divided foliage which sets off single, saucer-shaped flowers; light shrimp-pink filled with boss of purple stamens around the velvet-purple ovary. June. 90cm.

orientale 'Hula Hula'. Has large semi-double flowers with deeply shredded edges to the petals, which are a glorious vibrant salmon-pink with purple blotches inside and out. Tremendous impact in the garden or picked. Needs support. 90cm.

The next two oriental poppies are introductions from Germany. They are ideal for smaller gardens and do not flop about.

orientale 'Juliane'. Has pale salmon-pink flowers with ruched frilly petals. 60cm.

orientale 'Karine'. Has smooth petals forming perfect shallow saucer-shaped flowers in the same pale salmon-pink shade, held erect on 60cm stems.

orientale 'Laffeuer'. From Ernst Pagels in north Germany. Has brilliant scarlet, unmarked petals. Is an invasive but exciting perennial for sun and well-drained soil. 45cm.

orientale 'Lilac Girl'. A large flower, wavy-edged petals, deep lilac mixed with brown tones which ebb and flow from base to tip. Unusual and interesting when fresh. Damages in too much sun or wet. 90cm.

orientale 'Patty's Plum'. Medium sized flowers, deep lilac-wine fading to brownish tones. Beautiful and unusual, especially picked when you can admire its subtlety. Needs careful placing in the garden, not too much sun. Conversation stopping in a flower arrangement. 90cm.

orientale 'Roter Zwerg'. In our light soil this poppy remains upright when some others flop. Medium-sized flowers, bright scarlet, freely produced giving a long effect. 75cm.

orientale 'Silberosa'. Has a double row of wild-rose pink petals, wavy-edged centred with purple velvety boss and dark blotches, standing well above rich green foliage. 90cm.

orientale 'Sultana'. Large rose-coloured flowers on upright stems, much admired. June-July and second crop in September-October. 90cm.

orientale 'Tutu'. Brilliant orange-red silky petals form a large semi-double flower of great impact. 90cm.

orientale 'Wedding Day'. A seed raised strain with pure white flowers with a bold, crimson-black basal blotch on each petal. 80cm.

orientale 'Zuneigung'. Translates charmingly as 'Tender Affection'. Outstanding yet modest. Exquisite pale salmon-pink petals ruched in a double layer around dark purple stamens and seed box. Bleaches slightly to give a pretty two-tone effect. Medium-sized flowers freely produced, standing up well to wind and weather. 90cm.

rupifragum. A lovely perennial poppy and a rare colour in the garden. Semi-double, tissue paper petals of soft orange, in flower throughout the summer. 45cm.

spicatum. I enjoy this in bud as much as in flower. The leaves, stems and large gracefully drooping buds are heavily matted with fine felt. Pale apricot crinkled petals open in June-July. 60cm.

PARAHEBE catarractae. I call this the garden form. Makes more bushy growth than the type, and is a wonderful sight when smothered with light blue flowers in summer and again in autumn. 40cm.

catarractae white flowered. An excellent plant. Forms a tidy mound of evergreen leaves, completely whitened like snow by the thousands of tiny 'birds-eye' flowers in early summer. 50cm.

perfoliata. From a drought tolerant rootstock spring stout branching stems piercing through round grey-green waxy leaves reminiscent of the juvenile leaves of Eucalyptus. In midsummer, every shoot carries for weeks long, slender, drooping spires of soft blue, four-petalled flowers. We cut it well back after flowering, when new growth produces a second later flowering. 75cm.

PATRINIA scabiosifolia. Above clumps of coarsely-cut green leaves stand thin branching stems carrying sprays of clear yellow, tiny flowers, creating bright and fresh effect in late summer-autumn. Basal leaves turn reddish shades in autumn. 90cm.

PENSTEMON 'Alice Hindley'. Dark blue buds open large, soft blue flowers with white throats. Not reliably hardy, but one of the most lovely of garden plants. Mid-late summer. 75cm.

'Andenken an Friedrich Hahn'. Syn. *P.* 'Garnet'. Clear garnet-red tubular flowers, narrow dark green foliage. July to November. 75cm.

barbatus. Tall slender stems carry branched spires of narrow sealing-wax red tubular flowers, perfect contrast to pea-green stems and leaves. Irritates some with sprawling habit which is delightful in right place, over low wall or on a corner. Mid-late summer. 1m.

digitalis. I saw this in a garden in Portland, Oregon and was impressed. Tall stems carry heads of large, soft lilac chubby flowers. Needs no staking. Mid-late summer. 90cm.

digitalis 'Husker Red'. Clustered heads of green buds opening white flowers are enhanced by calyxes, stems and foliage stained beetroot purple. Early-midsummer. 90cm.

'Evelyn'. Forms neat bushy plants of very narrow leaves topped with slender spires of slim flowers, rose-pink with pale striped throats. In flower all summer till autumn frosts. 60cm.

'Hidcote Pink'. Narrow salmon-pink flowers with strong crimson veins in cream throat. Free-flowering, mid to late summer. 60cm.

'Sour Grapes'. I feel sentimental about this plant which was given me, under this name by Vita Sackville-West. I am told that it should be called 'Stapleford Gem'. Having sent out possibly thousands as *P.* 'Sour Grapes' I am reluctant to change and confuse many gardeners. *P.* 'Sour Grapes' (*P.* 'Stapleford Gem') is a beautiful plant, hardy on well-drained soil. The flowers are like unripe grapes or opals, soft green, amethyst and blue, opening from July till October. 60cm.

PEROVSKIA 'Blue Spire'. Russian sage. Makes a vertical feature as soon as the slender, whitened stems, lightly clad in fine-cut grey leaves, appear above the surrounding mounds in the dry sunny garden. In late summer they are topped with long spires of lavender-blue flowers. 1.2m.

PERSICARIA affinis 'Donald Lowndes'. Short stemmed, thick spikes of salmon-pink flowers over low mats of neat green leaves. Much admired from June-September. Not so vigorous as *P. a.* 'Superba'. 15cm.

affinis 'Superba'. Low spreading mats of neat green leaves, which turn rich russet brown in autumn, remaining all winter. Spikes of pale pink flowers deepen to crimson with age. Flowers midsummer-autumn. 25cm.

alpina. syn. *P. polymorpha.* Forms a tall columnar plant, composed of strong stems handsomely clothed in large pointed green leaves, topped, in midsummer with widely branched heads of small creamy-white flowers. Makes an important statement above lower plants, such as hostas, dicentras, ferns and ajugas. By September the flower heads become stained bronze-pink and green. For deep rich soil, sun or part shade, sheltered from wind. 1.8m.

amplexicaulis 'Alba'. Slim tapers of tiny white flowers smother tall bushy plants for months, lovely behind long flowering blue *Aster × frikartii* 'Mőnch'. 1.2m.

amplexicaulis 'Atrosanguinea'. Forms large branching bushy plants, which glow with slender tapers of tiny crimson flowers all late summer and autumn. 1.2m.

amplexicaulis 'Blackfield'. Selection with almost black tipped buds from which open dusky scarlet flowers. Like all the amplexicaulis knotweeds it is extremely long flowering, lasting from July till October. Best in a retentive soil in full sun or part shade. 1m.

amplexicaulis 'Firetail'. Similar to *P. amplexicaulis.* 'Atrosanguinea', perhaps slightly more intense. 1.2m.

amplexicaulis 'Inverleith'. Very attractive, makes a low leafy plant alight with crimson tapers for weeks from June-September. 45cm.

amplexicaulis 'Rosea'. Similar to *P. amplexicaulis* 'Atrosanguinea' with charming pale pink flowers. 1.2m.

amplexicaulis 'Rubie's Pink'. A stronger brighter pink that *P amplexicaulis* 'Rosea'. Found in the garden here many years ago by David Ward and named after his granddaughter Rubie. 1.2m.

bistorta subsp. carnea. Neater and narrower in leaf and flower spike than *P. bistorta* 'Superba' and needs less moisture. Flowers incessantly, with many stems carrying coral-pink pokers. 60cm.

bistorta 'Superba'. Best in a moist soil. Massed stems carry thick cyclamen-pink pokers, handsome dock-like foliage. Early summer. 75cm.

campanulata. Splendid weed smotherer in rich soil. Attractive, deeply veined foliage, with buff reverse. Tall branching stems are a mass of pink heather-like flowers all late summer and autumn. 1.2m.

milletii. A choice Chinese knotweed in the bistort class, but altogether more refined, where space is limited. It has narrow, dark-green leaves and heads of loganberry-like flowers in both colour and shape. Long flowering period mid-late summer. Needs good moist soil in sun or part shade. 45cm.

polystachya. A great shrub-like plant, in size and impact. Dies down completely in winter. In spring throws up many stout stems clothed in large ovate leaves on red leaf stalks, crowned in mid to late autumn with airy clusters of tiny white, honey scented flowers, scenting the air far and wide. It spreads and needs a large setting, in sun and retentive soil. Handsome near water. 2m.

vaccinifolia. This plant leafs very late in spring when its mats of russet-brown stems push out tiny shining green leaves. By late September it is smothered with spikes of tiny pink flowers. Exquisite. 8cm.

virginiana var. filiformis 'Compton's Red'. Collected by James Compton in Szechuan, China. Another eye-catching foliage plant for cool conditions. Bronze-tinted, branching stems support a mound of large, oval, pointed leaves marbled in shades of jade and moss green, overlaid with fine brown veins, which dissolve into a broad central, chestnut-brown V sign. Great contrast among ferns, tiarellas and heucheras. 90cm.

virginiana 'Painter's Palette'. Forms low branching plants covered with large oval leaves marbled in shades of cream and green, faintly brushed with pink. The centre of each leaf is marked with a strong 'V' sign which is brick-red when fresh but darkens to blackish-brown. Tiny rat-tail wisps of little brown flowers in late summer. 60cm.

virginiana Variegata Group. Is very like *P. virginiana* 'Painter's Palette' but without the 'V' sign and flushes of pink. It makes a beautiful cool feature among plain green companions in retentive soil. Both forms need shelter from sun scorch and wind. 60cm.

PETASITES japonicus var. giganteus. While flower-arrangers love the posy-like heads of green and white flowers which burst through bare clay in early spring, this is a plant for landscaping with its huge round leaves and invasive roots, making impenetrable ground-cover in heavy soil, even in solid clay. 1.2m.

PHLOMIS cashmeriana. This is a beautiful addition to this valued family. Branched stems above bold, rough-textured leaves carry whorls of soft lilac-mauve flowers. June-July. 1m.

chrysophylla. A woody framework is clothed to the ground with clusters of bold, simple leaves looking as if cut out of white felt. A splendid accent among small leafed plants such as helianthemum, lavendula, artemisia. Terminal clusters of claw-shaped yellow flowers in midsummer. 1.2m.

'Edward Bowles'. An attractive small sub-shrub with large floppy, downy heart-shaped leaves and whorls of sulphur yellow flowers in summer. Leave the seedheads for winter effect. A good plant for a sunny bank in free-draining soil. 1m.

italica. Smaller and more delicate than *P. chrysophylla*. A striking foliage plant, narrow, upstanding leaves covered with white wool. Clusters of lilac-pink, hooded flowers surround long stems at the inter-nodes, in late summer. Needs an open, sunny, sheltered site, in well drained soil. 1m.

russeliana. From large weed-smothering clumps of soft heart-shaped leaves rise stiff stems carrying whorls of rich-yellow hooded flowers in midsummer. The seedheads, whether green or dried, are equally effective. 90cm.

tuberosa 'Amazone'. From base of handsome large tooth-edged leaves rise dark purple branching stems carrying at intervals whorls of soft-lilac tubular flowers. A superb vertical for the dry sunny garden. Ornamental seedhead but is a mule, i.e. does not set seed. A rare plant selected by Ernst Pagels, north Germany. 1.6m.

PHLOX – Smaller Forms
The prostrate forms of Phlox are a delight, both for their weed-suppressing habit and for their flowers, individually beautiful, or in the mass, with breathtaking sheets of colour.

divaricata 'Blue Dreams'. Upright branching stems carry deep blue, long pointed buds opening soft light blue petals widely spaced. For cool conditions, leafmould soil. April-May. 40cm.

douglasii 'Boothman's Variety'. Cool lilac with a thin purple circle surrounding the centre. Mat-forming. May-June. 7cm.

pilosa. Slowly makes running clumps of small-leafed stems which carry clustered heads of mauve-pink flowers throughout summer. Easier than large border phlox in reasonable soil. 40cm.

x procumbens 'Variegata'. A remarkable plant, so robust in spite of its spectacular variegation. It quickly forms low cushions which in themselves are full of colour, green, cream and suffused pink, while the vivid rose-pink flowers add more glory and in no way detract, as most flowers do in variegated foliage. May, June and later. 10cm.

stolonifera 'Ariane'. Spreading mats of light green leaves are a background for large loose heads of snow-white yellow-eyed flowers. April-May. 20cm.

stolonifera 'Blue Ridge'. It makes good ground-cover, above which stands heads of lilac-blue flowers with a pin eye of orange stamens. April-May. 20cm.

subulata 'Lilacina'. Large pearly-blue flowers. A trim after flowering keeps it tidy. May-June. 15cm.

subulata 'McDaniel's Cushion'. Superb plant for sunny border edge or rock garden. Vigorous prostrate shoots closely-set with narrow green leaves form fresh live ground-cover all the year round. Smothered with large rose-pink flowers for weeks in early summer, the effect is stunning. 10cm.

subulata 'Scarlet Flame'. Bright cerise-red flowers cover vigorous mats of foliage. May-June. 10cm.

subulata 'Temiskaming'. Dense mats of small and narrow foliage. Vivid cerise flowers make a showy carpet for weeks. May-June. 15cm.

PHLOX – Border Forms

carolina 'Bill Baker'. Irresistible for the border edge. Almost horizontal stems clothed in narrow, pointed, evergreen leaves form low spread cushions. Above them short, branching stems carry clustered heads of scented lilac-pink flowers, in early summer. Reasonable soil, in sun or part shade. 45cm.

maculata 'Alpha'. Seems pretty free of mildew so far. Has narrow cylindrical heads of cool lilac-rose sweetly-scented flowers, producing a long succession from late summer, well into autumn. Needs no staking. 60cm.

paniculata 'David'. slightly larger flowers than the following with the palest of yellow eyes. 1m.

paniculata 'Harlequin'. Has less dramatic variegations than *P*. 'Nora Leigh', but makes up for that by having much more intense violet-purple flowers. 75cm.

paniculata 'Hesperis'. Coen Jansen selection. Pale violet, domed head, small flowers. 1m.

paniculata 'Mount Fuji'. Has remained healthy and robust over many years. Beautiful balanced heads of ivory-white scented flowers. Welcome in late summer, in the garden or house. 90cm.

paniculata 'Norah Leigh'. The most strikingly variegated form of border phlox, with leaves often more cream than green. Needs well-fed, retentive soil and some shade. Purple flowers in late summer. 75cm.

paniculata 'Rijinstroom'. Large bright rose-pink flowers on stiff stems. 1.2m.

PHUOPSIS stylosa. Super ground cover for dry sunny soil with refreshingly bright green, finely divided foliage, over which stand round pink pincushions stuck with pink pins. Early summer. 15cm.

PHORMIUM tenax. The New Zealand flax. A noble feature plant, winter and summer. Huge sword-like leaves arrange themselves in a perfect fan-like clump standing 2m or more. Above this soars a great flower spike whose dull red flowers are followed by black, curving seed pods held in clusters all along the stem. Provides an essential solid form where needed in any but the poorest of soils.

PHYLA nodiflora. A pretty trailing plant for paving, or ground-cover for small bulbs in warm, well-drained soil. Small oval leaves cover prostrate branching stems, set in late summer, with globular heads of tiny white and mauve flowers. Disappears in winter, but returns in spring. 10cm.

PHYSALIS alkekengi var. franchetii. Much valued in autumn for its stems of bright orange-red lanterns. Rather untidy habit, with underground running roots, but can be tucked into an odd corner. 60cm.
alkekengi var. franchetti 'Variegata'. Stems clothed from top to toe with pointed green leaves, irregularly patterned with creamy-yellow. This variegation is continued in the lantern-like seed cases, at first cream and green, ripening to orange. 60cm.

PHYSOSTEGIA virginiana. The Obedient plant. Has spires of curiously hinged tubular flowers which can be turned round on their stem without springing back. They prefer soil which does not dry out, in sun, when their running root stocks make dense mats of foliage. We offer the following varieties:-
virginiana subsp. speciosa 'Bouquet Rose'. I have come to rely on this plant in the garden and for the house, as it provides long-lasting spires of pale lilac-pink flowers for weeks in mid-late autumn. 90cm.
virginiana subsp. speciosa 'Variegata'. Provides leaves boldly edged with white, and stems of rich lilac-pink flowers. 45cm.
virginiana 'Summer Snow'. Similar habit, with pure white flowers-when those have dropped long spires of green bracts are still good for picking. Late summer. 90cm.
virginiana 'Summer Spire'. I love this plant for cool effect, whether cut, or in a damp sunny border. During late summer into autumn, 1.2m stems carry narrow, pyramidal heads of pale lilac flowers.
virginiana 'Vivid'. Autumn flowering, with luminous, light-purple, short spires. 40cm.

PHYTOLACCA – CAUTION: TOXIC IF EATEN.
americana. The Virginian poke weed. Sends up each year from a huge mangold-like root a stout plant with thick branching stems ending in spikes of close-packed white flowers which turn into shining maroon berries. Flowers midsummer. 1.2m.
polyandra. From China. Very similar in shape, this has bright rose-pink flowers followed by elderberry-black berries, contrasting with rhubarb-red stems and yellow autumn foliage. 1.2m.

PIMPINELLA major 'Rosea'. This enchanting cow parsley-like plant carries flat heads of rose-pink tiny flowers over several weeks in midsummer. Happy in ordinary soil, but preferring damp rather than dry conditions. 90cm.

PINELLIA cordata. Narrow, arum-like leaves, up to 12cm long, boldly veined surface, stained purple beneath, held on short purple stems, 5-8cm, which run through soft deep leafmould soil. They create an interesting foliage effect. Tiny green arum-like flowers with a very long antenna-like tip to the stigma.

pedatisecta. Larger in all its parts than *P. ternata*, with slim pale green flowers unstriped, the curving rat-tail tip to the spadix longer than the stem. 15cm.

ternata. Foliage makes interesting contrast, perhaps with mossy saxifrages, in cool shady places. Forms a colony of light green pointed leaves, joined in threes to top of the short 30cm stem. From spring to late summer very slim green Arum flowers appear, their long green spadix appearing like waving tails above the foliage. Much admired when picked.

PLANTAGO major 'Rubrifolia'. A handsome form of Rat-tail plantain. Large wide leaves of dark maroon-red are deeply veined. Strong contrast among silvers. Seedlings come true. The spiky brown seedheads are useful dried. 30cm.

PLATYCODON grandiflorus. The Japanese balloon-flower. The curiously angular inflated buds open to large flat, pale-blue flowers in late summer. 40cm.

POLEMONIUM caeruleum. Jacob's ladder. Held well above clumps of fresh green divided foliage are an endless succession of sky-blue small open bells, orange centred. Charming, especially in a cool situation, early to midsummer. 60cm.
caeruleum subsp. caeruleum f. albiflorum. A good white form, in flower for weeks, from late spring to late summer. 60cm.
carneum. In early summer produces sheaves of silky pearl-pink cupped flowers, lovely as an edging plant. 45cm.
'Lambrook Mauve'. Large heads of the prettiest silky lilac-mauve flowers, perfect among flowering ajugas, aquilegias and Bowles golden grass, *Milium effusum* 'Aureum' in spring. 40cm.

POLYGONATUM – HARMFUL IF EATEN. Watch out for grey sawfly caterpillars in late spring.
curvistylum. Slender arching stems clothed in narrow purple-tinted leaves carry clusters of little mauve bell-like flowers. June. 60cm.
× hybridum. This is the well known form of Solomon's seal. Close-set spreading rhizomes send up tall arching stems set with shining dark green leaves. In May they bear white and green-flushed bells on the lower side of the leafy shoots. Invaluable for flower arranging and for planting in shady places. 90cm.
× hybridum 'Betberg'. Given to me by Isbert Preussler, collected by him and named after a village in the Black Forest, near Laufen, Sulzburg. Emerging stems and young leaves stained chocolate brown, slowly fading as leaves mature. Produces purple berries. Still producing chocolate stained leaf tips while hung with clusters of flowers, up to five in a bunch, from leaf axils. 75cm.
× hybridum 'Striatum'. This seldom seen form has leaves boldly striped and edged creamy-white. Usually desired on sight. 60cm.
multiflorum. Distinct from *P. × hybridum*. Shorter, more upright stems hold leaves more closely set, standing upright on top side of slightly arched stems, to show wax-blue undersides. Beneath hang small cream bells followed by berries, at first dark bloom-coated green, finally almost black. 75cm.
odoratum. Has bowed leafy stems crowded with a fringe of scented cream bells. 40cm.
odoratum 'Flore Pleno'. Short, arched stems carry green-tipped, strongly scented flowers, consisting of two cream tubular flowers, one inside the other. Rare. 30cm.
'Silver Wings'. A dwarf form, distinctive in holding twisted leaves with greyish backs, upright, in pairs above sloping stems, the better to show off the fringe-like effect of cream bells hanging beneath them. 40cm.

verticillatum. For those who value a change in form and texture this plant slowly forms a slender column a metre tall of primly erect stems, clothed at intervals with whorls of very narrow pointed leaves. In spring clusters of small flowers hang along the upper ends, followed by small red berries. By autumn the whole plant glows like a lamp in shades of honey and amber. 1m.

PONTEDERIA cordata. Pickerel weed. Most handsome. Spreads slowly out into deeper water from the boggy edge. Standing above the water are crowded stems of beautiful leaves, spear-shaped marked with faint swirling lines and shadows, all topped with spikes of small blue flowers in late summer. 45cm above water.
cordata var. lancifolia. Has much longer spear-shaped leaves on smooth green stems standing proud above the water surface. A valuable contrasting vertical among sedges, water iris or water lilies. 1.5m.

POTENTILLA alba. Useful ground-cover for sun or light shade, formed by mats of soft grey-green lupin-like leaves, which are covered with white flowers, orange-eyed in spring and again in autumn. 10cm.
atrosanguinea. From a base of handsome green divided leaves come branching stems carrying intensely red, velvety-textured flowers, the colour of a fresh drop of blood. 45cm.
atrosanguinea var. argyrophylla. Neat clumps of heavily silvered strawberry-like leaves are a base for branching sprays of yellow flowers with orange centres, for many weeks in midsummer. 45cm.
calabra. Creeping woody stems are covered with small, finely cut, parasol-shaped leaves, silvery-white in drought, sprinkled with yellow, saucer-shaped flowers in midsummer. Good prostrate ground-cover for dry sunny sites. 5cm.
'Fireflame'. Good edge of border plant for sunny site. Neat clumps of fine-cut silvered leaves. Thin, branching stems carry many small red flowers with pale centres. 40cm.
'Gibson's Scarlet'. Hard to convey the effect of long sprays of brilliant velvet-red single flowers hung over healthy looking clumps of green divided foliage, lasting for weeks into autumn. 45cm.
× **hopwoodiana.** Charming pale pink herbaceous potentilla with a sprawling habit. Long flowering from mid to late summer. Lovely with eryngiums 40cm.
megalantha. Forms low mound of broadly trifoliate leaves, heavily veined like embossed leather, matt not shiny. Above them peer upwards shallow, cupped flowers, clear-yellow with orange centres. Leaves turn lemon-yellow in autumn. A good edge of the border plant, in sun or part shade. May-June. 15cm.
nepalensis 'Miss Willmott'. From among neat strawberry-leaves emerge long sprays of raspberry-pink flowers, dark-eyed, for weeks, mid to late summer. 30cm.
neumanniana 'Goldrausch'. A super plant. Neat mats of small dark-green leaves are edged with short sprays of bright yellow flowers like a doily. From spring until November frosts. 7cm.
rupestris. Quietly distinguished, for the front of a cool border. Small white flowers, yellow-eyed, are enhanced by daintily branching rose-pink stems. Early summer. 45cm.
× **tonguei.** From wide clumps of cinquefoil foliage are flung sprays of small flowers, apricot suffused crimson, of great charm. Mid to late summer. 25cm.

PRATIA angulata ' Treadwellii'. In cool soil quickly spreads its prostrate creeping stems, smothered all summer with stalkless starry white flowers, which by autumn have formed small rose-madder berries. 5cm.

pedunculata. Prostrate stems of tiny green leaves hug cool, moist soil, quickly forming dense mats, sprinkled in summer with small, pale-blue stemless flowers. 3cm.

pedunculata 'County Park'. A carpet of tiny green ground-hugging leaves set with dark gentian-blue, starry flowers. For sun or part shade, not dry soil. 2cm.

PRIMULA auricula 'Blue Velvet'. Exquisite blue with a white eye. 15cm.

auricula 'Old Red Dusty Miller'. Brownish-red flowers. White dusted foliage and stems. 15cm.

bulleyana. This Candelabra primula will grow in shade or in full sun if moist. Mealy stems bear whorls of rich orange flowers. Good seedheads. May and June. 45cm.

denticulata. Familiar Drumstick primula, with large round head of soft lavender flowers. Spring. 30cm.

denticulata var. alba. Beautiful form, white flowers, yellow eyes with luscious pale green leaves. Spring. 30cm.

florindae. The Himalayan cowslip. Must have moisture. Tall stems carry large drooping bells of softest sulphur-yellow. Beautiful seedheads dusted with luminous green. July to September. 90cm.

'Guinevere'. Crowded heads of pale lilac primrose flowers contrasting vividly with bronzy-purple foliage. Spring. 15cm.

japonica. The first candelabra primula to flower. Huge rosettes of lettuce-like leaves support thick stems carrying whorls of pink, magenta or white flowers, gold-eyed. Named forms include 'Miller's Crimson', 'Potsford White' and 'Appleblossom'. April to May. 60cm.

polyneura. Shades of pink to wine red over pretty deeply crinkled leaves scallop-edged and woolly backed. Likes cool shade. 20cm.

prolifera. Strong stems covered in white farina carry up to six whorls of clear yellow flowers. Has narrow leaves. Needs damp, rich soil which does not dry out. Midsummer. 60cm.

pubescens. Auricula. Soft shades of lemon, bright yellow, lavender, plum and bronze shades. All forms flower in spring. 15cm.

pulverulenta. Flowers after *P. japonica*. Crinkled green leaves, tall, slender mealy-white stems carry wine-red flowers. 60cm.

pulverulenta 'Bartley Strain'. Tiered spikes carry soft powder pink flowers. 60cm.

veris. Our native cowslip with rosettes of mid-green leaves. Stout stems bear clusters of nodding pale to deep yellow, fragrant flowers in spring. Needs a moist, but not waterlogged soil in semi-shade. 15cm.

vialii. Looking not unlike dwarf red hot pokers. Long tapering heads of closely packed red buds open lilac-purple primrose flowers, a dramatic colour combination, in midsummer. 30cm.

vulgaris. Perhaps the loveliest of all, the common yellow primrose. 15cm.

PRUNELLA. The following selected forms make good ground cover or edging plants, carpeting the soil with low clusters of leaves. They are sun lovers but not drought resistant, so need retentive soil with additional humus. All flower for several weeks in midsummer.

grandiflora. Has soft rose tinted flowers. 25cm.

grandiflora 'Alba'. Dense heads of white lipped flowers held in pale green calyxes on short stems. 20cm.

grandiflora 'Loveliness'. Has cool lilac blue flowers. 25cm.

PRUNUS tenella. Dwarf Russian almond. A wandering shrub with upright woody stems of dark green leaves. Pretty bowl-shaped salmon-pink flowers before the leaves in late spring. Best trimmed over after flowering. Deciduous. Hardy in full sun. 1m.

triloba. Dwarf cherry with bare branches carrying tight incurved buds which open into pale rose-pink double cherry blossoms well into the middle of April. Prune hard after flowering to encourage the production of long regrowth to flower the following year. 1.2m.

PULMONARIA. Lungwort. All these plants make excellent ground-cover in moisture-retaining soil, preferring partial shade. They are one of the first plants to flower, regardless of weather.

There is considerable variation, both from interbred seedlings and varying clones.

angustifolia 'Munstead Blue'. Making pools of clear true blue, the shortest and earliest to flower, with unspotted dark green smallish leaves. 15cm.

'Beth's Pink'. Broad leaves heavily spotted, good coral-red flowers with little hint of blue. 25cm.

'Blake's Silver'. A recent introduction with attractive silver leaves and pink flowers that are reputed not to fade out to blue. 30cm.

'Blue Crown'. Dark reddish buds quickly change, first to purple and then intensive violet-blue held above dark green leaves indefinitely mottled. 45cm.

'Blue Ensign'. Opens wide-eyed gentian-blue flowers. 40cm.

'Blue Hugel'. Very handsome producing quantities of vivid gentian-blue flowers of good size, opening wide, to good effect. 45cm.

'Cotton Cool'. Is an outstanding plant. The new basal leaves produced after flowering, make beautiful large rosette-like clumps of long, narrow, silvered leaves outlined against damp, leafmould soil in shade. 30cm.

'Diana Clare'. One of the best silvered pulmonarias. Forms striking rosettes of narrow, almost totally silvered, wavy-edged leaves with green rims. As a bonus has large, wide-open violet-blue flowers in early spring. 30cm.

ex Fran Patterson. Close clusters of dark blue flowers followed by striking clumps of long moss green leaves marked with pale green spots. 45cm.

'Glacier'. Barely pink buds open pure white flowers. 30cm.

'Little Star'. Makes a compact plant with narrow, slightly spotted leaves with short stems of rich blue flowers. 30cm.

longifolia. The flat basal rosettes form an eye-catching star shape against the soil, each dark green white-spotted leaf being long and narrow, tapering to a point. Rich blue flowers in dense terminal clusters. The latest to flower , often into early summer. 30cm.

longifolia 'Ankum'. Coen Janson, Holland. Very distinctive. 40cm stems carry dark heads of glistening, almost black buds opening first purplish tones quickly changing to indigo-blue, these dark tones enhanced by heavily silvered stem leaves. Basal leaves to following make large, eye-catching clumps of 30cm long, narrow wavy-edged leaves, heavily silvered.

'Mado'. Light sky-blue flowers, much spotted leaves. 40cm.

'Mawson's Blue'. Striking dark green leaves with taller sprays of gentian-blue flowers - flowering after *P* 'Munstead Blue'. 40cm.

'Majesté'. Curiously named I think. Flowers not nearly so effective as *P.* 'Excalibur', not opening so wide or such clean colours, maybe has better basal foliage. 30cm.

'Mary Mottram'. Another good blue, large light-blue flowers set off by rounded silver leaves narrowly margined with green, faintly peppered overall. 25-30cm.

'Netta Statham'. Narrow leafed form, has spaced pale green spots on deeper green. Exceptionally good gentian-blue flowers. Flowers held well upright, and flowering over long period. Stems 30-40cm.

officinalis 'Blue Mist'. Came from Amy Doncaster. Lavender-tinted buds open pale sky-blue flowers, creating a soft haze of colour in early March. 20cm.

Opal = 'Ocupol'. forms a bouquet packed with flowering stems carrying terminal clusters of palest blue flowers held above neat foliage so heavily spotted it contributes to the cool greyish tone overall. Lovely! 45cm.

rubra. Weed-smothering clumps of large light green leaves, unspotted, are preceded in very early spring by clustered heads of coral-red tubular flowers. 30cm.

rubra var. **albocorollata.** Large, unspotted, apple-green leaves set off drooping clusters of pure white flowers. 30cm.

rubra 'David Ward'. This beautiful form was spotted in my garden by David Ward. Forms huge, flower-like rosettes of long, pale green leaves with wide, white margins. Must have shade and soil that does not dry out. If exposed to sun or wind the delicate margins scorch and the leaves curl. Coral red flowers during March-April. 30cm.

saccharata. Has leaves up to 30cm long, rough textured, dark green, variously marbled in silver and grey-green. Most striking in shady corners. Likes cool soil. Masses of blue and rose flowers in March. 30cm.

saccharata 'Alba'. This fine form produces quantities of snow-white flowers, much larger than those of *P officinalis*, followed by rosettes of well-marked leaves for the rest of the season. 30cm.

saccharata Argentea Group. A large clump of these frosted silver leaves under the shade of shrubs is a lovely sight. Flowers in March. 30cm.

saccharata 'Dora Bielefeld'. Very attractive introduction from Germany, coral pink buds open soft, rose-pink flowers, leaves spotted pale green. 25cm.

saccharata 'Frühlingshimmel'. Remarkable for the open bell effect of its clear blue flowers, maturing from pale pink buds which contrast with reddish-brown calyxes. 25cm.

saccharata 'Reginald Kaye'. A well-selected form. Has large silvered spots in leaf centres, while broad borders are picked out in smaller spots. April-May. 30cm.

'Smoky Blue'. Good example of the old "soldiers and sailors" (*P. officinalis).* Good sized flowers open salmon-pink changing to blue, giving overall an amethyst effect of pink sliding into blue. Still making a show in early May. 30cm.

'Tim's Silver'. Another good form selected here. The silver surface coating gives a satiny sheen to the leaves, almost entirely covered, except for a fine green rim. Flowers a good mid blue. April-May. 30cm.

'Trevi Fountain'. Bright lavender-blue flowers on this form. Nicely spotted foliage. 30cm.

PULSATILLA vulgaris. Attractive in bud, flower and seed. A native of eastern England across northern Europe to the Ukraine. Best in a well drained soil in full sun. Good on chalk soils. From ferny green leaves in March emerge silk-wrapped buds, opening to huge purple flowers, each filled with golden stamens. No less beautiful are the common brown heads of feathered seed. 25cm.

vulgaris 'Alba'. Dusky white flowers after which develop fine seedheads. 25cm.

RANUNCULUS aconitifolius. Vigorous clumps of dark green divided leaves produce many branching stems carrying loose showers of single white buttercup flowers each with a yellow button centre. For retentive soil in sun. 90cm.

aconitifolius 'Flore Pleno'. The rare and exquisite 'Fair maids of France'. When well-grown, it carries bouquets of small, perfectly formed double-white buttercups, with green centres on widely branched stems. Early summer. 45cm.

acris 'Flore Pleno'. Deserves to be better known. Almost leafless branching stems carry multitudes of small tightly-double buttercups, lovely among blue *Iris sibirica*. June-July. 75cm.

acris 'Sulphureus'. From neat clumps of finely cut leaves, freckled brown, rise a shower of slender branching stems carrying creamy yellow enamelled saucers, with plenty of buds to follow, exquisite among blue forms of *Iris sibirica*. 50cm.

constantinopolitanus 'Plenus'. Non-invasive, a choice plant for damp soil, it produces many large tightly-double, glossy yellow flowers sharply green-centred. Early summer. 30cm.

illyricus. Provides showers of shining buttercups in May, above a ground-covering carpet of pretty velvety lobed leaves. These vanish in summer, returning in autumn to make cover between herbaceous plants which have died down. Thrives in well-drained soil and sun. 30cm.

repens var. pleniflorus. Most attractive in May-June when it forms golden carpets of small, shining, tightly double buttercup flowers with green centres. Long, wandering shoots root at the nodes, but are easily dislodged. Could be a menace in the wrong place, but lovely when space permits in damp soil, open site. 15cm.

RAOULIA australis Lutescens Group. Has grey-blue leaves so small the plant appears like a velvety mould creeping over gritty soil, powdered with minute yellow flowers in spring. Ideal tufa or trough plant. 1cm.

hookeri. Tightly-packed creeping mats of minute silver leaves spread over very well-drained soil. 1cm.

tenuicaulis. Forms a green river of moss-like minute foliage pressed flat between and over rocks in a scree bed, dusted with tiny yellow flowers in spring. Larger features like sempervivums or *Rhodiola rosea* look splendid growing out of it. 1cm.

REINECKEA carnea. Useful change of shape and texture, for ground cover in part shade, with slowly spreading clustered clumps of evergreen leaves like narrow lily-of-the-valley foliage. Tucked low among them may sometimes be found maroon-red stems carrying pale pink starry flowers, in late autumn. 30cm.

RHEUM 'Ace of Hearts'. Beautiful, grand foliage plant for small garden. Dark heart-shaped leaves, handsomely veined and backed with crimson create a focal point. Tall flower spikes of palest pink are light and dainty in early summer. 1.2m.

palmatum. Although not as colourful as *R. palmatum 'Atrosanguineum'*, this plant is worthy of a place in the wild garden, or in a bay in a shrubbery. The first year will see a huge weed-smothering mound of apple-green leaves 1-2m across, stout flower stems carry branched heads of frothy white flowers in June. 1.5m.

palmatum 'Atrosanguineum'. The crinkled young leaves are rosy-purple, which remains on the backs of the leaves, while the topsides turn dark green. The tall branching flower spires are massed with tiny cherry-red flowers while the seed cases are translucent rose-red. All these plants require plenty of humus. Early summer flowering. Flower stems 2m.

palmatum var. tanguticum. This scarce form has even larger leaves of more intense rosy-purple. It continues to produce new, freshly coloured leaves until late summer. Tall spires of tiny white flowers, early summer. 2m.

RHODANTHEMUM hosmariense. Finely fingered clusters of silver-grey leaves make a comfortably low mound, carrying in winter, hundreds of tight, black-pencilled buds which open a few large white daisies in mild spells, providing a glorious show in spring and early summer. 30cm.

RHODIOLA heterodonta. Similar in growth to *Rhodiola rosea,* but the colour of the foliage is fascinating. Waxy leaves, almost iridescent with lilac, amethyst, blue on grey. The bronze-pink flower buds and flowers make a fine contrast. Spring. 25cm.
rosea. Rose root. The whole development of this plant throughout the spring is a joy to watch. From a woody root-stock tight pinkish-bronze buds slowly elongate into close radiating stems of blue-grey leaves. Finally they are topped by sharp lime-green starry flowers bursting with anthers. 30cm.

RODGERSIA. These are among the finest foliage plants for marshy land, waterside or cool, damp soil. Will grow in sun if soil is moist, also in shade provided soil does not dry out. They make slowly spreading rhizomes.
'Badenweiler'. We are unsure of the name but having grown this for several years we are finally introducing it as a reliable damp loving plant. Large horse chestnut shaped leaves occasionally produce a spike of creamy-white flowers. Probably a form of *R. aesculifolia.* An excellent foliage plant. 80cm.
'Herkules'. Selection with Horse chestnut like foliage bronzed in early spring, green in midsummer. Flowers light pink in branched clusters. Best in sun or part shade and a moist soil. 1m.
pinnata 'Superba'. A treasure for cool and damp places from the moment its deeply pleated and divided bronze leaves start to unfold, until in midsummer, it flaunts a plume-like head of rose-red tiny flowers and finally leaves a bold seedhead. 90cm.
podophylla. The young unfolding leaves are rich dark brown in spring, turning green as they expand, often copper-tinted when mature. Each dramatically handsome leaf consists of five large leaflets, broadly triangular in outline, with jagged tips, arranged at the top of each stem. The head of creamy astilbe-like flowers is not remarkable. 75cm.

ROMNEYA coulteri. The Californian tree poppy. Although it dies down in winter, it creates a shrub-like effect in summer with many upright, branching stems clothed in glaucous-grey leaves, topped with fat buds, which open huge white poppies, 15cm across, with crumpled tissue-paper-like petals pinned together with a mass of yellow stamens. A spectacular site at the entrance to our dry garden. 1.8m.

ROSA pimpinellifolia double white. Makes a large thicket, of twiggy, spiny branches smothered in June with small bubble-shaped semi-double white flowers. Up to 1.5m.
pimpinellifolia 'Falkland'. I have taken this name from "Shrub Roses of Today" by Graham Stuart Thomas. This rose makes a dense twiggy framework furnished with tiny grey-green leaflets which set off clusters of small, in-curved semi-double roses, lilac with the palest hint of pink. 1.2m.
Both these forms of Burnet rose flourish in poor sandy soils where they slowly make large suckering thickets. A quick chop round with a sharp spade in early spring easily dislodges wanderers if space is limited.

ROSCOEA cautleyoides. From China comes this relation of ginger. Fleshy roots produce narrow blade-like leaves above which stand creamy-yellow orchid-like flowers. Looks and does well in woodland soil, among small ferns, corydalis, tiarellas. 30cm.

purpurea. This strangely attractive, orchid-like plant comes from India and Nepal. Fleshy roots produce clumps of lance-shaped, rich green leaves, while the purple flowers with large, drooping, lower lips are produced from a terminal spike for several weeks in midsummer. They need rich soil with adequate moisture, in sun or part shade. 30cm.

ROSMARINUS officinalis 'Sissinghurst Blue'. This much admired free-flowering variety originated as a self- sown seedling in the paving at Sissinghurst. It has good blue flowers, fine thin foliage and is remarkably hardy. 1.6m.

officinalis 'Tuscan Blue'. Makes upright growth with strong blue flowers, produced even in winter. Greatly admired at its best in early summer. 1.8m.

RUBUS idaeus 'Aureus'. Very attractive, among shrubs, or in the leaf litter beneath trees. Pale lemon-yellow leaves create a patch of sunlight where its underground shoots weave through fine leafmould. I have it running through blue hosta where it looks charming. 60cm.

spectabilis 'Olympic Double'. A thicket-forming shrub with glossy, dark green leaves. Pretty double, rose-like bright purple-pink flowers in April-May. Needs some space as it will sucker. Sun or light shade. 2m.

tricolor. Beautiful evergreen ground cover where something rampant can be appreciated. Prostrate bronze stems covered with soft reddish hairs carry shining polished green leaves which become bronze tinted when touched by frost. Can make over 2m of growth a season. 30cm.

RUDBECKIA fulgida var. deamii. Considered to be an improved form of *R. fulgida* var. *speciosa.* Flowering earlier, slightly taller in habit and with rougher foliage. Late summer to autumn. 75cm.

fulgida var. speciosa. Making a bright display in autumn, this very tidy daisy forms mounds of dark green foliage to set off large orange-yellow flowers, with a prominent black eye. 60cm.

fulgida var. sullivantii 'Goldsturm'. Another selected form, a seed strain flowering from July-September. 75cm.

laciniata 'Goldquelle'. A beautiful form low enough to look down onto the beautifully shaped flowers which although fully double when mature, have green shaded centres, opening from green dome shaped buds. Very effective in September border, lovely to pick. 75cm.

laciniata 'Herbstsonne'. A beautiful giant for the back of a large open border in retentive soil, or by pond-side. Strong leafy branching stems support a long display, in early autumn, of large, lemon-yellow daisies, the broad petals reflexed from upright central green knobs. Picks well, try a jugful by itself. 2m.

maxima. This plant has great presence. Large, simple leaves, wax-coated blue-grey, form a base for branching stems holding large, elegant, cone flowers; tall, narrow black centres are surrounded by long, languid, yellow petals. For sun and deep, damp soil. 1.2m.

subtomentosa. Earlier and taller than *R. fulgida*. Upright stems clothed in rough mid-green leaves carry branched heads of orange-yellow daisy yellow daisy flowers, buttoned with dark brown centres. 1.4m.

RUMEX acetosa. French sorrel. We have a specially delicate leaved form of this plant. Its large crisp pale green leaves give a sour tang to salads, or purée for fish and egg dishes. 45cm.

RUTA – CAUTION: SEVERELY TOXIC TO SKIN IN SUNLIGHT
graveolens 'Jackman's Blue'. Neat mounds of blue filigree foliage. Evergreen. Lovely under old-fashioned roses, with *Alchemilla mollis* or grey plants. 45cm.
graveolens 'Variegata'. In early summer this blue-green and white variegated rue has its uses, especially picked for foliage arrangements. 45cm.
Both forms of rue can cause blistering. Wear gloves and long sleeves when handling.

SAGINA subulata var. glabrata 'Aurea'. An immediately desirable little plant whose shredded golden leaves make vivid moss-like mats studded with tiny, white stars. For cool soil. 2cm.

SALVIA argentea. A fine feature plant to offset some of the fussy greys. In spring large flat crinkled grey leaves emerge completely whitened with soft silky down. This gradually disappears as stems of white hooded flowers appear in midsummer. Renewed growth in early autumn. 60cm.
guaranitica 'Blue Enigma'. Slender stems set with small dark green leaves carry branching spires of dark gentian-blue flowers forming a valued vertical accent in a warm garden in autumn. We cover the crowns with leaf litter. 1.2m.
'Indigo Spires'. Not reliably hardy, but makes a superb vertical feature in a tub combination. Tall dark-stained, branching stems are tipped with long spires, bearing almost navy blue buds, which open dark-blue lipped flowers lit with small white bee guides. Late summer-autumn. 1.4m.
lavandulifolia. Makes a compact bush of narrow grey leaves, and is conspicuous for the abundance of its rich purplish-blue flowers held upright well above the foliage in dense spikes in midsummer. 75cm.
lavandulifolia subsp. blancoana. This choice sage makes a low spreading bush covered with narrow silvery-grey leaves. From the tip shoots extend long curving sprays of soft lilac-blue flowers in midsummer. 30cm.
multicaulis. Makes a low clump of spoon-shaped, whitish-grey leaves. Thin stiffly-upright stems carry, at spaced intervals, conspicuous clusters of bracts which stick out pale-blue tongues of flower, then drop them as they turn themselves into glowing maroon-red seed cases, as showy and exciting as any gardener or flower arranger could wish, from summer to autumn. 30cm.
nemorosa 'Caradonna'. A more recent acquisition with distinctly dark stained stems of violet blue flowers. Shorter growing and will repeat flower if cut down after first flowering. For sunny front or mid border in any reasonable soil. 50cm.
nemorosa 'Ostfriesland'. Very similar to *S.* × *superba* but shorter. 40cm.
nemorosa 'Pusztaflamme'. This curiously attractive plant has triangular shaped heads of densely-packed flowers of mournful purple hue, chenille velvet in texture. Makes good accent on border edge, dries well. Aromatic leaves. Mid-late summer. 50cm.
nemorosa subsp. tesquicola. From a neat base come many upright branching stems narrowly set, like pipe cleaners, with reddish bracts holding small pink and blue flowers. The effect is very light and very pretty, lasts for weeks when the flowers fade but the bracts remain. For dry well-drained soil. Mid-late summer. 60cm.
nemorosa 'Wesuwe'. A well selected form, produces many spires of intense violet-purple flowers, accented with dark reddish bracts. Cut down halfway after first flush will give second performances in late summer-autumn. 60cm.

officinalis 'Berggarten'. Forming a substantial sub-shrub with extra large grey-felted leaves, this sage makes much needed contrast among the filigree foliage of artemisia and fennel. Has larger blue-purple flowers than the type. 60cm.

officinalis 'Icterina'. Golden sage. A variegated form of the culinary sage. The new foliage is beautifully marbled, primrose, gold and sage-green. Remains all winter. Best in a warm site. 60cm.

officinalis 'Purpurascens'. Purple sage. The young summer foliage is a delight, soft greyish-purple velvet, with spikes of purple-blue flowers. Occasional shoots are variegated pink, cream and purple. Will form a lax bush, but can be kept under control by careful pruning in spring. 60cm.

officinalis 'Tricolor'. No need for flowers with this mound of velvety foliage vividly variegated white, cyclamen-pink and purple. Tender in cold districts. 40cm.

patens 'Cambridge Blue'. Gaping mouthed tubular flowers 5cm long, in pale sky-blue, open in pairs over many weeks, on slender spires, with more to come from the base. Mid-late summer. 45cm.

patens 'Royal Blue'. Makes contrast with dark gentian-blue flowers. 60cm.

pratensis Haematodes Group. Very flat rosettes of crinkled grey-green leaves veined purple, send up numerous stems bearing long spires of lilac-blue flowers. A haze of soft colour above the greys. Midsummer. 90cm.

pratensis 'Rosea'. A form with more sprawling stems and pink flowers. 75cm.

sclarea var. turkestanica. Biennial Clary sage. An erect perennial or biennial with hairy wrinkled, mid-green leaves. Spikes of large white flowers with pink bracts from spring to summer. Hardy. Will seed freely. Tolerant of any reasonable soil in full sun. 1m.

× **superba.** Much admired in late summer. Clumps of rich green crêpey leaves send up stiff spikes of intense violet-purple flowers with crimson bracts. 90cm.

× **sylvestris 'Blauhügel'.** Forms neat short bushy plants crowded with long spires of rich-blue lipped flowers. Makes an eye-catching display for weeks. Smothered with bees. 40cm.

× **sylvestris 'Mainacht'.** A German hybrid between *S. pratensis* and *S. nemorosa*, makes bushy plants crowded with dense heads of deep purple flowers, enhanced by dark stems and reddish bracts, very effective singly or in groups for landscape effect. 45cm.

× **sylvestris 'Rose Queen'.** Neat bushy plants of aromatic leaves crowded with spikes of dark buds opening bright rose-pink lipped flowers. Its long season can be extended if flowers are removed before seeding. Early-late summer. 45cm.

× **sylvestris 'Schneehügel'.** A neat plant for border edges, stiffly upright, much branched stems create a dense effect when each spire is thickly clothed with pure-white lipped flowers. 50cm.

uliginosa. Worth protecting underground shoots with a bit of bracken or straw. In late September slender leafy stems carry head high loose spires of pure sky-blue flowers. Needs a warm site, yet soil that does not dry out. 1.5m.

verticillata. A plant of character, makes a large clump of healthy-looking foliage well into late summer when it produces long arching spikes of small, but vivid, violet flowers set in crimson-tinted calyxes. 75cm.

verticillata 'Purple Rain'. Closely-set whorls of small, bright purple, lipped flowers held in dark purple calyxes on low branching stems creating valuable dark vertical shapes among paler flowers. 60cm.

SANGUISORBA canadensis. Handsome in early autumn topped with branching stems which carry narrow cylindrical heads of greenish-white fluffy flowers. Autumn frosts turn the leaves red and copper. 1.5m.

hakusanensis. Above a base of pinnate leaves stand a crowd of upright stems bearing many drooping pink catkin-like flower heads. Overall effect enchanting. 75cm.

obtusa. Above blue-grey pinnate leaves rise branching stems carrying large fluffy bottle brushes of soft rose. Late summer. 1.2m.

tenuifolia 'Purpurea'. A most striking plant. From a leafy base spring many tall stems topped with branching heads carrying hundreds of wine-coloured, small catkin-shaped flower heads. The delicate form combined with dancing shapes of deep colour is very unusual and effective. Needs some support. 1.5m.

SANTOLINA chamaecyparissis. Forms round dense bushes of silver-grey closely feathered foliage. Small yellow button flowers in July. 60cm.

chamaecyparissus var. nana. Very desirable, much smaller, much whiter foliage. 30cm.

pinnata subsp. neapolitana. Foliage more delicately feathered, the button flowers are cool sulphur-yellow. A splendid background plant. 45cm.

rosmarinifolia subsp. rosmarinifolia. Another fresh green, to plant among silver plants. Forms a neat round bush of vivid green aromatic foliage, a bright setting for the lemon-yellow button flowers. Midsummer. 45cm.

rosmarinifolia subsp. rosmarinifolia 'Primrose Gem'. With button flowers of pale primrose-yellow these two santolinas make a good combination. 45cm.

SAPONARIA ocymoides. A vigorous trailer smothered with bright pink campion flowers, for a sunny wall or hot dry bank. Early summer. 30cm.

ocymoides 'Alba'. White campion flowers smother prostrate trailing stems in early summer. Useful edging for the sunny, dry garden. May-June. 20cm.

officinalis 'Alba Plena'. Commonly called Soapwort. The lather made from its leaves was used to clean delicate fabrics. A plant with invasive roots to tuck among shrubs or an odd waste corner. I love its quantities of large, double, white campion flowers. It makes a show for weeks in late summer-autumn, fresh and bright, good for mixed posies. 75cm.

SAXIFRAGA 'Aureopunctata' (× urbium). Variegated version of London pride. Makes attractive ground cover all year round with spreading rosettes of leathery leaves speckled with gold. Sprays of little pink flowers on 40cm stems in May.

'Black Ruby' (fortunei). A dwarf version with darkest purple, almost black leaves and short stems carrying clusters of rich pink starry flowers well into November. 20cm.

'Cloth of Gold' (ex arata subsp. moschata). Tiny rosettes of finely-cut yellow leaves are tightly clustered to form low spreading cushions in cool damp soil. 5cm.

'Dentata' (× polita). Evergreen rosettes of dark green spoon-shaped leaves whose edges look as if they had been cut with pinking shears. Sprays of small, almost white flowers in May, similar to London pride. 25cm.

fortunei 'Rubrifolia' (fortunei). A choice and rare plant for cool soil in a sheltered corner. Round varnished leaves, bronze-red above, carmine beneath, form a succulent looking clump. In October wide sprays of white starry flowers stand well above on rose-pink stems. 30cm.

× geum Dixter form. Makes carpeting rosettes of small evergreen leaves. Bronze-tinted branching stems carry airy sprays of white-petalled flowers appearing pink because of their crimson centres. Not too dry soil, sun or part shade. Early summer. 40cm.

'Ingeborg'. A low, mossy, cushion saxifrage, smothered in May with bright ruby flowers that fade to a striped pink, all shades seen on the plant at the same time creating a pretty two-tone effect. 15cm.

SCABIOSA caucasica 'Clive Greaves'. This justifiably popular old variety produces soft-lavender-blue flowers over several weeks. 75cm.

caucasica 'Miss Willmott'. In flower for months throughout the summer, large pale cream, almost greenish-white flowers on tall stems, endlessly till the frosts. 75cm.

caucasica 'Moerheim Blue'. Deep blue frilly petals, darker at the edges, surround pale central dome of fertile flowers. Long season-mid to late summer. 90cm.

caucasica 'Staffa'. A deeper blue form of this well established summer flowering perennial. Flowering for weeks. Divide every few years as growth emerges in the spring to maintain vigour. 90cm.

columbaria var. ochroleuca. A dainty plant. Crowds of wiry stems lightly clad in finely-cut leaves carry cool, lemon-yellow flowers for weeks in late summer. Sun and fertile soil. 75cm.

'Pink Mist'. Above low tuffets of finely-cut leaves appear a forest of bare stems each topped with a pale mauvish-pink pin-cushion. Continuing the display for weeks throughout summer. Excellent for border edge, loved by bees and butterflies. 60cm.

SCILLA peruviana. A fine dark metallic blue form this low growing but leafy almost evergreen bulb. It hails from south west Europe and North Africa not Peru. Nice warm, sunny spot to flower well. 30cm.

peruviana 'Alba'. Above clumps of strap-shaped, fleshy leaves stand large, pyramidal-shaped heads of star-shaped flowers, opening pale grey-blue from deeper blue buds. Spring. 30cm.

SCROPHULARIA auriculata 'Variegata'. This variegated figwort makes a conspicuous feature plant. Its broad basal leaves, waved and crimped, have wide cream margins, with centres marbled in shades of green. Stiff, branching stems carry smaller variegated leaves, sometimes totally cream. Needs retentive soil. 75cm.

SCUTELLARIA altissima. A lively skull-cap which seeds around, producing spires of small blue and white, snapdragon-like flowers. A charming vertical among the smaller perennials. 60cm.

scordiifolia. Curious little bead-like white tubers spread themselves through light soil to send up masses of dark blue-lipped flowers. Very effective in a mass among thymes. Midsummer. 15cm.

SEDUM acre 'Aureum'. Pale green mats glow for weeks in early spring as new young growth becomes butter-yellow. 5cm.

aizoon 'Euphorbioides'. Heads of warm yellow starry flowers fade to handsome bronze seedheads, reddish stems, green leaves, overall interesting effect. Midsummer. 30cm.

anacampseros. A strong ground cover with whorls of closely packed blue-grey leaves. The ball-like flower heads are blue-grey in bud, developing to pinkish-brown. Midsummer. 30cm.

'Bertram Anderson'. Similar to *S.* 'Vera Jameson', prostrate stems up to 30 long, clothed in small purple leaves, carry loose heads of wine-coloured starry flowers. The overall dark effect very good with a pale plant such as *Gypsophila* 'Rosenschleier'. 15cm.

'Carl'. Excellent for border edge. Short, close packed stems carry bun-shaped heads of lively, rose-pink flowers above blue-grey leaves. An unusual shade for sedums. Early flowering. 45cm.

cauticola 'Lidakense'. Trailing stems with bluntly rounded leaves, a wonderful grey colour. Flower heads of pinkish-red during August-September. Effective ground cover. 15cm.

'Evening Cloud'. Dense hummocks of grey, succulent leaves are smothered in August with clustered heads of grey buds opening rich, rosy-red flowers, humming with bees. 25cm.

'Herbstfreude'. syn. *Sedum* 'Autumn Joy' and still one of the best garden plants, in all stages. First the early rosettes of fleshy grey-green leaves, then large heads of waxy buds exactly the same colour as the leaves, next opening to rich pink starry flowers which deepen to brick red and finally warm brown seedheads. Crowns need dividing occasionally to produce best results. 60cm.

hispanicum var. minus 'Aureum'. A neat growing little plant which in autumn changes to soft creamy-yellow, making attractive contrast among low grey or bronze foliage plants. 2.5cm.

'Joyce Henderson'. Elegant eye catching stems and leaves tinted with soft purple blooms. Carry dome-shaped heads of pale beige-pink buds opening starry flowers, rose-pink and white. 75cm.

middendorfianum. A most attractive low ground cover. The neat leaves, not fleshy form small greenish-bronze rosettes, whilst the little yellow star-like flowers have a reddish tinge. 8cm.

oreganum. Improves the drier it becomes with close-packed clusters of fleshy fat leaves turn rich bronze-red in summer. Flowers are flat stems of small bright yellow stars. Midsummer. 5cm.

pluricaule. Makes very close round cushions of fleshy grey-green leaves smothered in October with bright pink flowers. 4cm.

populifolium. Forms a dwarf woody shrub, smothered in late summer with heads of greenish pink flowers. 30cm.

'Purple Emperor'. Selected by Graham Gough. Matt leaves, grey-purple when young, intensifying to rich purple. Differs from *S. telephium* 'Mohrchen' in having paler flowers contrasting with dark buds and calyxes, with new flower buds in every leaf axil, prolonging season. Late summer. 60cm.

'Red Cauli'. Aptly named unusual form with dense red flower heads during late August through to September. Attractive purple-grey foliage on dark stems. Full sun and a well drained soil. 40cm.

'Ruby Glow'. Forms a rosette of lax stems, which carry purple-grey succulent foliage, topped with clusters of wine-red starry flowers in late summer. 25cm.

spathulifolium. Forms close mats of fleshy purple-red rosettes, covered with a waxy bloom. 8cm.

spathulifolium 'Cape Blanco'. Identical except for colour. The fleshy rosettes, silver-grey in winter become blue-grey in summer, overlaid with white bloom which intensifies with drought. Both have heads of soft yellow flowers. 8cm.

spectabile 'Brilliant'. Large flat heads of bright mauve-pink flowers, humming with bees in late summer. 45cm.

spectabile 'Iceberg'. Clumps of palest-green, fleshy leaves stand out on the border edge from spring onwards. In late September each stem is topped with wide flat heads of greenish-white starry flowers. 45cm.

spurium 'Atropurpureum'. There are several red-leafed forms, this one seems extra good, wine-red foliage scarcely needs the rose-red flowers. 10cm.

spurium 'Green Mantle'. I value this for the fresh effect it makes with bright green rosettes of fleshy leaves forming dense ground cover on poor soil in open situations. 10cm.

spurium 'Variegatum'. Trailing stems are studded with rosettes of round, succulent leaves strongly variegated pink, cream and green. 10cm.

'Stewed Rhubarb Mountain'. Creamy dark and light pink flowers are the feature of this aptly named stonecrop. Grey-green foliage is often purple tinted. Full sun. 50cm.

telephium 'Hester'. Similar to *S. telephium* subsp. *maximum* 'Atropurpureum', but more compact, with densely flowered heads. 60cm.

telephium 'Karfunkelstein'. Roughly translates to mean glimmering stone. A wonderful name for one of the best of the more recent cultivars. Young growth with a purple-pink sheen. Masses of small individual pink flower heads during late summer. Best in full sun. 50cm.

telephium 'Matrona'. Selected from a batch of seedlings by Ewald Hugin, first class plantsman from Freiburg, Germany. Stout upstanding stems stained maroon, clothed in fleshy, purple-flushed leaves, carry wide, flat heads of pale rose-pink starry flowers. The colour of the entire plant and fresh succulent effect in dry summer conditions is outstanding. August. 75cm.

telephium 'Matrona' Darker form. A sport which appeared here on a clump of S. 'Matrona' with a distinctly darker shade of pink flower heads 70cm.

telephium subsp. maximum 'Atropurpureum'. From spring to autumn a dramatic feature plant. Thick fleshy leaves of a bloomy purple-brown make a dark accent. In late summer the flat heads of small starry flowers combine a rosy-pink and brown, while the chocolate-brown seedheads still add interest. 75cm.

telephium 'Mohrchen'. Glossy young, olive-green leaves mature to shining purple, when they are almost smothered in August with dense heads of dark buds opening creamy-pink flowers fading to deep coral pink. Lovely contrast with dark foliage. Makes shorter, more compact plants than *S. t.* subsp. *maximum* 'Atropurpureum'. A splendid plant in August, loved by bees. 40cm.

telephium 'Munstead Red'. Purple stained stems clothed in blue-grey leaves carry wide flat heads of raspberry-red flowers first opening in mid-August. Quantities of new shoots bearing unopened buds appear from leaf-axils, from ground-level upwards, to make a continuous show well into late autumn. By late September plants look like glowing coals, with many shades of red, from bright tones of fresh flowers to deep bronze-red of mature heads. 30cm.

telephium 'Strawberries and Cream'. A lovely variety with dark tinted, sharply toothed foliage and clusters of starry, dark pink and white flowers in late summer. 50cm.

telephium subsp. ruprechtii. A superb plant for a sunny site in any well drained soil. Fleshy grey-purple leaves flushed pink, pink stems and flower buds open clusters of creamy-yellow flowers and maturing to reddish-brown seedheads. Handsome for months, from spring to autumn. 40cm.

telephium subsp. ruprechtii 'Pink Dome'. Differs from *S. t.* subsp. *ruprechtii* in that the pewter foliage is suffused with warm tones, as are the flowers, which are a combination of soft cream and pink. As the terminal flowers fade to brown seedheads fresh flowers are produced all along the stems making an attractive effect into autumn. 60cm.

'Vera Jameson'. Short, gracefully arching stems carry bloom-coated purple, fleshy leaves, with heads of dusty-pink flowers in late summer. A most fortunate hybrid introduced by Joe Elliot. 25cm.

SELINUM wallichianum. A tall erect cow parsley-like perennial with finely cut, bright green leaves. Tiny star shaped, white flowers in flat umbels from midsummer to early autumn. Best in a well drained, yet reasonably moist soil in sun or light shade, a dark background helps define the flowers. We have two forms of this, one of which sets seed and it is from this form we offer seed grown plants. 1.2m.

The other form we grow and rightly or not call *S. tenuifolium* is sterile and has to be propagated by offsets which it frugally produces. It is much more refined, maybe it is E.A. Bowles's "Queen of the Umbellifers" as quoted by Graham Stuart Thomas. We sometimes have it available if you ask.

SEMPERVIVUM. We have an interesting and wide selection available on the Nursery. Most are named although for a few I have not yet found reliable names to fit; some grow as wide across as a saucer, making handsome feature plants, others are tiny, suitable for sink, trough gardens, or crevices in the rock-garden. Among the larger ones the texture is mostly waxen or smooth as marble, apple-green rosettes tipped mahogany, shadowed with purple, bronze-red or green-tipped rose. The small ones are also found in warm shades of bronze and mahogany. But there are, as well, the 'cobweb'-covered forms, and those with incurved leaves edged with bristly hairs.

SENECIO cineraria 'White Diamond'. A fine feature plant for dry sunny places in well-drained soil. Makes a low shrub-like plant clothed in handsome broadly-cut leaves which look as if they were cut from greyish-white felt, becoming whiter as the soil gets drier. Heads of yellow daisy-like flowers are best removed to encourage new leafy shoots. 60cm.
viravira. Fern-like white foliage on lax white stems, with heads of groundsel-like flowers, the palest sulphur-yellow. Needs a protected, warm site. 1m.

SERRATULA seoanei. This little knapweed comes as fresh as a daisy at the end of autumn. Small, wiry plants clothed in finely-cut leaves, produce exquisite mauve-pink fuzzy heads when there is little else to please. Attractive seedheads when left standing into the winter. Full sun, fertile soil. 40cm.

SIDALCEA 'My Love'. This elegant plant forms upright, branching stems crowded with pale-pink silky flowers, much like small single hollyhocks, flowering for weeks, produced from a succession of side branches. Mid-late summer. 1m.
'Rose Queen'. Strong self-supporting, branched stems are furnished with round scalloped leaves at the base, changing to finely cut, hen's foot-shaped leaves towards the top, crowded with long spires of deep rose-pink translucent flowers. In flower for weeks, produced from succession of side branches. Mid-late summer. 1.4m.
'William Smith'. Dusky redish-pink flowers on tall upright stems during July-August. Best cut down when over as it tends to flop. Full sun and a good soil. 1.2m.

SIDERITIS syriaca. For warm, well-drained gardens. Low woody stems support rosettes of white woolly leaves from which emerge in midsummer, long, graceful flower heads rather like *Stachys byzantina*, but with small lemon-yellow flowers tucked among white 'cotton wool'. 30cm.

SILENE dioica 'Flore Pleno'. Deep rose-pink campion flowers, lightly double unroll to reveal white centres during June-July. Average soil, in sun. 45cm.
dioica 'Minikin'. Another selected form of pink campion. Tight healthy rosettes of slightly woolly leaves, crowded in early summer with short-stemmed pink campion flowers form an eye-catching border edge. 40cm.
keiskei. Forms a mesh of wiry branching stems smothered with dark-tipped pointed leaves and buds, opening vivid, rose-pink campion-like flowers. Late summer into autumn. 25cm.
schafta. Easy and valued small plant for late summer into autumn. Low mounds of small green leaves carry 15cm stems of rose-pink flowers for weeks.
schafta 'Shell Pink'. Deserves to be more widely grown. Forms a low cushion of tangled stems set with small, pointed, hairy leaves, transformed in mid-late summer when smothered with pale pink flowers, whose widely spaced petals create a starry effect. Durable and hardy, for well-drained soil in sun. 15cm.

uniflora 'Druett's Variegated'. Each tiny rosette of grey-blue leaves is firmly edged cream, creating a bright effect where contrast is needed. Single white flowers in early summer. 5cm.
uniflora 'Robin Whitebreast'. Pure double white flowers, large as carnations and not unlike, tumble from spreading mats of waxy-grey foliage. Best when flopping over an edge. Early summer. 5cm.

SINACALIA tangutica. Dark, almost black-stained stems carry prettily carved leaves topped in August-September, with long pyramidal shaped heads of small, cool-yellow flowers which develop into pale fluffy seedheads. Invasive, but where space permits, one of the pleasures of autumn. 1.4m.

SISYRINCHIUM angustifolium. Blue-eyed grass. Clumps of little grassy leaves are topped by satiny deep-blue flowers clustered on short stems, in midsummer. 10cm.
'Californian Skies'. Large sky-blue flowers, free-flowering. 15cm.
idahoense. Impressive, with good-sized, deep blue flowers on erect stems, produced for weeks on end in midsummer. 20cm.
'Quaint and Queer'. Curiously attractive chocolate and cream flowers spangle stiff, branching, sprawling stems for months, throughout midsummer to autumn. 40cm.
'Sapphire'. Beautiful blue eyed grass with lovely large sapphire blue flowers held above evergreen clumps of short iris-like foliage, from late spring to early autumn. 20cm
striatum. Valued for the contrast of grey-green iris-like leaves among grey and silver plants. Attractive too are slender spires of small pale-yellow flowers which rise above the leaves. 60cm.
striatum 'Aunt May'. Originated at Chevithorn, Tiverton, Devon. The iris-like leaves are boldly striped with creamy-yellow, making a perfect foil for blue flowers such as the shorter veronicas. Brightest when freshly divided. 45cm.

SOLANUM crispum 'Glasnevin'. Forms a fast growing semi-evergreen shrub against a warm wall. Every new shoot tipped with a large loose cluster of violet-blue flowers, like those of the potato. In flower from midsummer to autumn. Long unwieldy shoots need to be shortened back after main flowering, the basic framework secured against a wall. 3m.
laxum 'Creche ar Pape'. Grown to perfection in the Exotic Garden at Great Dixter and now for several years on a south wall facing our nursery this hardy form will flower all summer long given a sunny sheltered wall, fence or other support. Might need a hard spring prune if gets out of hand or damaged by winter. Lovely chalky white, blue shaded flowers drip from the plant during late summer. 3m plus.

SOLIDAGO. Is the Latin name for Goldenrod. I am not keen on the tall gawky ones which grow wild with Michaelmas daisies in north west America but I do find good use for some of the smaller, neat-growing forms.
caesia. An unusual Goldenrod, producing many dark tinted stems, set with tiny pointed leaves, and small bundles of fluffy yellow flowers, like mimosa, almost the entire length of the stems, in late summer-autumn, part sun-shade. 75cm.
glomerata. In deep rich soil forms a fresh looking light green leafy plant carrying spires of yellow daisy-like flowers. A good vertical mid-border. August-September. 90cm.
× luteus 'Lemore'. Has larger individual florets in its massed flower heads, of a lovely shade of pale lemon-yellow, attractive for cut flowers in late summer. 75cm.
'Queenie'. A good edging plant for late summer, dense heads of bright yellow. Late summer. 20cm.

rugosa. From north eastern America. 1.2m sturdy stems support arched lateral branches which subdivide to form huge airy sprays of tiny yellow daisy flowers, creating an elegant fountain-like effect in late autumn. Needs retentive soil.

STACHYS byzantina 'Big Ears'. Has broader, bolder leaves than the type, not so heavily felted, so has a less 'frosty' appearance. A good hard wearing carpeting plant in poor sunny conditions. 30cm.

byzantina 'Cotton Boll'. (My name for this unusual form as I cannot trace another) produces round, silvery-white velvety bobbles along a stiff tall stem. Dries perfectly, unusual and lovely for dried arrangements. 60cm.

byzantina 'Primrose Heron'. The new leaf clusters in spring and early summer are pale yellow, making very effective contrast in the Gravel Garden, slowly becoming grey when dry conditions oblige the plant to protect itself with fine, soft pile. 40cm in flower. Introduced by Sue Gemmell.

byzantina 'Silver Carpet'. This non-flowering form spends its energy creating carpets of velvet-textured, silver-grey 'Lambs Ears', ideal edging for a sunny border, or planted beneath roses. 12cm.

macrantha. Makes slowly spreading clumps of rich green, scallop-edged leaves, while rosy-mauve funnel-shaped flowers in whorls are held on erect brancing stems in June. A lovely plant for retentive soil. 60cm.

macrantha 'Alba'. Above light-green leaves stand whorls of lovely pure-white flowers, creating a good vertical effect. Long flowering, cuts well. Midsummer. 60cm.

officinalis 'Rosea Superba'. Basal leaves make dense mats of bright green crinkled leaves. Above them stand many stems topped with close-packed heads of small rose-pink flowers, in midsummer. An edging plant for retentive soil. 45cm.

STEMMACANTHA centaureoides. syn. *Centaurea pulchra* 'Major'. A most beautiful plant. From a base of strong silver-grey cut leaves, rise stiff stems bearing large knobbly buds of overlapping transparent silver scales which open into striking cyclamen-pink flowers, midsummer. 90cm.

STERNBERGIA lutea. Often mistaken for an autumn flowering crocus this Mediterranean bulb requires full sun and good drainage for the large yellow goblet-like flowers to emerge in September quickly followed by glossy deep green foliage. Slow to establish. 15cm.

STOKESIA laevis. Large, cornflower-like blooms soft blue with creamy-white centres. Good edge of border plant in sun. Mid-late summer. 40cm.

laevis 'Alba'. Out of a batch of white seedlings we selected this as being the finest form and propagate it vegetatively. Its large white, cornflower-shaped flowers make it a fine feature for the border edge. Sun, retentive soil. 40cm.

STROBILANTHES atropurpurea. A handsome and unusual plant. Thriving in sun and any soil it sends up many branching stems clothed with dark green hairy leaves. In late summer it becomes a mass of purple-blue hooded flowers remaining a feature for weeks. 1.2m.

STYLOPHORUM diphyllum. A north east American woodland plant for leaf-mould soil and semi-shade. Has divided leaves, oak leaf in shape, slightly mottled above, grey beneath. Just above them hang four-petalled, silky, yellow poppy-like flowers in May. Large green, prickly seed pods, rather like gooseberries, hang hidden beneath the leaves in late summer. 45cm.

SYMPHYOTRICHUM. The new name for this group of former Asters.

ericoides 'Esther'. Is irresistible during October and into November. Each plant makes a low, loose bouquet, composed of thousands of small lilac-rose flowers lit with a green eye. 75cm.

ericoides f. prostratus 'Snow Flurry'. I originally brought this home many years ago after a lecture tour of the eastern United States. Although I sent plants back for identification, no one could source it. Subsequently, by a consensus of opinion, it became 'Snow Flurry', since it produces ground-hugging stems, much-branched, to form a low sprawling cushion, smothered in autumn with tiny white daisies, resembling a snow drift. Perfect edge of border plant in retentive soil in sun. 20cm.

novae-angliae. From damp sunny meadows and along swamp edges in the north east United States and Canada. This is the hairy parent of many garden hybrids, needing sunlight to open its in-curved petals, but producing healthy disease-free offspring with tall stiff sturdy stems, up to 2m. The type has mauve flowers.

novae-angliae 'Andenken an Alma Pötschke'. Stiff leafy stems carry heads of bright cherry-red flowers with slightly curling petals, an outstanding colour in the autumn garden. 90cm.

novi-belgii. From swampy places where it is frequent near the Atlantic from Newfoundland to Georgia. It has smooth green leaves on slender elegant stems (1.2m) topped with large pyramidal sprays of cool blue flowers. Self-sown seedlings vary; some are rather wishy-washy. Modern named varieties tend to have developed the flower at the expense of the plant - too large, too double flowers proving overweight for the stems which have to be supported. But the colours are often lovely, from white through shades of pink to lavenders and blue.

novi-belgii 'Heinz Richard'. Forms low compact clumps of foliage smothered in late summer with large semi-double, cyclamen-pink flowers with fresh yellow eyes. 30cm.

novi-belgii 'Kristina'. A favourite cushion plant for the border edge. Densely set clusters of dark green leaves are buried beneath pure white double daisy flowers. 45cm.

novi-belgii 'Purple Dome'. Makes a compact, long-lasting display of rich purple flowers. 60cm.

pilosus var. pringlei. Is similar to *A. pringlei* 'Monte Cassino', but taller and more erect, forming a bouquet of stiff, wiry stems, much branched, spangled with white stars, the latest of autumn treasures. 90cm.

pilosus var. pringlei 'Monte Cassino'. With starry white flowers obliterating tiny narrow leaves on much branched wiry stems. This creates a snowy effect in late autumn. 60cm.

SYMPHYTUM asperum. A stately plant set with leafy branching stems, each weighted with drooping clusters of dark ruby-red buds opening intense gentian-blue bell-like flowers. For retentive soil, sun, or part shade. 90cm.

caucasicum. Clusters of grey-green pointed leaves, colonise by underground stems, horribly invasive in the wrong place, but where allowable it is one of the delights of spring, with arching stems carrying clusters of sky-blue tubular flowers. 60cm.

'Goldsmith'. Selected by that observant plantsman Eric Smith, this form has low mounds of dark green leaves, handsomely suffused with cream and yellow. 25cm.

'Hidcote Blue'. I value this form and the following one highly, as ground-cover between shrubs. Each makes weed-proof clusters of rough-textured green leaves. In late spring-early summer. *S.* 'Hidcote Blue' produces branching stems which unroll croziers of red buds changing to blue and white tubular flowers. 45cm.

'Hidcote Pink'. Has no blue in it, pink and white flowers only. A grouping several feet across, in full flower, is a lovely sight. 45cm.

ibericum. This is a most useful plant making impenetrable weed-cover in shade among shrubs. It forms mounds of rough dark green leaves, spreading by underground shoots. In spring before the new leaves are fully developed the fiddle-neck clusters of flowers change from burnt-orange buds to creamy-yellow bells. 30cm.

ibericum 'All Gold'. Handsome feature plant for woodland conditions, or between shrubs. Large dock-shaped leaves 45cm long are entirely suffused yellow when young, gradually maturing to a big green mound. Branched stems carry lilac tubular flowers early midsummer. 45cm.

ibericum 'Blaueglocken'. From Herr Pagels, Germany. Forms spreading clumps of fresh green, heavily veined leaves. Upright branching stems tipped with croziers of coral-red buds open narrow tubular flowers of light Cambridge blue. For retentive soil among shrubs, or in the wild garden. May-June. 40cm.

TANACETUM corymbosum 'Festafel'. Above neat mounds of finely-cut, fern-like leaves stand stiff stems carrying open bouquets of yellow-green-eyed white daisies, good to pick and in the border. Flowers in midsummer and a few in autumn. 75cm.

densum subsp. amani. A most charming spreader in dry sunny places. Forms low mounds of silvery-white foliage like tiny Prince of Wales feathers, or finely cut jersey cloth. 20cm.

niveum. Is a delight in hot, dry, sunny situations. It overwinters as seedlings or as a mature woody framework bearing much divided aromatic leaves. In summer as conditions become drier, the leaves turn grey, as they become coated with fine grey hairs. By midsummer the plant erupts into a large bouquet of small, white, daisy-like flowers. Lovely scattered among purple and white campions, *Lychnis coronaria*, and other grey plants. 50cm.

parthenium 'Aureum'. Lime-yellow, finely divided foliage throughout the year, charming to grow or pick. Sprays of tiny white daisies, throughout summer. 30cm.

parthenium 'White Bonnet'. Charming cottage garden plant. Sprays of small double white daisies, green eyed. Lovely to pick from midsummer to autumn. 60cm.

ptarmiciflorum 'Silver Feather'. The whitest of all drought-tolerant plants. A woody framework supports the lacy effect of narrow, fern-like leaves and stems all whitened with dense felt. Yellow daisy flowers a bonus. Treat as annual in cold districts. Has survived several winters here in well drained soil. 45cm.

vulgare. Tansy. I have found this such a reliable performer in making running patches of finely cut, aromatic foliage soon producing stout stems carrying heads of double yellow flowers. 1.2m.

TELLIMA grandiflora Odorata Group. Scented form. Foliage not so deeply coloured in winter as the other tellimas, but the flowers smell deliciously of old-fashioned pinks, scenting the air for yards around. 60cm.

grandiflora 'Purpurteppich'. Differs from *T. grandiflora* Rubra Group in that the leaves become veined and stained with maroon in summer, while the flowers have dark stems and pink-stained rims to slightly larger green bells. May-June. 60cm.

grandiflora Rubra Group. An all-the-year-round foliage plant. Spreading clumps of round scalloped leaves, green above, purple beneath, changing to rich red-purples and bronze in winter. In early summer there are tall spikes of pink-fringed green bells. 60cm.

All tellimas need humus-rich soil in part shade.

TEUCRIUM hircanicum. Caucasian germander. A useful vertical for virtually any soil or situation. Rather course, sage-like foliage. Each stem producing a spike of dusky purple-red flowers during mid to late summer. Associate well with silvers and greys of different shapes and textures. The seedheads stand well although at the risk of over abundant seeding. 60cm.

× **lucidrys.** Low bushy plants clothed in dark green glossy leaves carry short spires of small pink flowers in early summer. A fresh-looking accent plant among greys in dry situations. 30cm.

scorodonia 'Crispum Marginatum'. Making ground-cover under shrubs, this unusual form of the Wood sage has green suede-textured leaves whose ruffled edges are rimmed with white. The spikes of tiny cream-lipped flowers are another charm in midsummer. 30cm.

THALICTRUM aquilegiifolium. From a basal clump of grey-green leaves, finely divided, slender purple stems ascend carrying pretty fans of leaves, topped with large heads of fluffy, rosy-lilac flowers. Seed heads are good, green or dried. Early to midsummer. 1.4m.

aquilegiifolium var. album. The white flowered form often with dark stems. Comes true from seed. 1.4m.

delavayi. This very elegant plant needs a cool place sheltered from wind, perhaps supported among shrubs. Small deep lilac flowers, enclosing tufts of cream stamens dangle in airy-fairy fashion from wide, branching heads. Exquisite in late summer. 1.5m.

delavayi 'Album'. Beautiful white form of *T. delavayi*, with paler green finely divided leaves. Both need rich soil. 1.4m.

delavayi 'Hewitt's Double'. From a base of divided grey-green leaves purple-tinted stems hold aloft huge airy sprays of tiny mauve pom-pom-shaped flowers in late summer. The effect is magical but needs a little care to protect it from battering wind. Plant where it can be supported or sheltered by neighbours. 1.4m.

'Elin'. Attractive, dark foliage emerges in early spring and the plant soon races up above head height as the foliage settles down to a more glaucous green. Flowers create a haze of dusky lavender-pink flowers. Might need support if grown in part shade but seems sturdy enough in an open sunny position. 2m.

flavum subsp. glaucum. A strong stately plant with blue-grey foliage and stems topped with fluffy pale yellow flowers. Looks good in contrast with miscanthus and ligularia by the water-side. Midsummer. 1.5m.

kiusianum. This little woodland plant from Japan will thread itself through light leaf-mould soil, or a cool raised bed in part shade. Sprays of tiny rounded leaves and heads of fluffy rosy-mauve flowers stand only a few inches above soil level. This improved form originated in Kew. 15cm.

pubescens. Tall strong stems carry throughout their length much divided side branches bearing fluffy bundles of creamy-white flowers, altogether a delightful vertical effect rising above lower plants. Needs careful placing to avoid being toppled by wind, but worth the effort. Midsummer. 1.2m.

THERMOPSIS lupinoides. A lupin-like plant, with almost black, slightly hairy stems carrying narrow heads of pale lemon-yellow pea-flowers held in conspicuous dark green calyxes. The stems are clothed in trifoliate leaves. The total effect is very handsome. 60cm.

THYMUS 'Coccineus'. Dark neat foliage, rich crimson flowers. 2.5cm.

doerfleri. Grey narrow wedge-shaped leaves arranged in stiff rosettes, flowers pink. 2.5cm.

'Doone Valley'. An exceptionally attractive thyme. Close mats of dark green foliage heavily marked with gold. Large heads of mauve flowers in late summer. 8cm.

'Golden King'. Bushy upright thyme, brilliant with golden-edged leaves. 30cm.

'Hartington Silver'. Spreads a pale carpet of tiny leaves with yellow margins, making a bright contrast to other thymes. 2cm.

herba-barona. Caraway-scented thyme. Wiry mats of dark green leaves heavily scented of caraway seed. Pink and mauve flowers. 10cm.

herba-barona 'Lemon-scented'. Collected by us in Corsica. The strongest of fresh lemon scents. 10cm.

longicaulis. Quickly forms wide spreading mats of thin wiry stems, with small scented green leaves forming total ground cover. Completely covered in early summer with clustered heads of rosy-mauve flowers, much admired. 10cm.

neiceffii. Tantalisingly lovely, will fall over a rock or wall like water, making long lax prostrate shoots covered with narrow blue-grey leaves. Smothered with mauvy-pink flowers, it is enchanting. 2cm.

polytrichus subsp. britanicus. syn. *T. pseudolanuginosus*. Wooly thyme. Grey-green prostrate mats of minute woolly leaves, irresistible to touch. 5cm.

pulegioides 'Bertram Anderson'. Makes sprawling mats of the brightest gold leaves. Regular trimming encourages fresh growth. 5cm.

'Redstart'. Forms a mat of dark evergreen leaves, with rosy-red flowers from late spring to midsummer. 5cm.

serpyllum var. albus. Dense flat mats of emerald green, starred with white flowers. 2.5cm.

serpyllum 'Minor'. Minute woolly leaves pressed to the ground like moss, speckled with silvery-pink flowers. 2cm.

serpyllum 'Pink Chintz'. Less prostrate, making loose cushions of soft woolly leaves smothered in heads of pale pink flowers. 10cm.

'Silver Queen'. Makes attractive small bushes of prettily variegated grey-green and silver leaves. 30cm.

vulgaris. The scented cooking thyme, makes low dense bushes of dark green leaves, very handsome when full of pale flowers and humming bees. 30cm.

TIARELLA cordifolia. Running trails of pretty pointed green leaves form complete cover. In spring a mass of foaming creamy-white flowers spikes. Early summer. 30cm.

cordifolia 'Slick Rock'. Appears to be a diminutive form of *T. cordifolia*. Tiny green heart shaped leaves with serrated edges form a ground covering carpet beneath ferns, woodland grasses, etc. Has short spires of pink buds opening white starry flowers in spring. 5cm.

'Iron Butterfly'. Deeply dissected green leaves with a distinctly fingered pattern of dark maroon. Flowers are scented, white with a hint of pink and are borne prolifically above the foliage during spring and early summer. Makes clumps of year round interest, lovely with spring bulbs. 30cm.

'Jeepers Creepers'. Lovely neat plant with a trailing, creeping habit. It has pretty white foamy flowers on long spikes during late spring and from then, the deeply cut maroon foliage turns to red with pink tones in the autumn. Another useful runner for shady areas. 25cm.

'Ninja'. Has bronze-tinted leaves with deeply cut edges, producing throughout summer spires of fluffy white flowers opening from pink buds. 30cm.

'Pinwheel'. Has marked lobed leaves with veins lightly picked out in dark brown. Clump forming. 40cm.

'Tiger Stripe'. Has light green palmate leaves variously blotched along the veins as if with a sponge dipped in brown paint, fading with age to warm rosy shades in winter. Clump forming. 40cm.

wherryi 'Bronze Beauty'. Was collected in the wild by Chris Brickell. He gave it to Elizabeth Strangman who first introduced it. Maple-shaped leaves with serrated edges show both pale green and deep reddish-bronze colouring. Dusty-pink buds on dark stems open palest pink starry flowers. Not invasive like *T. cordifolia,* this plant and *T. wherryi* 'Green Velvet' make slowly-spreading clumps. May-June. 25cm.
wherryi 'Green Velvet'. This also has delicate spires of starry white flowers, but the leaves are like shadowed green velvet, exquisite for months. Midsummer. 25cm.

TOLMIEA menziesii. Another ground-cover plant among shrubs. Tiarella-like in foliage with spires of small coppery-brown flowers, while the leaves have the endearing habit of forming new little plants sitting on top of the old leaves, which root when pressed into the soil. 30cm.
menziesii 'Taff's Gold'. Random speckling is not always attractive but in this case each leaf is so lightened by the irregular freckling of green and primrose it is a delight in shady places. Good in hanging baskets or on window sills. 30cm.

TRACHYSTEMON orientalis. Superb spreading ground-cover in dense shade. Makes an important feature with large healthy-looking rough green leaves forming overlapping mounds. Curious blue borage-like flowers on pink naked stems, in spring, before the leaves take over. 60cm.

TRADESCANTIA. Spiderwort. A will grow anywhere plant with lush green stems carrying curving strap-shaped leaves which form a cradle where they meet the stem. Out of this tumble an endless succession of three-petalled flowers all summer. Be quick to cut down as they tend to self seed.
Andersoniana Group 'Blue Stone'. A clear bright blue. 45cm.
Andersoniana Group 'Charlotte'. A new introduction with clusters of extra-large, soft-amethyst flowers, freely produced. 60cm.
Andersoniana Group 'Innocence'. Pure white. 45cm.
Andersoniana Group 'Osprey'. White with blue centre. 45cm.
Andersoniana Group 'Zwanenburg Blue'. Large deep blue flowers. 45cm.
virginiana 'Brevicaulis'. Under this name I have a charming coloured form which is soft cyclamen-pink. 45cm.

TRICYRTIS 'Empress'. This Toad lily hybrid makes a tall upright clump, topped from late July-September with branched spikes of flowers with a white background heavily covered with dark purple speckles. 75cm.
formosana. A fascinating plant for shady places. Its stems are clothed with corrugated oval leaves topped in autumn with sprays of small lily-like flowers, pale purple, freckled with dark purple spots. 75cm.
'Hototogisu'. This form has unspotted flowers of an intense light mauve-purple. Requires a retentive soil in full or part shade. Running habit. Interestingly hototogisu is the Japanese common name for all tricyrtis. 1m.
ohsumiensis. An exotic-looking plant for cool, shady conditions and damp leaf-mould soil. Pairs of rich-green, pointed leaves facing opposite ways are wrapped round the stem, each forming a cradle for butter-yellow, lily-like flowers 5cm across, faintly peppered with red. Lovely with *Adiantum pedatum* 'Imbricatum' the prettiest, low-growing, lacy fern. 60cm.
'Shimone'. Many stems clothed in deeply veined, pointed leaves carry a profusion of upturned white flowers lightly speckled with purple, creating a lilac effect. Still good in mid November. 90cm.

'**Tojen**'. Another handsome form. Branched, arching, purple stems, clothed in rich-green, deeply veined leaves, carry multitudes of unspotted flowers which open wide mauve-tipped petals to show a white centre marked with yellow dots. Long succession of buds to come. September. 1m.

'**White Towers**'. Green felted leaves are set alternately along 75cm stems. Each leaf base holds short-stemmed buds, opening unspotted creamy-white flowers with yellow ring at base of petals.

TRIFOLIUM pratense 'Susan Smith'. When I first began my garden, Susan and Harry, (with his camera) were soon regular visitors. This pretty clover has emerald-green leaves so finely netted with yellow, they appear quite pale, creating good contrast in a cool place, preferably heavy soil. Pink clover flowers midsummer. 12cm.

repens 'Purpurascens Quadrifolium'. This clover is valued for its foliage, mostly four-leafed, and of a striking chocolate colour. Quickly makes effective ground-cover in retentive soil. 10cm.

TRILLIUM. These lovely woodland treasures need cool shady conditions with plenty of leafmould in soil that does not dry out. They are so called because each stem carries three leaves, three calyxes, and three petals, all joined together at the top of each bare stem.

chloropetalum. Selected form from Edinburgh Botanical Gardens. Poised above its platform of three softly mottled green leaves stand upright 3 petalled flowers, a beautiful soft beetroot red as the light falls through them. 30cm plus, when established.

chloropetalum rubrum. Short green stems support dark mottled leaves centred with long narrow calyxes and narrow purple tinted petals. 40cm.

chloropetalum white. We are proud to offer this plant, since my first stock from seed took 8 years to flower! Three broad, wavy edged, plain green leaves form a handsome 'collar' more than 25cm across, setting off the large creamy-white three- petalled flower. It makes a dramatic feature where contrast is needed among small-leafed plants, such as *Tiarella*, or the golden-leafed Creeping Jenny. Spring. 40cm.

cuneatum. Mixed forms. Seedlings vary considerably in size, leaf colour and flower quality. They have large triangular leaves variously marbled in shades of green, centred with short narrow purple stained calyxes and stemless wine coloured petals fiercely upright. Effective contrast above mat plants in a shady garden. 30cm.

cuneatum. Beth's special form. Has the most beautiful leaf of all trilliums. Poised on top of 25cm stems are three large leaves marbled in shade of chocolate, olive and sage-green, the colours slowly fading with age. Like a half closed tulip, three deep-plum petals complete a perfect combination.

erectum f. albiflorum. Strongly scented, nodding white flowers with conspicuous pointed bracts, are pinned together with a dark purple ovary. 35cm.

erectum Beige. Longer than the type. Strongly veined green on outside petals, more faint within, a pale beige effect. 30cm.

grandiflorum. The Wake robin, the best known Trillium. It makes a dome-shaped plant of ribbed and shining leaves which set off the pure white funnel-shaped flowers poised above them. 30cm.

grandiflorum 'Flore Pleno'. Breathtaking, perfectly formed double flowers of pearly whiteness are poised above three rich-green, pointed leaves. Our stock came from Alan Bloom of Bressingham in Norfolk. A treasure for cool damp shade. 30cm.

luteum. 40cm stems, dark brown at the base carry three faintly mottled pointed leaves pinned together with a three-petalled yellowish-green flower, effective among the small fern, *Cystopteris fragilis* and the hardy purple orchid, *Dactylorhiza foliosa.*

rivale. Another gem for the right conditions. Exquisite shell-pink flowers nod above a carpet of green pointed leaves held on short stems. Needs cool, moist leaf-mould soil and adequate rainfall. Dies down in midsummer. Where suited spreads and seeds. 15cm.

TRITONIA disticha subsp. rubrolucens. Enchanting rose-pink flowers, like tiny lilies on fine wiry branching stems, lovely to pick or enjoy in the garden, from late summer to autumn. 75cm.

TROLLIUS. Globe flower. Elegant moisture loving perennials, wonderful with the blue Siberian iris.

chinensis. This very distinctive globe flower has a mass of orange stamens, and slashed petals filling orange bowls. Midsummer. 90cm.

× **cultorum 'Alabaster'.** This globe flower has cream flowers. Exquisite but not so robust as the yellow forms. 60cm.

× **cultorum 'Feuertroll'.** Forms strong clumps of handsome cut leaves. Tall branching stems carry a long display of warm orange flowers in early summer. 90cm.

× **cultorum 'Helios'.** Another robust variety with clear yellow globular flowers. May-June. 90cm.

europaeus. The wild form of globe flower is unbeatable with its exquisite pale lemon globes over mounds of glossy, cut foliage. Early summer. 75cm.

pumilus. Glossy, open, cup-shaped flowers stand on short stems above neat clumps of rich-green, divided leaves. Lovely in midsummer on a damp edge, with blue *Mysotis scorpioides* 'Mermaid'. 25cm.

stenopetalus. Magnificent large flowers, semi-double, clear shining yellow, with central ring of yellow stamens set off by bold healthy green foliage. Retentive, moist soil, sun. Flowering much later than those above. June-July. 75cm.

TROPAEOLUM pentaphyllum. An unusual perennial relative of the nasturtium. It makes lengthy trails of tiny round leaves, deeply scalloped. Festooned in midsummer with small spurred flowers in soft rose-pink and green. When established travels underground searching for a wall or shrub to scramble over. Needs a warm well-drained site in full sun.

polyphyllum. Rare and covetable. Long trails densely clothed with small blue-grey, deeply lobed leaves with clusters of small yellow nasturtium-like flowers creating a garland along its entire length. Prefers light soil which its underground runners can penetrate and full sun.

tuberosum var. lineamaculatum 'Ken Aslet'. Long trails of small, round, lobed leaves carry long-spurred orange and scarlet flowers in autumn. For a warm wall or fence or shrub that can be spared as a support, in well-drained soil. 2m.

TULBAGHIA violacea. Above upright clusters of narrow strap-shaped leaves stand bare stems carrying allium-like heads of soft lilac-mauve flowers throughout summer until autumn. For a warm site, well-drained soil. Pot up a clump to keep safe for winter, cover the rest with protective mulch. 60cm.

violacea 'Silver Lace'. This is the variegated form. Its grey-green, strap-shaped leaves are veined with white creating a pretty pale effect together with allium-like heads of soft, lilac-mauve flowers throughout summer and into autumn. Not reliably frost hardy and best treated as a pot-plant. 40cm.

violacea var robustior. Of greater vigour and height than *T. violacea.* soon forms clumps of narrow greyish green leaves and has a very long flowering season with agapanthus-like stems of fragrant lilac flowers. Frost hardy here over many years. 60cm.

TULIPA sprengeri. The last wild tulip to flower, opening end of May, beginning of June. Slim olive-green buds go unnoticed, until one sunny morning you are startled to see wide-open, dazzling scarlet, pointed petals on 40cm stems. Good near acid green euphorbias. After several years they are now seeding around, taking approx four years to flower.

UROSPERMUM dalechampii. Beautiful large lemon-yellow dandelion flowers are poised above rosettes of grey-green, toothed leaves. Good in spring and again in late summer. Has long lasting silky seedheads. 30cm.

UVULARIA. Merrybells. North American woodland plants, related to Solomon's seal, (Polygonatum), needing cool leafy soil. They look right standing above carpets of *Tiarella cordifolia,* or *Phlox stolonifera,* in dampish places, in part shade.
grandiflora. From arching stems dangle daffodil-yellow, bell-shaped flowers with long twisting pointed petals held well above leaves clasping the lower part of the stem in late April. 45cm.
grandiflora var. pallida. A choice treasure. Pale primrose-yellow dangling flowers twist and open more widely than those of *U. perfoliata.* 45cm.
perfoliata. Comes into flower as *U. grandiflora* is fading, with pale creamy-yellow flowers, pale green leaves, on shorter stems. 30cm.

VALERIANA officinalis. Forms a delicate column 1.3m tall of branching stems topped with panicles of tiny white star-like flowers. Planted here in heavy but not wet soil it has made an arresting picture reflected in one of my ponds, together with the silvery-green plumes of the tufted hair grass, *Deschampsia cespitosa* 'Goldschleier', a delightful partnership for weeks throughout summer.
phu 'Aurea'. Spring foliage is clear yellow, a feature for weeks while daffodils come and go. By June the foliage has turned green, supporting almost bare branching stems topped with clusters of fluffy, creamy-white flowers, making a graceful vertical. Best colour in the sun. 75cm.
pyrenaica. Above clumps of large heart-shaped leaves stand maroon-stained stems carrying lacy heads of tiny lilac flowers which produce clouds of fluffy seedheads creating a screen-like effect. For moist soil or a rich border in part shade. May-July. 1m.

VANCOUVERIA chrysantha. From thin, wandering underground rhizomes appear wiry stems carrying shield-shaped leaves edged and stained with reddish-brown. Above them in May-June, on hair-thin stems float little yellow flowers. For light soil, leafmould and part shade. 30cm.

hexandra. Epimedium-like foliage tinted purple in the spring with dainty white flowers held above the foliage in later spring-early summer. For light soil, leafmould rich and part shade. Slowly spreading habit. 30cm.

VERATRUM – CAUTION: TOXIC IF EATEN.
album. Takes up to seven years to produce flowering sized plants from seed! A fat tap root produces clusters of hosta-like leaves, finely pleated, like a fan. (Guard them from slugs!) In late summer a tall flower stem emerges, carrying a pyramidal head of densely set flowers, little white cups, shadowed with green. We sell stout plants, at least four to five years old. 1.5m.
californicum. Much earlier into leaf than *V. album,* forming impressive clumps of pleated foliage reliably producing looser branched spikes of creamy white flowers. Do not cut down to early as seedheads are an attractive bonus. Likes a good rich soil in part shade. 2m.

VERBASCUM bombyciferum. A giant mullein. Huge rosettes, a yard across, of great grey-white felted leaves. Sends up a tree-like stem covered in white wool, supporting a candelabra head of yellow flowers. Biennial. Mid to late summer. Over 2m.
chaixii. Good perennial, scarcely branched stems tightly massed with yellow or white flowers, with mauve eyes. Mid to late summer. 75cm.
'Gainsborough'. From a basal rosette of crinkled grey-green leaves emerges a tall branching spire studded with pale lemon-yellow flowers, from June till late summer. Not long lived, but easily propagated from root cuttings. 1m.

VERBENA bonariensis. For hot dry positions, tall rigid branching stems are topped with tight-packed flat clusters of small, mauve, scented flowers. Standing high above the silver plants they make summer 'screens' to view the garden through. Late summer to autumn. 1.4m.
corymbosa. Surprisingly likes moist soil, which it colonises with tangles of low feathery shoots topped all summer with violet-blue clusters. Useful among trollius, rudbeckia or small bushy willows. Flowers for weeks from midsummer. 30cm.
hastata. Upright stems clothed in narrow willow-like leaves topped with clustered heads of light purple flowers. 1.4m.
'La France'. Forms a low mound of much branched stems clothed in small deep green leaves setting off a constant display of light violet-blue flowers from early summer to autumn. For warm, well-drained soil in sun. Has stood recent winters outside but not reliably hardy so overwinter a few cuttings. 45cm.
officinalis var. grandiflora 'Bampton'. A recently introduced vervain. We have been busy propagating an especially fine form (inferior plants, grown from seed produce less intense foliage colour). Purple tinted foliage all summer long, complimenting the airy, lavender-pink flower spikes. Must have full sun and ideal in patio container displays. 75cm.
rigida. Neat and low growing with jewel-like colour, intensely vivid violet-purple, very good among silvers. Both this and *V. bonariensis* are reputed to be not very hardy, but in warm, well-drained soil neither are damaged. Both seed, often placing themselves better than I would have done. Late summer to autumn. 45cm.

VERNONIA arkansana. Stiff stems, clothed in narrow pointed leaves, make a large clump, suitable for big borders or the wild garden, in retentive soil. In late autumn they carry flat-topped clusters of small, tightly packed daisy-like flowers, in brilliant reddish-purple. Plant it with late asters or surround it with colchicums. 2m.

VERONICA austriaca subsp. teucrium 'Crater Lake Blue'. This popular plant produces soft spikes of intense gentian-blue flowers in midsummer. Irresistible and easy. 30cm.

austriaca subsp. teucrium 'Kapitän'. Outstanding in the dry sunny garden. Forms upright bushy plants smothered with spires of deep gentian-blue flowers in early summer. 40cm.

gentianoides. In good soil makes spreading rosettes of green glossy leaves, with graceful spires of pale washy-blue flowers in early summer, lovely beside the hot tomato-red of *Geum* 'Borisii'. 45cm.

gentianoides 'Variegata'. Foliage variegated green and white. Spires of pale blue flowers. 45cm.

longifolia. Makes slowly increasing clumps, crowded in midsummer with spires of deep, pure blue flowers, a good mid-border plant in retentive soil. 75cm.

longifolia 'Rose Tone'. Branching spires of tiny silvery-pink flowers provide an attractive vertical, loved by bees. Has a long season in retentive soil. Early-late summer. 75cm.

longifolia 'Schneeriesen'. A good mid-border vertical for late summer, with stiffly upright stems encrusted with ivory-white flowers. Needs retentive soil and sun. 75cm.

peduncularis 'Georgia Blue'. Introduced from Georgia by Roy Lancaster. Forms a low cushion plant, ideal for sunny or part-shady border edge, giving year round effect. Stems and young foliage tinted reddish-bronze, crowded with intense blue flowers for weeks in midsummer, continuing intermittently into autumn. 15cm.

spicata 'Erika'. Above compact clusters of grey-green leaves stand dense spires of sugar-pink flowers in midsummer. 25cm.

spicata 'Heidekind'. Delightful edging plant, provides a long succession of spikes of raspberry-pink flowers in midsummer. 25cm.

spicata subsp. incana 'Nana'. Very distinctive mats of almost white felted foliage contrasting with spires of deep purple-blue flowers make this very desirable. Midsummer. 25cm.

VERONICASTRUM virginicum 'Album'. Valued for its elegant form, creating contrast among mounds and domes of plants such as border phlox or *Rudbeckia speciosa*. Erect stems, carrying whorls of horizontal, dark green leaves are topped with tapers of tiny close-set flowers white flowers showing a hint of lilac in late summer. 1.6m.

virginicum f. roseum. Stout erect stems 1.5m tall. Clothed with each node a star-shape of narrow pointed leaves which are topped with narrow pyramidal spires of tiny shell pink flowers. Excellent contrast in shape to border phlox. Full sun and retentive soil. July to August.

virginicum 'Lavendelturm'. Creates a most beautiful vertical effect. Strong stems clothed in whorls of pointed leaves are topped with long spires of pinkish-lilac flowers, much visited by honey bees and bumble bees. Midsummer. 1.5m.

virginicum var. sibiricum. Forms an elegant column of stems clothed in whorls of narrow pointed leaves topped with spires of closely set tiny, lilac-blue, tubular flowers thrusting out anthers on silvery stems, creating a fuzzy effect. Attractive in seed too. For retentive soil. Midsummer. 1.2m.

VINCA. The periwinkles make excellent evergreen ground-cover in shade. Mulch with crushed bark to check weeds until ground-cover is formed. All do spread.

difformis. Lovely throughout winter when starry-white periwinkle flowers peep from among trails of fresh-looking evergreen leaves. Needs shelter from icy blasts. Mine is trained through wire netting on a wall alongside an oil tank. Flowers in late spring and autumn are washed with palest blue. 60cm.

major 'Variegata'. A beautiful variegated form boldly splashed with cream and gold, spreads by runners. 45cm.

major var. oxyloba. We used to call this *V.* 'Dartington Star'. A much more informative if incorrect name. Always noticed here with its 5 narrow-petalled flowers and covering large areas under the oaks in our woodland garden. Evergreen with arching stems of dark green foliage. Dark starry violet-blue flowers from late spring to autumn. Spread indefinite. 30cm.

minor f. alba. White flowers with small leaves marbled light and dark green in spring and early summer. 20cm.

minor 'Argenteovariegata'. Small leaves variegated green and white on dwarfed plants. Pale blue flowers. 15cm.

minor 'Atropurpurea'. Plum-purple single flowers. 20cm.

minor 'Azurea Flore Pleno'. This dwarf periwinkle has pale-blue flowers, a closer look reveals outer petals surrounding a pinched collage of inners. Makes good ground cover almost anywhere. A light trim in late summer allows the flowers to be seen better the following spring. 20cm

minor 'La Grave'. syn. *V.* 'Bowles Blue'. This small-leafed, neat growing periwinkle smothers itself with large blue flowers. Spring. 20cm.

VIOLA. Violas do not like being scorched, the following thrive in cool but not too shady conditions. Most violas will grow in sun or part-shade but do best in retentive soil enriched with a little humus.

'Alice Witter'. Is smothered with quantities of chubby white flowers marked with deep pink centres above carpets of rounded green leaves. 10cm.

'Bowles Black'. Quantities all summer and into winter of tiny, midnight-black velvet pansies. Magnetic. True from seed if not allowed to intermarry with other violas. 15cm.

cornuta Alba Group. Long succession of chalk-white flowers in spring and early summer with a late flush in autumn. 15cm.

cornuta Lilacina Group. Mound-like mats of fresh green foliage covered with china-blue flowers on very long stalks. 15cm.

cornuta Purpurea Group. A dark purple-blue or violet-coloured form. 15cm.

cornuta. 'Rosea'. Little unsure of the correct name but this is a charming form with the same lax habit of other *V. cornuta*. Mauve-pink flowers in abundance during late spring to early summer. Best cut back after flowering. 30cm.

'Etain'. Exquisite creamy-pansy faces 5cm across are edged with narrow blue borders, held together with tiny orange eyes. Scented. 10cm.

gracilis. This delightful Viola makes tidy mounds of foliage, above which float a profusion of pansy-violets of deep purple velvet. Early summer. 15cm.

'Irish Molly'. A small pansy whose velvet brown petals are shadowed with lime green. Flowers for weeks in midsummer. 13cm.

'Jackanapes'. Hard to pass by, this little pansy is bicoloured, bright yellow and rusty-red. Long display of flowers from spring to midsummer. 10cm.

'Maggie Mott'. The small, evocatively scented, pale-blue pansy of my childhood , planted out then by the thousand as bedding beneath roses. Flowers on and off all summer. 13cm.

'Martin'. Carpets of small leaves embroidered all summer with continuous display of royal purple velvety flowers, the size of a ten-penny piece, with tiny yellow eyes. 18cm.

'Molly Sanderson'. Medium sized velvety-black pansies freely produced from spring until autumn. 15cm.

'Moonlight'. Irresistible, fragrant little pansy flowers. 4cm across, soft creamy-yellow with tiny yellow eye, faintly whiskered. Main flowering May-June, spasmodically thereafter. 13cm.

'Priceana'. Is similar to *V.* 'Alice Witter', but with centres veined and stained deep blue. 10cm.

riviniana Purpurea Group. syn. *Viola labradorica*. Might be a nuisance if it weren't so lovely! It makes a running mass of small dark purple leaves which set off the quantities of light coloured, scentless flowers. Beautiful with yellow grasses and snowdrops. 15cm.

sororia. Makes fat rhizomes just beneath the soil surface, slowly enlarging its low mounds. In spring before the leaves grow large, there are quantities of big pure white violets, scentless, but none the less desirable. 15cm.

sororia 'Freckles'. Pale blue ground freckled with purple spots. Early spring. 13cm.

VITIS 'Fragola'. Familiar to visitors to the nursery in the autumn as it fruits on the south wall of our nursery building. We encourage people to taste in order to appreciate the unusual fruity flavour of this "Strawberry Vine". Needs a warm wall, support and cultivation as other fruiting vines.

WALDSTEINIA ternata. A beautiful and valuable carpeter which will flourish in sun or shade, spreading its dark-lobed leaves, evergreen and glossy to contrast with sprays of bright yellow strawberry flowers in spring. 10cm.

YUCCA filamentosa 'Variegata'. A small yucca with short, wide concave leaves fairly soft to touch, edged with long curling threads, making large rosettes at ground level. Makes a winter picture with the small *Bergenia* 'Wintermarchen'. 50cm.

ZANTEDESCHIA aethiopica 'Crowborough'. Has wide spathes of pure white flowers held above handsome dark green leaves marked with a swirling pattern of veins. Strong clumps of overlapping leaves form a distinctive feature when flowers are finished. Grows well in deeply prepared soil kept moist in summer. Crowns must be protected in winter with a mulch. Thrives in deep mud in natural ponds. 75cm.

aethiopica 'Green Goddess'. Large green flowers with white throat, magnificent foliage. Perfect for flower arrangers. Cultivation as above. 1m.

aethiopica 'Little Gem'. A dwarf form of arum lily, useful in smaller gardens where the type might be overwhelming. Needs winter protection, i.e. heavy mulching if in border. If container grown in small pond, better to remove and put in frost-free shelter until spring. Flowers in midsummer. 60cm.

'Lime Lady'. A smaller form of arum lily, with slender light-green flower spathes, and leaves irregularly marked with silver spots. Actually they are white lesions, without chlorophyll, showing up well when sunlight passes through them. 70cm.

All flower from mid to late summer.

ZAUSCHNERIA californica subsp. cana. Hummingbird trumpet. Will stand the hottest drought, spreading by underground runners. It sends up wiry stems covered with narrow ash-grey leaves, topped in late summer with brilliant scarlet tubular flowers. 30cm.

californica 'Dublin'. syn. 'Glasnevin' (which is Dublin's Botanic Garden). Massed with scarlet tubular flowers for weeks in autumn, this splendid form has small matt-green leaves. 40cm.

californica 'Ed Carmen'. Given to us many years ago by its namesake with grey-green foliage and bright orange-scarlet flowers on neat clumps. Loved by bees. For full sun in a well drained soil. 40cm.

californica 'Olbrich Silver'. Was selected by Marshall Olbrich whose nursery I have visited near San Francisco. It was selected for its particularly ashen leaves which became almost white in very dry conditions, setting off bright scarlet trumpets in autumn. 30cm.

californica 'Western Hills'. This is a specially free-flowering form of scarlet Hummingbird trumpet. Wiry, bushy plants are clothed in tiny felted leaves, smothered in late summer-autumn with brilliant scarlet, tubular flowers. With good drainage and full sun it thrives in very dry conditions. But remember not to cut down any untidy top growth until the spring. 45cm.

ZIGADENUS elegans. From bulbous plants come grassy leaves while above them stand open spires of pale green, star-shaped flowers, each petal spotted with dark enamelled-green in midsummer. For enriched soil, in sun. 40cm.

Ferns

In the garden ferns immediately create the peaceful atmosphere of cool woodland. Districts harassed by drought, with low rainfall and drying winds provide few suitable sites for ferns, but provided they are sheltered from desiccating wind, and every effort is made to conserve moisture in the soil by adding plenty of compost or leafmould, several can be grown tolerably well.

Shady places make the best sites, under north walls, or beneath the shade of trees. A woodland character is easily achieved in the smallest garden with suitable ferns and other shade-loving plants such as hosta, polygonatum (Solomon's seal) with soft ground-cover like tiarella, or ajuga, and perhaps the lovely golden grass, *Milium effusum* 'Aureum'. Add to these any, or all of the following, *Dryopteris filix-mas* and *Polystichum setiferum* Acutilobum Group and you will almost imagine yourself gardening in the damp counties of the north and west.

Polystichum setiferum Plumosum Group needs rather damper conditions, of atmosphere, rather than very wet soil, to produce the most luxuriant fronds.

Matteuccia struthiopteris, called both Shuttlecock or Ostrich plume fern, needs a regular supply of moisture and protection from damaging winds. Its delicacy and form are breathtaking, in cool moist hollows, beneath the shade of trees. It will tolerate really wet soil, as will *Onoclea sensibilis,* the Sensitive fern, which spreads its rhizomes over soggy wet soil by the water's edge, weaving a pattern among strands of iris, trollius, and bog primulas.

ADIANTUM pedatum. Slowly increasing root-stocks send up black wiry stems topped with finger-shaped fronds of maidenhair fern-like delicacy. Needs a sheltered position among low woodland plants. A treasure for good humus-rich soil sheltered from drying wind. 40cm.
pedatum 'Imbricatum'. Makes low congested mounds of delicate foliage. Short, black, wiry stems carry 5 or 7 fronds threaded with tiny pinnae arranged like the fingers of a hand. 15cm.

ASPLENIUM scolopendrium. The Hart's tongue fern. Broad, undulating, strap-shaped leaves, provide essential contrast to the feathery ferns, or rounded leaves, like hosta or bergenia. Hardy and easy in any soil, but intolerant of drought. 30cm.
scolopendrium 'Angustatum'. Is the narrow, ruffle-edged form, given to me by Helen von Stein Zeppelin, of Laufen, Bavaria. 30cm.
scolopendrium Crispum Group. Has most beautifully crimped margins to the leaves. Rare, since it is sterile and must be increased vegetatively. Needs a choice site, shelter from wind, rich humus soil which never dries out. 30cm.
scolopendrium Undulatum Group. Is one of several varieties which have arching fronds which show off crimped wavy edges. 30cm.

ATHYRIUM. Provided the following three ferns have a cool situation, plenty of humus, and shelter from drying wind they will thrive and increase very satisfactorily.
filix-femina. The Lady fern. A fern of lace-like delicacy, preferring moist soil but will make do with less. Can grow 1m plus according to conditions.
filix-femina 'Frizelliae'. The Tatting fern. A popular fern here with narrow fronds with many pinnae, which are reduced to a string of little green beads, resembling tatting (a type of hand-made lace). Best in a moist woodland soil, in light shade. Height 30cm.
filix-femina 'Minutissimum'. Forms slowly increasing dense clumps of small lacy, typical fern leaves, attractive for edge of shady border with a blue leafed hosta and yellow Creeping Jenny. 20cm.

niponicum var. pictum. Japanese painted fern. This lovely fern spreads its leaves almost horizontally to show off its beautiful colouring. Each frond of tiny pinnae is so pale it appears to be silvery-grey, flushed with maroon on either side of the central vein which is pinkish-brown. 30cm.

BLECHNUM chilense. From damp woods of central Chile; a magnificent evergreen fern for a cool, damp site. The great fronds look as if they were stamped out of dark, matt-green leather. Handsome in rich soil or by waterside. The roots are slowly invasive. 1m.

penna-marina subsp. alpinum. Creeping rhizomes produce crowds of small ladder-shaped fronds, making very attractive ground cover in shade. Good contrast with round-leafed plants like asarum, saxifraga or geum. 25cm.

spicant. Found in forests and damp moors around the temperate world. One of the prettiest of hardy ferns. Neat clumps of narrow, ladder-shaped fronds, of a lively shining green, make way for taller, upright, fertile fronds, which are green at first, but when they have scattered their spores, they wither, remaining all winter as handsome curling brown skeletons. Size depends on moisture, from 30-60cm, or more. For lime-free soil.

CYSTOPTERIS fragilis. Forms low dense clumps of wiry stems carrying dainty lace-like foliage. Makes compact edging plant. Prefers cool leaf mould in Scotland but makes do with less in Essex, producing a succession of new growth when weather turns cooler or damper. 25cm.

DRYOPTERIS affinis. Golden green when young this beautiful fern stands out early in the year. Later the great fronds, richly green, remain a feature until severe frost. Although vigorous, varies in height according to conditions. 1m.

dilatata. A robust fern for naturalising in woodland, with dark green broad-based fronds on bright green stalks. 1m.

erythrosora. A rare fern found in China and Japan. The young fronds are glossy, rosy-brown, becoming green later. For sheltered site and plenty of humus. 45cm.

filix-mas. The Male fern. Deserves a place in every garden, being beautiful and tolerant of any soil (except bog), thriving in hedge bottoms or other mean places. Each spring new fiddle-necks emerge from the tumble of collapsed fronds that endured the winter. Perfect with Solomon's seal and hostas. 90cm.

goldiana. This fern has large light green fronds. The fresh growth of the plant is covered in light brown scales which can be rather impressive when the plant is mature. Dryopteris and will grow well in any moist to dryish soil. Will form a good sized clump in a few years. 75cm.

wallichiana. From a tight cluster of copper scaly knobs, golden green fiddle-necks unfold to become tall stately fronds forming a plant of noble aspect. A most distinctive fern. 1m.

MATTEUCCIA orientalis. The oriental Ostrich plume fern is slightly more compact than *M. struthiopteris* and, with a longer leaf stem, gives a slightly more open and lighter appearance in a sheltered position in cool moist soil, slowly spreading via runners. 90cm.

struthiopteris. Ostrich plume fern. Perhaps the most beautiful fern for damp, even boggy conditions sheltered from drying winds and sun. The dainty fronds emerge from the top of a short stem to form an open, pale-green shuttlecock of breathtaking lacy design. In winter you may find dark brown fossil-like fruiting fronds left behind, decorative in left standing in the garden or cut for 'drieds'. 1m.

ONOCLEA sensibilis. Sensitive fern. Another fern for waterside, or beneath trees where soil never becomes dry. Arching, broadly segmented fronds are freshly produced throughout summer from a running rootstock, so making attractive ground cover, or edging to a pond, beautiful with water iris and golden Creeping Jenny, *Lysimachia nummularia* 'Aurea'. 45cm.

OSMUNDA regalis. The Royal fern. Nothing quite like it. Unfolding fronds are tinted coppery-brown, becoming green, tall and elegant until autumn when they develop shades of tan and snuff brown. Must have moisture all summer, cool conditions and plenty of humus. 1.2m.

POLYPODIUM vulgare. Common polypody. An attractive evergreen fern with deep cut leathery fronds. Excellent for dry shade. Spreading slowly. 30cm.

POLYSTICHUM aculeatum. Hard shield fern. In spring the unfurling fronds curl over backwards like reversed crosiers, then form a perfect shuttlecock shape of fresh glossy daintily-cut plumes from the centre of the previous years ruff of overwintered leathery fronds. 75cm.

minitum. Western sword fern. Aptly named with long sword-like fronds which, given good conditions, can reach a metre long. A rich moist soil is best. Evergreen so only trim off dead leaves. 1m.

setiferum Acutilobum Group. This easy fern has narrow, daintily set fronds of great elegance. Grows almost anywhere, even in drier shade but responds with great luxuriance in cool semi-shade. Grows taller in damp climates, usually 60cm.

setiferum Dahlem Group. I collected this fern and *P.* 'Herrenhausen' from a German nursery. *P.* Dahlem Group produces tall, upright, elegant fronds, making it a perfect companion for hostas in shady places. Individual fronds may exceed 90cm.

setiferum Divisilobum Group 'Herrenhausen'. Differs from *P.* Dahlem Group in producing much more finely-cut fronds which lie more horizontally, creating a large rosette of exquisite lacy design perfect by the edge of a shady walk. Individual fronds up to 75cm.

setiferum Plumosodivisilobum Group. There are several variations of these very feathery forms. We think this is the best, each overlapping segment so frilled and fluted, the entire frond has an almost parsley-like effect in bright green. The back shows the strong mid-rib heavily 'furred' with pale chestnut-brown scales. 60cm.

setiferum 'Pulcherrimum Bevis'. Was pulled out of a hedge alongside a ploughed field by a farm labourer, John Bevis, found at Hawchurch, in Dorset, in 1876; a most distinct and elegant fern. Upright lacy fronds are slightly lopsided, as if you had gently pulled each one through your half-closed hand. 90cm.

Grasses and Grass-like Plants

I think we are all missing opportunities to make our garden designs more exciting by not using grasses as effectively as we might. For so long our minds have been fixed on conventional flowering plants, those plants which provide plenty of colour, not always considering the brief time some of these displays may last.

Well chosen grasses add grace and elegance, provide ground-cover, contribute many shades of green, grey, bronze or yellow throughout spring and summer and finally, wonderful autumn tints at the end of the year. Personally I do not care for a mass of grasses lumped together, unless it be done on a large scale and in the right setting. In a mixed border I love to see a few tall grasses, such as the miscanthus group rising from among mounds and cushions of other perennial plants, partnered perhaps with tall and stately campanulas, filipendula or the noble eupatorium. These columnar grasses, which need no staking, might be used to make a feature in mown lawns, or planted in groups by the waterside, where the light caught in their fluttering, ribbon-like leaves can suggest a fountain. Do not feel excluded if you have no pond margins. Miscanthus will grow in any reasonable garden soil, and add atmosphere to even a small garden. In much drier gardens blue-leafed grasses make a welcome change of texture among the woolly white and silvered leaves of drought-resisting plants. The longer the drought lasts, the more powdery-blue grasses like festuca and helictotrichon become. For summer-long display *Stipa gigantea* with great airy heads of metallic oat-like flowers quivering on stiff 2m stems, is one of the most decorative grasses, taking up surprisingly little room on the ground.

No other plant gives the same effect as grasses do in the landscape, be they large and imposing, small and tufty, or graceful and fountain-like. And let us not forget their flowers, which might be feathered plumes, delicate sprays of tiny beads on thread-like stems, or sheaves of upright spikes for contrast. Throughout the whole growing season grasses add style, substance or delicacy to a design.

Autumn brings glorious shades of yellow, copper, tan, bronze and red in many, especially in forms of molinia. They are like a sunburst on dull, grey autumn days when you are drawn irresistibly towards them as towards a light. Flower arrangers do not need to be reminded of the value of grasses in home decoration. A similar awareness of texture, movement, elegance, and longevity of ornamental grasses will help you make some experiments in the garden. Both garden and landscape designers should take the opportunity to display grasses in association with the kinds of plants with which they would be found in natural conditions. When chosen to suit the site, these neglected plants make exciting accents among other ground covering plants.

Grasses, or grass-like plants, are available to suit all conditions, whether in sun, dry and dusty, in cool-shaded woodland, in deep rich soil in sun, or in damp boggy soil by water. Together with species plants that naturally prefer these diverse conditions, they create a totally harmonious atmosphere for much of the year.

It is important not to divide grasses in autumn. The golden rule is to divide and replant in spring.

ALOPECURUS pratensis 'Aureus'. The Golden fox tail grass makes striking low clumps of foliage, vividly striped gold and green. Very useful and bright for edging. The fox tail-like flower-spikes rise to 50cm.

AMPELODESMOS mauritanicus. This large elegant grass has made a fountain-like feature in my dry well-drained soil from June to November. From a base of arching green leaves spring tall pale stems carrying long drooping flower heads, beautiful in outline. For a sunny spot in mild districts. 2m.

ANEMANTHELE lessoniana. syn. *Stipa arundinacea.* Pheasant's tail grass. Forms arching clumps of fine foliage with long trailing flower heads, like tresses of shining brown hair. In winter the foliage develops tints of red, orange and yellow. Needs rich soil that does not dry out. 60cm.

ARUNDO donax var. versicolor. This is the variegated form of the Giant reed which comes from the Camargue, southern France. Tall, strong stems are clothed in drooping ribbon-like leaves striped more cream than green making a dramatic feature plant for late summer-autumn. It must be cosseted, soil not too dry and needs winter protection. Worth potting up in autumn, keeping under cover for winter, and planting out again when safe to do so, or it may be used in a cool conservatory. 1.4m.

CALAMAGROSTIS × **acutiflora 'Avalanche'.** Feather reed grass. Clump forming grass with arching pale yellow leaves, fading to pinkish white, with green margins and stripes. The reverse variegation to *C.* × *acutiflora* 'Overdam'. Purple flowers that fade to greyish pink. 1.2m.
× **acutiflora 'Karl Foerster'.** An outstanding vertical especially in autumn and winter. Narrow flower panicles held bolt upright on needle-like stems form a slender column. They bleach straw colour, standing firm without support or damage throughout winter. 1.5m.
× **acutiflora 'Overdam'.** Very impressive. Quickly makes arching mounds of freshly striped green and white grassy leaves topped with feathery plumes in late summer. A welcome addition for the garden designer. 1.2m.
brachytricha. An appealing grass feature. Needle-like flower stems carry pyramidal-shaped flower heads, like elegant bottle-brushes; grey-green with a touch of mauve when fresh, fading to buff, a shape tempting to stroke. A fine vertical above lower plants. Autumn flowering. 1m.

CAREX comans 'Frosted Curls'. Soft bundles of pale-silvery-green thread-like leaves curl as they touch the ground, bunched like the end of a ponytail. 30cm.
conica 'Snowline'. Forms an outstanding silvery effect seen from a distance. Soft arching mounds of narrow grass-like leaves boldly edged white. For retentive soil, sun or part shade. 30cm.
elata 'Aurea'. Bowles's golden sedge. A lovely sight by the water's edge or in a sunny place in damp soil. This graceful sedge has bright golden, grass-like foliage with pointed clusters of brown flowers held stiffly upright in June. 60cm.
oshimensis 'Evergold'. This eye-catching sedge makes a focal point on the edge of a dampish border. The grass-like, evergreen foliage is bright gold with narrow green margins. Spiralling out from the centre of the clump, it fans out to show off each leaf. 25cm.
pendula. Good by the pond, or as contrast among shrubs. From grassy tufts long curving stems end in graceful fox-tails. 90cm.
petriei. Forms eye-catching clumps of pinkish-brown grass-like leaves, effective as a dot plant, dramatic in drifts, particularly with blue flowers or grasses. Will grow in any situation, in acid or alkaline soil provided it never dries out. 30cm.

riparia 'Variegata'. Long narrow arching leaves are dramatically variegated white and green. In spring many are totally white. Although one of the most attractive grassy plants in the right place, it could be troublesome, being invasive. Needs moist soil. 60cm.

CHASMANTHUM latifolium. Forms a loose column of flowering stems softened by broad-bladed leaves curling round them. They are topped with curious and attractive flower heads, each individual spikelet being totally flat as though it had been pressed with a flat iron. Dries well, remaining green shaded with bronze and purple tints. Needs humus-rich soil and full sun. 90cm.

CORTADERIA selloana 'Pumila'. A more restrained form of Pampas grass, yet impressive still with beautiful arching foliage and dense erect plumes of creamy-white flowers resembling feather dusters. About 1.5m.
selloana 'Sunningdale Silver'. Pampas grass. A superb landscape grass for autumn effect. From a base of long, arching leaves, like layered skirts, emerge stout stems bearing huge, graceful, feathery heads of silky, creamy-white flowers. Magnificent near water, near red stemmed dogwoods or isolated in mown grass. Flower heads 75cm long, stems can be up to 3m tall.

DESCHAMPSIA caespitosa 'Goldschleier'. The Tufted hair grass is one of the loveliest for effect, either grouped in a bay among shrubs, or as a specimen rising above lower plants. It forms large dense tussocks of narrow arching green leaves. By midsummer many tall flower stems rise well above the foliage carrying large airy plumes of tiny silver-green flowers. Gradually flowers and stems turn bright straw-yellow, creating a golden veil. Needs retentive soil in sun. 1.2m.
flexuosa 'Tatra Gold'. Forms low arching tufts of needle-fine grass, brilliantly yellow-green most of the year. In midsummer carries light-catching silky bronze flower heads of stiff pale stems. For sun or shade, acid soil, not too dry. Flower stems. 45cm.

ELYMUS magellanicus. In hot dry soils this grass looks as if cut from thins strips of aluminium, it is so silvery-white. Needs grooming in spring to set off the fresh young growth. 45cm.

ERAGROSTIS curvula. Forms tussocks of very narrow leaves over-topped in late summer-autumn with delicate curved sprays of tiny flowers fading to pale fawn. 90cm.
curvula 'Totnes Burgundy'. This handsome new introduction has leaves which turn deep burgundy red from the tips down, contrasting with long arching sprays of beige flowers. For full sun. 75cm.
elliottii. Distinctly greyer foliage than *E. curvula.* This form of Love grass excels in hot dry conditions producing arching stems of smoky-grey flowers. 75cm.
tricoides. From tufts of very fine green leaves spring a mass of stems, erect at first, but later bowed by weight of dark green brown seedheads. It is a bad seeder. 75cm.

ERIOPHORUM angustifolium. The Cotton grass of bogs. Quickly runs in wet soil, sending up its spikes of white cotton-wool flowers in late summer. Best planted in large pots if you wish to contain its enthusiasm. 40cm.

FARGESIA nitida. This graceful bamboo forms an arching shower of purple flushed canes carrying narrow dainty leaves which are winter hardy. Best in deep soil and part shade. Canes can reach 4m. I use mine for runner bean sticks.

FESTUCA glauca 'Elijah Blue'. Looks wonderful in hot dry weather, this strong form has needle stiff rolled leaves in vivid grey-blue. 30cm.
glauca 'Golden Toupee'. Forms wide tufts of luminous yellowy-green tightly rolled leaves. Makes great impact among flat thyme mats. For sun or part shade. Feathery flowers stand 30cm high.
mairei. Hailing from North Africa this plant has been at home in our hot dry gravel garden for many years, never failing to show off its slender flowers on straight, upright stems. 1m.
punctoria. Again for driest soils and full sun, this curious grass is hard and spiky, steel-blue and comes from hot rocks in Spain. Plant it with sempervivums. 15cm.
valesiaca 'Silbersee'. In full sun, on dry soil this neat compact grass is powder-blue. A wonderful contrast among thymes, or as edging. 25cm.

GLYCERIA maxima var. variegata. A handsome plant for the water-side or heavy soil. Broad strap-like leaves striped with white and yellow and warmly shaded with pink in spring and autumn. 60cm.

HAKONECHLOA macra. Hakone grass. Arching mounds of greenery provide a perfect foil for other showy neighbours. Best in a humus rich soil and part to full shade. Good in pots. 30cm.
macra 'All Gold'. The golden form of Japanese forest grass, hence it thrives in the shade but must have enough light not to turn a pale green. So perhaps sun till midday then shade. Once the right position is found it produces a dramatic clump of summer long brightness. Also retains its dying foliage in winter which is best cut back by March. 45cm.
macra 'Aureola'. This represents a grass that never fails to cause comment. It makes soft clumps of foliage with each ribbon-like leaf vividly variegated gold and buff with touches of bronze. In good soil the leaves can be 60cm, but they arch over into overlapping mounds, so overall height is nearer 45cm.

HELICTOTRICHON sempervirens. Forms arching clumps of vivid grey-blue foliage and sends up oat-like plumes of the same colour. Useful contrast in form among other grey foliaged plants. Evergreen. 1m.

HOLCUS mollis 'Albovariegatus'. Creeping rhizomes carry tufts of soft leaves with broad white margins centred by a narrow green strip, giving the effect of a white carpet in spring, and again when new growth appears in autumn. Although invasive, it is easily dislodged. Succeeds in shade or open borders, in light or heavy soil. 15cm.

IMPERATA cylindrica 'Rubra'. Has done well in hot dry summers in gravel soil and full sun. Has clumped well, coloured well and produced a continual display of fresh new leaf. 1cm wide ribbon-shaped leaves stained deep maroon, colour intensifying towards the tip. 50cm.

KOELERIA glauca. Is not unlike Festuca but with more substance. Low dense tussocks of very blue-grey leaves carry attractive upright flower heads of the same shade. Looks well closely grouped as ground cover, or used as a feature plant through low mats. 20cm.

LEYMUS arenarius. Lyme grass. In full bloom stands 1.4m high. Stiff wheat-like flowers, stems and leaves all a vivid grey-blue. This is a handsome feature plant in poor, hot, dry soil. Not a grass for small gardens unless in a container. The 'wheat' is splendid for drieds.

LUZULA nivea. This graceful wood rush has wide sprays of tiny parchment-coloured flowers in midsummer, pretty contrast in form with ferns and violets. Dries well. 45cm.
sylvatica 'Aurea'. An exceptionally good plant for foliage effect. Broad-bladed leaves of overall golden-yellow, form handsome arching clumps that command attention, especially in winter. Easy in any soil, but best in retentive soil, in the open or part shade. 30cm.
sylvatica 'Marginata'. A handsome wood rush forming dense tufts of rich green leaves edged with white, making impenetrable ground-cover. Tolerates dry shade but grows more lushly in damp conditions. Drooping sprays of gold and brown spikelets in early summer. 45cm.

MELICA altissima 'Atropurpurea'. This non-invasive grass forms clumps of soft green foliage topped in midsummer with heads of soft chaffy flowers stained purple fading to pinkish-buff when dried. Ideal to put with dried annuals like Helipterum. Each tassel-like head looks as if the individual papery flowers were threaded then pushed to the tip of the wire-fine stems. 75cm.
uniflora f. albida. Quietly attractive. Above neat clumps of soft green foliage float sprays of pale little buds looking rather like tiny grains of rice, such a dainty effect planted among ferns, hostas, or the grey-leafed *Dicentra* 'Langtrees'. 60cm.
uniflora 'Variegata'. Tuffets of narrow ribbon-like leaves are striped cream and green, their dainty curving habit contrasts with the green rosettes of *Saxifraga* 'Dentata' in part shade. 30cm.

MILIUM effusum 'Aureum'. Bowles's golden grass. Non-running clumps of soft foliage, bright yellow in spring and early summer, make patches of sunlight in shady places. Many fine stems support a cloud of tiny golden flower-like beads, in early summer. 40cm.
effusum 'Yaffle'. A taller, more robust version of Bowles's golden grass, standing almost 1m tall. A cloud of filmy flowers shimmer above ribbon-like leaves, all in Green Woodpecker shades and tones of yellowy-green; lovely contrast for the chestnut tones of *Heuchera americana.*

MISCANTHUS. This species, including many improved varieties contains some of the most beautiful and valued ornamental grasses. From a nurseryman in north Germany, Ernst Pagels, have come a number of forms specially selected to flower regularly in our northern summers. The range in size is also considerable. For imposing specimen plants, or for use as a windbreak, some are well over 2m but there are also delights for the small garden, flowering at about 1.2m. The species are found wild in Japan and China, in wet meadow lands, or hillsides. In gardens they make strong, non-invasive clumps in any soil which does not dry out. They need careful placing to show off their beautiful columnar form.

Standing among my stock beds of miscanthus in mid-December I watch the constant movement of shimmering corn-coloured stems festooned with bleached, rustling, ribbon-shaped leaves, topped with frothy flower heads looking like feather dusters. Against the pale green background of my neighbour's winter corn, and the black lace effect of leafless oaks and birches, these beautiful grasses create a warm living effect. They look very well in my garden, reflected in the ponds, or as a feature in mixed borders.

nepalensis. An unusual and beautiful miscanthus that has delicate airy, golden flower plumes held high above mounds of green foliage. Flowers from midsummer onwards. A sunny sheltered spot is needed for winter protection or use in pot displays. 1.5m.

'Purpurascens'. Is much shorter than the others. By late summer the upper surface of the leaves shows warm brown, enhanced by the shining central vein which is pink. Narrow pinkish-brown flower heads appear in October when the whole plant becomes suffused with shades of red, orange and buff. 1.2m.

sacchariflorus. Magnificent feature grass for retentive soil or the waterside, a perfect partner for massive *Gunnera manicata* or ornamental rheum. Not invasive, slowly increasing clumps send up, each year, bamboo-like canes hung with long fluttering ribbon-like leaves. Can be used in large gardens as summer windbreak or shading. Flowers only after hot summers. 3m plus.

sinensis 'Ferne Osten'. This grass opens even darker plumes than *M. sinensis* 'Malepartus', but is shorter with leaves correspondingly narrower. Wonderful autumn colour, bright copper and dark red tints on leaves. 1.5m.

sinensis 'Gracillimus'. Forms a clump like a slender bamboo. Very narrow leaves curling gracefully as they lengthen are topped by plumey inflorescences, in autumn. Bleaches palest straw colour to form a striking winter feature. 1.5m.

sinensis 'Grosse Fontäne'. Forms an upright column of purple stems supporting a cascade of ribbon-shaped leaves accentuated with wide white mid-ribs. Shuttlecock-shaped feathery plumes are freely produced, silvery buff stained with purple, drying to long curling plumes. 2.5m.

sinensis 'Malepartus'. Imposing columns of arching, broad, ribbon-like leaves, with conspicuous central silver vein. Large feathery plumes, silky and mahogany red when fresh, drying to pinkish-buff. 2m.

sinensis 'Morning Light'. Forms a column of stems clothed in very narrow arching leaves lit with silver central veins, creating overall a delicate hazy effect. 1.2m.

sinensis 'Punktchen'. Developed from a stock of *M. sinensis*. 'Zebrinus', this plant has yellow dots instead of zebra stripes. The prolific foliage and succession of autumn flowering make it a very worthwhile garden plant. 1.5m.

sinensis 'Rotsilber'. Narrow green leaves with strong silvery mid rib, enhanced in autumn by reddish tinge which seeps into flower stems and sheath holding silky feather plumes. 1.2m.

sinensis 'Silberfeder'. A columnar feature plant, tall stems swathed from top to bottom in narrow ribbon-like leaves carry upright slender shuttlecocks of feathery plumes silver-pinky beige to stand among autumn flowers. 2m plus.

sinensis 'Strictus'. Differs from *M. sinensis*. 'Zebrinus' in its narrower, more upright habit, making it a useful specimen grass for smaller gardens. The distinctive yellow bars across the leaves appear more numerous and brighter than those of *M. sinensis* 'Zebrinus'. 1.8m.

sinensis 'Undine'. A column of stems bearing very narrow white-veined leaves creates a light effect. Above flutter shimmering flower heads strongly tinted purple, maturing as upstanding fluffy plumes. Flowers freely. 1.8m.

sinensis 'Variegatus'. Quite distinct. The strap-shaped leaves, strongly variegated green and white, fall from rigid stems, making a fountain all summer in a moist border. 1.5m.

sinensis 'Yaku-jima'. Makes slowly increasing clumps. Very free-flowering. Whole plant bleaches to warm caramel colours in late autumn. Suitable for small gardens. 1.2m.

sinensis 'Zebrinus'. Graceful stems in dense clumps carry narrow green leaves strongly banded at intervals with yellow, very striking as a contrasting form in the border, marvellous by water. Easy anywhere in good soil. 1.8m.

MOLINIA caerulea subsp. arundinacea. A tidy grass, an arresting sight, in autumn, when its strong clumps of foliage and stiff needle-like flower stems blaze with autumn colour, honey-gold. 1m.
caerulea subsp. arundinacea 'Transparent'. Above low neat clumps of narrow ribbon-shaped leaves stand tall, rigid, knitting-needle-like stems topped with lace-fine heads of tiny rice-like seed cases less densely set on hair thin stems creating a more gauzy effect. The whole making an exquisite screen when still, or when seen bowing and dancing in the wind. Autumn. 1.6m.
caerulea subsp. arundinacea 'Windspiel'. A column of strongly upright stems support a firmly shaped inflorescence of tiny bead-like seed cases held vertically, bold enough to make impact, delicate enough to create a hazy screen through which to view the sky. By November the whole plant glows in rich shades of honey. 1.8m.
caerulea subsp. caerulea 'Claerwen'. Forms attractive tussocks of strongly variegated green and white foliage, each narrow, ribbon-like leaf variously striped green and white, flowers on stiffly upright stems. 50cm.
caerulea subsp. caerulea 'Edith Dudszus'. Very effective vertical among flat mat plants, i.e. thymes. From a neat base of narrow leaves spring stiff needle-like flower stems creating a charming ray-like effect, best in autumn. 60cm.
caerulea subsp. caerulea 'Heidebraut'. Creates its own sunshine on grey autumnal days. Narrow columns of stiff, warm, straw-coloured flowering stems are topped with light dainty seedheads. They create a glistening screen, each tiny pointed seed case catching the light, the non-invasive basal clump of foliage already spent. 1.4m.
caerulea subsp. caerulea 'Moorhexe'. Forms a prim, narrow column of stiffly upright foliage with needle-like flower stems rising unbowed above. Most effective as an accent among low plants, or an outcrop in the rock garden. 45cm.
caerulea subsp. caerulea 'Variegata'. One of the loveliest variegated grasses. Short neat tufts of vividly coloured green and cream leaves send up feathery plumes, the whole making a shower of pale buff in autumn. Sells on sight. 45cm.

ORYZOPSIS miliacea. Indian rice grass. Like most grasses looks best in a void surrounded by lower plants where its showers of exquisitely dainty flower heads are not interrupted. Does seed, so best if cut back after first flush of flower when it quickly grows back to give a late summer-autumn display, still looking good in winter in shades of buff and brown. Stands really dry conditions. 1m.

PANICUM virgatum 'Dallas Blues'. A wonderful feature grass, bolt upright wide, blue foliage topped with airy panicles of tiny red-brown flowers. Best in full sun. 1.4m.
virgatum 'Rubrum'. Non-invasive, clump-forming grass. Lovely massed, perhaps on a bank, or seen individually against some solid feature, perhaps a wall or thrusting through railings where clouds of tiny chestnut brown seedheads in wide airy panicles make wondrous contrast, caught in low sunlight. Narrow ribbon-like leaves, tinted red in autumn complete a plant that is a must for the garden, or in flower arrangements. 1.2m.
virgatum 'Shenandoah'. A lovely form of Switch grass with thin blue-grey foliage the tips of which become stained red as autumn approaches. Airy fawn-brown panicles of flowers add to the charm. Full sun. 90cm.

PENNISETUM alopecuroides. Has the largest, most handsome, bottle-brush-like flower heads, dark green, shadowed with black, softened with long, fine hairs. Forms much admired feature at mown grass edge of a damp, sunny border, every hair caught in low sunlight, or gilded with hoar frost. 90cm.

alopecuroides 'Hameln'. Over narrow grassy leaves stand fan-shaped sheaves of thin wiry stems carrying caterpillar-like flower heads in autumn. Green at first, fuzzy with fine dark hairs, fading to pale brown in winter. Free-flowering in open site, retentive soil. 60cm.

macrourum. Above mounds of grassy leaves stand tall stems carrying long narrow, cat-tail-like flower heads, a very distinctive and attractive vertical feature among lower plants in the dry sunny border. This plant has remained compact in our garden, but needs watching. Late summer-autumn. 1.2m.

orientale. For this grass I welcome a warm, dry summer when dense hummocks of fine, narrow leaves become crowned with flower heads. They dangle, fat and hairy, like soft grey-mauve caterpillars suspended from thin, wiry stems. 45cm.

villosum. Will not stand many degrees of frost, but so beautiful it is worth the trouble to pot it and protect inside over winter. Above fine, grassy leaves there appears a constant display of furry white caterpillar-like flower heads that no-one passes by. Do not divide until spring. 60cm.

PHALARIS arundinacea var. picta 'Feesey'. Luckily not so invasive as the usual form of Gardener's garters because you will covet it on sight. Clumps of white or green stems carry ribbon-shaped leaves beautifully striped, more white than green. Any soil, not too dry, in sun or shade. 75cm.

PLEIOBLASTUS auricomus. The loveliest dwarf bamboo with fluttering, ribbon-shaped leaves, rich yellow, sometimes lightly pencilled with green. Looks freshest and best on new canes, old ones cut to ground each spring. Appreciates dressings of well-rotted compost. Up to 1.2m.

POA labillardieri. Above strong tussocks of needle-thin, blue-green leaves stands a great fan of plume-like flower heads. As mature heads fall outwards, new ones replace them, retaining a beautiful transparent screen of flower-heads. One of the best grasses for dry soil. 1m.

SACCHARUM ravennae. Superb shape, strong, purple stained stems support a columnar shape formed by long, white veined, ribbon like leaves arching down from top to bottom. Catching the light the effect is both strong, yet graceful. Our summers not quite hot enough to mature the inflorescence which forms too late in autumn. 2m.

SASA veitchii. This ground-covering bamboo has wide blade-shaped leaves, plain green all summer, but by autumn the leaf margins become blanched, straw-yellow, giving a bold variegated effect throughout winter. Makes dense colonies of invading stems so only suitable for large gardens. Useful to bind clay banks of reservoirs or lakes. 1m

SORGHASTRUM avenaceum. Gold stem, one of the main grasses of the tall grass prairie, makes a beautiful specimen grass in gardens. From a neat base of narrow soft leaves, rise tall rigid stems carrying drooping panicles of bronze-tinted flowers dangling with yellow anthers in late summer. 90cm.

SPARTINA pectinata 'Aureomarginata'. Another prairie grass. Arching ribbon-like, olive-green leaves are margined with yellow, topped with narrow flower spikes dangling purple stamens. Invasive, preferring moist soil. 2m.

SPODIOPOGON sibiricus. A very distinctive grass. It creates a compact bamboo-like effect with fresh green broad-bladed leaves clothing the flower stems, diminishing in size as they meet the long, stiffly upright heads of shining chestnut-brown flowers, all turning to warm shades of maize in winter. 1m.

STIPA barbata. Feather grass. Above tussocks of very narrow grassy leaves, stand stiff, knitting needle-like stems, which carry long, silky flower heads, pale silvery green floating in a soft breeze. As they ripen they become white and feathery, curled into corkscrew shapes, the better to twirl each pointed seed into the ground. Full sun and well-drained soil. July-September. 1.2m.

calamagrostis. A handsome grass for dry soil. Graceful fountains of narrow green leaves are topped with large feathery plumes of soft buff. 90cm.

extremiorientalis. Broad ribbon like leaves fall from stiff flower stem. Flowers bronze tinted green when fresh fading to fawn, creating open feathery effect, very effective vertical see-through screen. August. 1.8m.

gigantea The Golden oat grass. From dense basal clumps of fine narrow leaves spring many tall stems carrying truly superb heads of oat-like flowers which shimmer and shine as if made from beaten gold. A long lasting feature for months, throughout summer. 2m.

grandis. Charming grouped or singly. From base of very narrow leaves rise a column of flower stems, 1.2m tall which carry a haze of flower heads, distinguished by long cat whisker-like awns, turning buff when ripe, creating soft hazy effect.

splendens. Has given many years of pleasure in our gravel garden. Producing a large clump above which thin flower spikes shoot out in all directions. Trimmed back each spring. 1.2m.

tenacissima. Quite different from *S. tenuissima*. The flower heads are shaped like slender cat's tails poised on tall stems 1.6m tall. Interesting verticals against blue sky, in a void, among lower plants.

tenuissima. These clumps of hair-fine foliage wave an endless display of silver-green flower heads, each seed tipped with a long silky filament. The overall effect of delicate plumes and foliage waving in the slightest breeze is magical, among daisy flowers especially. Needs well-drained soil and sun. Midsummer-autumn. Effective all year, until cut down in spring. It does seed but is easily removed. 60cm.

UNCINIA uncinata. From New Zealand, this beautiful sedge varies in colour tone. We offer a particularly well-coloured clone. It forms arching tussocks of mahogany-brown, narrow grass-like leaves, brightest when young, the whole effect very striking among other foliages. We have overwintered it outside for several years, but it could be affected by specially cold winters. For rich retentive soil, in sun, or part shade. 30cm.

NOTES

NOTES

NOTES

NOTES